SHOW AND TELL

SHOW

AND

TELL

Identity as Performance

in U.S. Latina/o Fiction

Karen Christian

University
of New
Mexico Press
Albuquerque

© 1997 by the University
of New Mexico Press
All rights reserved.
FIRST EDITION

Library of Congress
Cataloging-in-Publication Data
Christian, Karen, 1960–
Show and tell: performing identity in U.S. Latina/o
fiction / Karen Christian. — 1st ed.
p.   cm.
Includes bibliographical references and index.
ISBN 0-8263-1796-0. —
ISBN 0-8263-1831-2 (pbk.)
1. American fiction — Hispanic American authors —
History and criticism.   2. American fiction — 20th
century — History and criticism.   3. Hispanic
Americans — Intellectual life.   4. Hispanic
Americans in literature.   5. Group identity in
literature.   6. Ethnic groups in literature.   I. Title.
PS153.H56C47   1997
813'.509868 — dc21   97-4875
CIP

For my mother, who was my first teacher;
and my sister, who always listens

In memory of my father,
who had most of the answers

CONTENTS

ACKNOWLEDGMENTS

I wish to express heartfelt thanks to all the friends and colleagues who directly or indirectly participated in this project. My deepest gratitude goes to Juan Bruce-Novoa, who introduced me to Chicana/o literature and helped me develop powerful tools with which to read and appreciate the works. Many of my ideas on cultural identity grew out of challenging discussions with the University of California Humanities Research Institute Minority Discourse Initiative. I am particularly grateful to Marta Sánchez, Irit Rogoff, Jeff Belnap, Alycee Lane, and Elena Tajima Creef for thought-provoking conversations and perceptive suggestions for my work. I am greatly indebted to Linette Davis; without her fortuitous introduction to Judith Butler's work I would not have been able to produce this "performance." I also wish to thank Lillian Manzor, who provided me with exceptionally insightful criticisms and whose enthusiasm for Latina/o literature is an inspiration. At the University of Maryland, I have had the good fortune to work with Lázaro Lima, Michael Horswell, and Virginia Bell; their encouragement and thoughtful comments were most helpful. I would like to express my sincere appreciation to Andrea Otáñez, my editor at the University of New Mexico Press, for her belief in the importance of this project, and to the two anonymous readers who made such insightful comments and suggestions.

Personal thanks go to Polly, for her love, support, and life-saving sense of humor; and to Phyllis and Reggie, for gently offering positive reinforcement. I owe my greatest debt of gratitude to Miguel — companion and anchor, craftsman of the written word whose editorial comments and suggestions infuse the pages of this book.

In Drag

In the Midwest, where I grew up, a conversation with a person you have just met usually begins with a brief exchange about the weather. In Los Angeles, where I attended graduate school, you "bond" with new acquaintances by commiserating about that day's traffic. In such conversations, these preliminaries are generally followed by a discussion of careers. I say that I'm a teacher; explaining what I teach, however, is a challenge when talking to someone not connected to academia. In some situations I simply add that I'm a Spanish professor at a university. If I'm feeling chatty, I'll mention that my area is Latin American literature, to which most people tend to react with something like, "Ah, García Márquez . . . magical realism . . . Ah, yes." Only when I'm in the mood to go into a long-winded explanation do I describe my work more accurately: I specialize in U.S. Latina/o literature. This statement frequently confounds the person with whom I'm conversing; I've learned to quickly elaborate, "You know, works by Mexican-American writers, U.S. Cubans, that sort of thing." The dialogue often continues with a superficial discussion of *The Mambo Kings Play Songs of Love,* or moves off in a completely different direction: "Did you see the movie *Mi familia?* What did you think of it?," or "Do you study graffiti too?"

These exchanges invariably leave me feeling dissatisfied, annoyed with myself for the roundabout, almost apologetic way I talk about my work. Yet I sense that there is something difficult to comprehend about my career choice. Part of the problem has to do with who I am, with the identity that is visibly inscribed on my body and is immediately apparent to the people I meet: a blonde, blue-eyed *gringa* whose English is marked by a faint midwestern twang. What possible connection could I have with Latino culture — a culture that "mainstream America" associates primarily with stereotypes, a few successful entertainers, and sensationalized news releases?

This book is in some ways my testimonial that such a connection can and does exist. It is a declaration, albeit in scholarly form, of my enduring passion for and fascination with U.S. Latina/o literature. This relationship began over ten years ago in the unlikely place of Wichita, Kansas. One of my professors, Elías Miguel Muñoz — born in Cuba, "exiled" for a second time in the Land of Oz — presented me with a copy of his recently published first novel, *Los viajes de Orlando Cachumbambé,* and introduced me to a wealth of other U.S. Cuban writers. The affair continued in southern California, where I became an avid reader of Chicana/o literature thanks to Juan Bruce-Novoa. The five years I spent studying at UC-Irvine and living Los Angeles-style multiculturalism were tremendously exciting and stimulating. I will always remember my year with the UC Humanities Research Institute Minority Discourse Initiative as one of the most significant times in my academic career. My colleagues, who were involved in fascinating projects on topics as diverse as ethnic beauty pageants and Nike shoes as cultural fetish, helped me to begin thinking about Latina/o literature and culture in ways that I had never considered.

Those were unsettling times as well, for many of my unquestioned assumptions about identity, race, and culture were being challenged at every turn. I was constantly struggling to find adequate ways to talk about ethnic identity without homogenizing or relying on standards of ethnic authenticity. There were too many wonderful works by Latina/o writers that didn't fit within these standards, that failed to include the "right" themes or characters. At the same time, I became acutely aware of my own outsider status, as an Anglo critic working on Latina/o texts. How could I offer insights into writing that was so distant from my own life experience? How could I avoid becoming an ethnographer and simply appropriating the literature to support my theories? I married a Latino and had the perfect opportunity to acquire a more suitable-sounding last name, but I knew that to do so would make me no less an impostor, a *gringa* cross-dressing as Latina spokesperson. After all, at the end of the day I can take off my "costume" and return to middle-class white invisibility; history and society do not mark me as ethnic or racial Other.

Inadvertently, I have followed in the footsteps of the countless academics who use their writing to work out their personal problems/agendas. I have gradually come to see this book as a way of indirectly acknowledging the shifting identities that my work entails, of recognizing that *all* identity is to some extent a drag show. I am fully aware of the implications and possible dangers of making the metaphors of performance and drag central to this project. There is the inevitable skepticism, if not outright rejection, that may be evoked by my argument that the divisions between identities — between ethnic and mainstream, gay and straight, people of color and whites — are fluid, and that the identities themselves are illusory. But I have met too many people who defy easy categorization — the friend who was born in Taiwan, raised in Brazil, works with Latinos in Los Angeles, and prefers to speak Portuguese, even though his physical appearance proclaims that he is Asian; the woman who was fired from her job because she refused to shave off her mustache; the colleague, born in Spain to Dutch parents, who confesses that he isn't sure what identity he should claim; the divorced father of two children who is now a gay activist. Perhaps we are all drag performers whose "core" identity would be a challenge to define.

I do not presume to be an anthropologist, or a sociologist, or a philosopher, although I "cross-dress" as all of these in my role as a literary and cultural critic. This project was motivated by my desire to gain greater understanding of the identity issues that intrigue me, issues that come up time and again in the U.S. Latina/o literature that I read and teach. I have brought together nine novels by outstanding U.S. Latina/o writers; these works have proven to be both enlightening and provocative in my endeavors to discover more about culture and identity. I owe my deepest appreciation to the writers themselves, for their artistic vision and devotion to their craft. Indeed, my identity as critic depends upon their "performances." These writers' work — their exploration of human existence — is joyous affirmation of the infinite possibilities of identity.

SHOW AND TELL

ONE

BETWEEN STANDING STILL
AND MOVING

Reading U.S. Latina/o Identity

I am nothing and no one
I am the possibility
of everything . . .
— VÍCTOR HERNÁNDEZ CRUZ, *"Side 32"*

Cubano-americano: ¿dónde soy?
son que se fue de Cuba
corazón que dejé enterrado
rinconcito de mi tierra
pedacito de cielo: ¿dónde soy? . . .
cuba: no
america: no
— GUSTAVO PÉREZ-FIRMAT, *"Filosofías del no"*

Finally you must choose between
standing still in the one solid
spot you
have found, or you keep moving
and take the risk . . .
— JUDITH ORTIZ COFER, *"Crossings"*

my feet
recognize
no border

no rule
no code
no lord

for this
wanderer's
heart
— FRANCISCO X. ALARCÓN, *"Mestizo"*

What does it mean to be "the possibility of everything" but also "nothing and no one"? To be rooted neither in Cuba nor in America, to stand still or "keep moving and take the risk," to possess a "wanderer's heart"? These images of movement, of uprootedness, of identity in flux, offer partial answers to the questions at the heart of this book: What insights do literary works lend into the complexities of U.S. Latina/o identity? How can Latina/o literature illuminate the processes through which the self is constructed?

Since the 1960s, Latinos have made substantial achievements in the American cultural and political spheres.[1] The last fifteen years in particular have seen a "boom" in U.S. Latina/o cultural production, both in quantity and complexity. Readers of U.S. Latina/o literature, no longer limited to well-known texts by Chicano writers and the occasional Nuyorican author, now have access to an expanding body of noteworthy works by immigrants from Cuba, the Dominican Republic, and Central and South America. The growth has been accompanied by rising numbers of mainstream reviews of Latina/o fiction and college-level courses offered in this literature. In turn, the amount and theoretical sophistication of scholarship on Chicana/o, mainland Puerto Rican/ Nuyorican, and U.S. Cuban literatures have increased steadily since the first studies were published in the early 1970s.[2]

A survey of U.S. Latina/o literary criticism indicates that the prevailing tendency has been to regard Chicana/o, Nuyorican, and U.S. Cuban literatures as distinct cultural phenomena. The most recent comprehensive scholarly studies continue this trend,[3] in spite of evidence that the literatures are frequently grouped together under the rubric of U.S. Latina/o (or U.S. Hispanic, or Chicano/Latino) in both anthologies and college courses.[4] With rare exceptions, this move to treat writings by Chicanos, Nuyoricans, U.S. Cubans, and other Latinos as part of the same literary corpus has not been accompanied by critical studies on Latina/o literature as a whole.[5]

The apparent reluctance on the part of critics is understandable, for Chicana/o, Nuyorican, U.S. Cuban, and other Latina/o literatures emerge from widely diverging historical, political, and economic contexts. Some critics trace the origins of Chicana/o writing to Alvar Núñez Cabeza de Vaca's *Naufragios* (1542), which chronicles his shipwreck and eight-year journey from what later became Florida to northwestern Mexico.[6] In 1848, the Treaty of Guadalupe Hidalgo — which annexed 918,000 square miles of Mexican territory to the United States — created a Mexican-descent minority in the United States. Chicana/o literature gained recognition as a U.S. ethnic literature fol-

lowing the civil rights struggles of the 1960s, particularly the cultural affirmation efforts of Luis Valdez's Teatro Campesino, Quinto Sol Publications, and
the Chicano Movement.[7]

In contrast to the Chicana/o historical trajectory, the growth of Nuyorican
and U.S. Cuban communities has been influenced more by migration and
immigration than by shifting national borders. A Latino community composed of both intellectual elites and working-class Puerto Ricans and Cubans
began to form in New York in the late nineteenth century. As a consequence of
large-scale migrations, this ethnic community became predominantly Puerto
Rican in the twentieth century. One such migration occurred after 1917, when
Puerto Ricans were made U.S. citizens; a second took place during the 1950s,
when the industrialization program called "Operation Bootstrap" produced a
mass migration of displaced rural Puerto Ricans. The term *Nuyorican* was
coined in the early 1970s by a group of writers who perceived the need for the
community to assert its cultural autonomy.[8]

In addition to the New York Puerto Rican community, there are also size-
able numbers of Puerto Ricans in New Jersey, Illinois, Florida, and other
states. Ongoing back-and-forth migration between the island and the United
States lends mainland Puerto Rican communities a uniquely dynamic character that is evidenced by the widespread bilingualism in such communities.[9]

Literary works by Puerto Rican migrants and Cuban émigrés to the eastern
United States date back to at least the nineteenth century. At present, critics
nevertheless tend to treat U.S. Cuban literature as a relatively new corpus that
has emerged from exiles who began arriving in the United States after the 1959
Cuban Revolution.[10] The majority of the approximately 650,000 Cubans who
settled primarily in south Florida and New Jersey during the 1960s and 1970s
were members of the middle and upper classes. Deemed political refugees
fleeing a Communist regime, these exiles received considerable assistance from
the U.S. government, including emergency housing, medical care, English-
language training, and educational support. For these and other reasons, the
U.S. Cuban community is often portrayed as having little in common with
working-class Chicana/o and Nuyorican communities.[11]

Treating the literatures of these Latina/o groups as essentially distinct from
one another is to some degree justifiable. However, by doing so critics may
inadvertently perpetuate a view of ethnic writing as sociohistorical documentation of a particular community's experience. In the late 1980s, Werner Sollors observed that ethnic literature in the United States was traditionally assumed to reaffirm a preestablished conception of identity associated with the
ethnic community, while simultaneously rejecting Anglo-American culture.
Sollors indicated that the numerous scholars who viewed ethnic literature in

this way based their readings of texts "on static notions of descent and on primordial, organicist, sometimes even biological — but in all cases largely unquestioned — concepts of ethnic-group membership" (1986, 11). Ethnicity, then, has typically been articulated through reference to ancestry and to traditional practices — language, customs, religious practices, and so forth — that differ from those of the national majority.

In *The Invention of Ethnicity,* Sollors discusses a number of premises upon which such views are founded. Each distinct group is seen as possessing "an essential continuum of certain myths and traits," along with a focus on survival of the group, which is faced with the threat of the encroaching dominant culture (1989, xiv).[12] Yet criticism that seeks a direct correspondence between the ethnic writer and his/her community ultimately imposes thematic limitations on the literary works. When the "authenticity" of ethnic texts is judged by their adherence to a set of thematic and/or ideological standards, the result is ghettoization of the literature.

Criticism based on such standards can act as a sort of straitjacket for Latina/o writers who choose to avail themselves of "nonethnic" thematic material and forms. In novels by Chicano/a writers John Rechy, Luis Urrea, Sheila Ortiz Taylor, and Cecile Pineda, for example, allusions to an identifiable Chicana/o problematic are subtle or nonexistent. Likewise, mainland Puerto Rican author Sandra Benítez sets her 1993 novel *A Place Where the Sea Remembers* in coastal Mexico, and U.S. Cuban writer Ibis Gómez-Vega's *Send My Roots Rain* (1991) takes place in a Chicana/o community in the desert of the southwestern United States. As these works make clear, critics of Latina/o literature must acknowledge that the ethnic group encompasses diverse ideologies and modes of artistic expression.[13]

A move away from the ghettoizing tendencies of earlier ethnic literary criticism is reflected in David Palumbo-Liu's *The Ethnic Canon: Histories, Institutions, and Interventions* (1995), which considers various ethnic literatures together. Palumbo-Liu's approach suggests that ethnic writing shares common theoretical concerns and should not be treated solely as a product of a specific sociohistorical context. In his introduction to the essays by critics of different U.S. ethnic literatures, he critiques the use of ethnic texts "as authentic, unmediated representations of ethnicity" (11). Palumbo-Liu emphasizes the need to interrogate the discourse employed in criticism of a particular text. This makes it possible to theorize "the (often tenuous) *nature* of [the text's] relation to dominant discourses" (22–23, n.4), that is, how the text has been appropriated as exemplary of minority resistance or a homogenized ethnic experience. The editors of *Memory, Narrative, and Identity: New Essays in Ethnic American Literatures* (1994) likewise highlight possibilities for theoretical dialogue among ethnic literatures. They point out that recent studies of a variety of ethnic texts raise many common questions — of authenticity and representation, innovation and experimentation, narrative and identity — that offer new perspectives "on larger issues of nation and culture" (Singh et al., 16).

These comments by Sollors, Palumbo-Liu, and Singh et al. support the development of a theoretical model that could accommodate the array of writings comprising U.S. Latina/o literature. At the same time, when theorizing about such a diverse corpus it is crucial to avoid relying on generalizations, totalizing definitions, and/or essentialisms. Introductory remarks to two recent anthologies of U.S. Latina/o literature allude to the challenges that await critics who attempt to study this literary corpus as a whole. In *Iguana Dreams: New Latino Fiction*, Delia Poey and Virgil Suárez observe that such an approach has potential dangers insofar as "in the eyes of many Anglos, the diverse Latino cultures are interchangeable" (xvi). Poey and Suárez stress that while the anthologized writers all offer perspectives on "the Latino experience," the editors' intention is to showcase distinct voices, styles, experiences, and "definition[s] of what being Latino means" (xix). Ray González, editor of *Currents from the Dancing River: Contemporary Latino Fiction, Nonfiction, and Poetry*, similarly refers to "a Latino perspective on the world," stating that "[a]lthough cultural differences remain between Mexican Americans, Puerto Ricans in the United States, and Cuban Americans, Latino writers are coming together in a cohesive yet exciting and unpredictable whole" (xiii–xiv).

The contradictions and conundrums implicit in these editors' observations suggest a valid question for critics: Is it possible to formulate a global approach to U.S. Latina/o writing that does not perpetuate a reductive, totalizing view of the literature? In the foreword to the 1993 anthology *Growing Up Latino: Memoirs and Stories*, which contains excerpts from many of the best-known works of U.S. Latina/o fiction, Ilán Stavans attempts to contextualize the recent boom in fiction by U.S. writers of Latin American descent.[14] His assessment all but erases differences between the works of writers as dissimilar as Chicanos Tomás Rivera and Gloria Anzaldúa, mainland Puerto Ricans Piri Thomas and Judith Ortiz Cofer, Cuban-American Oscar Hijuelos, and Dominican-American Julia Alvarez. Describing the anthologized writers, Stavans proclaims:

Although diverse in backgrounds and nationalities, their collective identity is one. And indeed this volume, the result of twenty-five different pens, despite its variety of styles and subjects, has an amazing autobiographical homogeneity, as if one supreme creator, a writer of writers, were responsible for every one of its pages. (xii–xiii)

The unsubstantiated essentialism underlying Stavans's vision of U.S. Latina/o literature stems from his failure to acknowledge the profound differences within a large and multifaceted ethnic group.[15] Yet as early as 1982 Juan Bruce-Novoa had called homogenizing tendencies the product of an illusion of a monolithic Hispanic character; he argued that "the groups are diverse and their literature cannot be reduced to simple generalizations without doing each violence" (1990, 28).

Other critics have sought to identify common attributes of U.S. Latina/o fiction by emphasizing its connection to Latin American literature. In a *New York Times* review of U.S. Cuban writer Roberto Fernández's novel *Raining Backwards* (1988), critic Andrei Codrescu pronounces a sweeping value judgment based on this relationship between the two literatures. He declares that "North American Latino fiction is a poor cousin of its Southern Hemisphere relation" (27), a statement that clearly demonstrates the confusion produced by U.S. Latina/o literature's complex intercultural status. While a Latin American influence may be evident in some works by U.S. Latina/o authors, this literary tradition is not the only one available to Latina/o writers, nor is it necessarily their most important influence.

Codrescu's view of U.S. Latina/o fiction as an inferior outgrowth of Latin American literature has implications similar to Stavans's postulation of a U.S. Latina/o "collective identity." Both are uninformed attempts to identify the U.S. Latina/o character or "essence" that distinguishes the works from other bodies of literature. Yet such broad descriptive endeavors are rarely successful, for U.S. Latina/o culture has never been monolithic or homogeneous. Ethnic markers such as traditions, language, and religious practices cannot be consistently traced across generations, gender, and class within an ethnic group. The social imaginary that Latina/o literary works are often assumed to portray has been continually contested by an array of "counternarratives." Postcolonial critic Homi Bhabha describes counternarratives as cultural texts that "disturb those ideological manoeuvres through which 'imagined communities' are given essentialist identities" (149). The Chicano Movement and other minority group political movements of the 1960s and 1970s, for example, demanded revision of the prevailing notion of American identity. In a similar fashion, a number of Chicana writers produced counternarratives that challenged the androcentric bias of Chicano cultural nationalism.[16] Richard Rodríguez's 1982 autobiography *Hunger of Memory*, which has been denounced by Chicana/o critics for its proassimilation stance,[17] could also be viewed as a counternarrative to dominant Chicano cultural discourse.

Criticism of U.S. Cuban writing has likewise had to respond to the emergence of counternarratives. The editors of the first anthology of Cuban-American literature ever published, *Veinte años de literatura cubanoamericana: Antología 1962–1982*, claimed that in contrast to the "ethnic activism" of Chicano and Nuyorican writers, Cuban-American writers "se muestran apacibles y nostálgicos" (Burunat and García 1988, 13).[18] In a 1985 article Eliana Rivero declared that literature by Cuban immigrants could not be considered ethnic because of its assumed sympathetic ideological stance toward middle-class American values (1985, 187). Now, however, U.S. Cuban literature can no longer be accurately depicted as affirming middle-class Anglo-American values. Recent works by younger writers born in Cuba (Elías Miguel Muñoz, Cristina García, Achy Obejas) raise issues of social class and cultural identity and operate as counternarratives to conservative U.S. Cuban discourse. Gay and lesbian voices further problematize exclusionary views of U.S. Cuban and Latino/a identity by challenging culturally coded gender constructs.[19]

In this book, I argue that a single theoretical model can be applied to diverse U.S. Latina/o texts without essentializing Latina/o cultural identity. My project is to some extent an outgrowth of the generalized displacement of a stable sense of identity that has taken place in Western thought during the twentieth century. In "Ethnicity: Identity and Difference," cultural critic Stuart Hall attributes this decentering to four major intellectual shifts: the de-authorization of Western rationality as the source of universal knowledge and truth; the theoretical postulations of Marx regarding the historical construction of the subject; Freud's grounding of identity in psychic processes; and Saussure's concept of subjectivity as a construct of language (1989, 10–12). These challenges to the stability of the subject have resulted in identity being reconceptualized as a process of identification, as "something that happens over time, that is never absolutely stable, that is subject to the play of history and the play of difference" (Hall 1989, 15). Identity is thus an ongoing narrative that can never be outside representation.

Recent theoretical projects on Chicana/o culture and literature indicate that a number of critics are grappling with these questions of essentialism and the social construction of identity. Perhaps the best-known articulation of de-essentialized Chicana/o identity is that developed by cultural critic Gloria Anzaldúa in *Borderlands/La Frontera: The New Mestiza* (1987). Anzaldúa characterizes the self, which is necessarily nonunitary, by what she calls *mestiza* or border consciousness: a multiple subjectivity constructed at the intersection of gender, class, race, culture, and sexuality. As Anzaldúa declares, "I, a *mestiza*, continually walk out of one culture and into another, because I am in all cultures at the same time" (77), thus portraying Chicana/o identity as what Yvonne Yarbro-Bejarano terms "a constantly shifting process or activity of breaking down binary dualisms" (1994, 11). Yet in spite of Anzaldúa's desire to emphasize "the breaking down of paradigms" (80), her project tends to rely on images that evoke Chicana/o cultural essence — "indigenous like corn" (81), "We are the *chile colorado*" (82), "we have such love of the Mother, the good mother" (84) — and claims that U.S. Latinos and Latin Americans share a "common culture" (87). *Borderlands/La Frontera* nonetheless offers a provocative response to the need to recognize that "all identity is constructed across difference," expressed by Hall and other cultural critics in the 1980s (Hall 1987, 44).

In "Chicana/o Cultural Representations: Reframing Alternative Critical Discourses," Angie Chabrám and Rosa Linda Fregoso further challenge notions of monolithic Chicana/o identity by critiquing the discourse of Chicano cultural nationalism. A fundamental shortcoming of the nationalist ideology, according to Chabrám and Fregoso, arose from its insistence on an essential Chicano identity rooted in Aztlán, the legendary Aztec homeland and mythical origin of the Chicano nation. The discourse thus portrayed Chicano cultural identity as static and one-dimensional and failed to acknowledge historical differences and diversity among Chicanos (204–5). Rafael Pérez-Torres's 1995 study of Chicana/o poetry, *Movements in Chicano Poetry: Against Myths, Against Margins,* convincingly shows how Chicana/o cultural production has always been characterized by internal contradictions. Pérez-Torres asserts that Chicano literature does not manifest "a singularly fixed, original, authentic configuration" of identity but rather compels readers to consider the processes of identity construction. In short, claims to Chicana/o identity "reveal themselves . . . to be finally involved in an endless project of becoming, rather than being, Chicana/o" (30).

Feminist critic Norma Alarcón's theoretical writings reflect a similarly anti-essentialist stance toward Chicana/o cultural identity. In "Chicana Feminism: In the Tracks of 'the' Native Woman," Alarcón observes that "the story of Chicanas/os has not turned out to be a 'definitive' culture as some dreamed" (1990, 248). She notes that, as critics of Chicana/o cultural production have acknowledged, there is no fixed identity, and "the term [Chicano] itself . . . has become a critical site of political, ideological and discursive struggle" (1990, 248). In the place of a presumed unitary Chicana/o self, Alarcón proposes a "subject-in-process" — characterized by shifting identifications or "provisional identities" — who produces hybrid cultural narratives (1994, 135–36). Through their readings of Chicana/o culture, Anzaldúa, Chabrám and Fregoso, Pérez-Torres, and Alarcón support a view of a heterogeneous, multidimensional, and dynamic subjectivity that has implications for the cultural production of other ethnic communities as well.

The social constructionist arguments of the foregoing critics are compelling, as are efforts by literary critics to formulate anti-essentialist approaches to Latina/o texts. Since the 1970s, Bruce-Novoa has called for recognition of the diversity and dialogical character of Chicana/o voices and cultural production.[20] With respect to writing by Puerto Ricans in the United States, Juan Flores emphasizes the literature's "growing diversity and sophistication" as evidenced by a wide range of language usage and the publication of works by women and writers from areas other than New York (43). Flores's description of this writing as "a literature of 'mingling and sharing,' of interaction and exchange" with other cultures (44) resonates with Alarcón's observations on hybrid cultural narratives. In general, however, even the most recent theoretical studies of Latina/o literature do not consistently assimilate the notion of nonunitary identity, and many ultimately reinscribe a binary model of identity (ethnic/nonethnic) and resistance. Edna Acosta-Belén's 1992 essay on Nuyorican literature exemplifies this tendency to assert the plurality of Latina/o identity and literary expression while assuming clearly definable difference from a monolithic Anglo-American "mainstream." Acosta-Belén concurs with Werner Sollors that ethnicity is an ongoing process of invention, and she affirms the "changeable nature of identity" (985). This position appears to contradict her claim that Nuyorican and other ethnic writers articulate "a distinctive collective identity" and that being Puerto Rican (or Hispanic/Latino) "implies a separation from the dominant society" (987).

Similar tension can be detected in Ramón Saldívar's much-cited study *Chicano Narrative: The Dialectics of Difference*. In this work, the author's critical perspective on Chicana/o literature calls into question the anti-essentialist intentions he declares in his introduction. Saldívar proposes to "test the usefulness" of an array of literary theories — structuralism, poststructuralism, deconstruction, psychoanalysis, Marxist criticism, feminist theory, and "other nontraditional forms of literary analysis" — for the interpretation of Chicano narrative (3). His ostensibly eclectic approach nevertheless remains clearly focused on the material aspects of culture and identity, as indicated by the critic's emphasis on Chicano literature's "opposition and resistance to mainstream social, historical, economic, and cultural modalities" (3) and its "foregrounding of sociopolitical themes" (5). Saldívar's move to show that Chicana/o identity is subjectivity in process, dialectical but "without coalescence or synthesis" (174), is made less convincing by essentialist statements like "Chicanos and their narratives . . . [reflect] in no uncertain terms the forms and styles of their folk-base origins" (25) and "Chicano narrative presents subjects acting according to . . . ideologies in active resistance to the existing material apparatus of American society" (213). *Chicano Narrative: The Dialectics of Difference* thus relies heavily on materialist readings of the texts without engaging the "immaterial" aspects of identity — memory, desire, shifting individual identifications — that are also fundamental to the conception of subjectivity in process.

Challenges to essentialist notions of Chicana/o identity have coincided with a move by critics to recognize and explore the diversity of Chicana subjectivity and writing. Both *Infinite Divisions: An Anthology of Chicana Literature*, edited by Tey Diana Rebolledo and Eliana S. Rivero, and Rebolledo's study *Women Singing in the Snow: A Cultural Analysis of Chicana Literature*, articulate this objective. In their introductory comments to *Infinite Divisions*, Rebolledo and Rivera observe that Chicana literature "has blossomed into a rich and complex body of work" (xx) and that the "Chicana experience" depicted by the anthologized writers involves "contradictory and multiple realities" (31). By showcasing a wide array of writings produced by Chicanas from 1848 until the present, this anthology presents a greatly expanded view of Chicana literature.

Rebolledo's *Women Singing in the Snow,* a thematic analysis of many of the works included in *Infinite Divisions,* could be read as a theoretical companion volume to the anthology. The following quote from the preface, which refers to Chicana writers in general, underscores Rebolledo's desire to avoid essentializing Chicana subjectivity:

Having multiple identities in various cultures also allows for shifting perspectives in all areas: since the subject need not be stable, then it can become multiply voiced — that is, it no longer has to be unified and static but is free to be complex and disparate. (xi)

Yet this statement evokes more questions than it answers: What does it mean to have "multiple identities in various cultures"? When was the subject ever required to be unified and static? What is a "disparate" subject? Rebolledo nevertheless succeeds in identifying numerous themes, archetypes, and stereotypes found in Chicana literature and contextualizes them with a wealth of cultural background. This broad, inclusive portrayal of Chicana writing provides convincing evidence of the diverse subject positions from which the writing emerges.

Considerable strides have been made in the development of nonessentialist critical approaches to Latina/o texts, as shown by the theoretical and scholarly projects that I have mentioned. Indeed, U.S. Latina/o literary criticism currently depends on criteria of ethnic authenticity to a far lesser degree than did the "culturalist" criticism produced during the 1970s and early 1980s.[21] Nevertheless, the theoretical positions of many ostensibly anti-essentialist critics — including Anzaldúa, Acosta-Belén, Saldívar, and Rebolledo — remain grounded in the notion of clearly identifiable Chicano/Latino experience represented through writing. In my project, I endeavor to engage and grapple with this contradiction: How can U.S. Latina/o literary production be treated as a definable corpus while allowing for multiple and shifting subjectivities and the ongoing transformation of Latina/o culture?

My study of Latina/o fiction, like the recent scholarship I have discussed, promotes a de-essentialized view of identity, but I also recognize that essentialist categories cannot be avoided entirely. As Diana Fuss notes in *Essentially Speaking: Feminism, Nature and Difference*, anti-essentialist theories of identity tend to assume that essentialism and constructionism are mutually exclusive, binary opposites of one another. Fuss argues that "essentialism, when held most under suspicion by constructionists, is often effectively doing its work elsewhere, under other guises" (1). The constructionist stance insists that identities are socially and historically constructed. This position ostensibly precludes the notions of unchanging "essence" (feminine, masculine, racial, cultural, and so on) and "natural" givens that precede social processes. Yet constructionism is grounded in social categories — woman, man, black, Latina/o — that remain constant, such that "it is difficult to see how constructionism can *be* constructionism without a fundamental dependency upon essentialism" (Fuss 4). Thus even as I strive to deconstruct limiting paradigms of cultural and gender essence throughout this project, I must acknowledge that a certain degree of essentialism is implicit in the categories Latina/o, Chicana/o, Nuyorican, U.S. Cuban, and so forth.

The impossibility of completely freeing identity theory of essentialisms need not, however, imply a return to earlier conceptions of monolithic and clearly definable ethnicity. By the same token, U.S. Latina/o literature's status as "minority" or resistance literature should not require a historical materialist approach to the texts, to the exclusion of other theoretical strategies. If literature is, among other things, the exploration of human identity in all its fullness — its historical, social, psychological, spiritual facets — reading ethnic literary texts through the lens of history and material relations can render only a partial view of the dynamics of identity. Such interpretations tend to reiterate a binary model of resistance that ignores the constantly shifting boundaries of communities and the complex interactions between groups and individuals.

As Peggy Phelan observes in *Unmarked: The Politics of Performance*, theories of cultural production that focus solely on the material conditions influencing identities fail to engage "questions about the immaterial construction of identities — those processes of belief which summon memory, sight, and love" (5). Identity is undeniably rooted in history, but it is also inflected by ahistorical forces, "the huge unknowns of our psychic lives" highlighted by Freud, Lacan, and others (Hall 1989, 11).[22] In this sense, the essays in *Memory, Narrative, and Identity* make an important contribution to ethnic literary criticism. The editors assert that the complex interplay between individual, psychological processes and the sociohistorical is apparent in memory insofar as "all memories—individual, family, ethnic, or racial—are socially constructed" (Singh et al. vii).[23] My readings of Latina/o fiction likewise suggest that sociohistorical forces are not the only factors that determine identity, and that immaterial processes of identity formation must be taken into account as well.

Homi Bhabha's concept of "nation as narration" (142) offers a dynamic model for the relationship between ethnic literature and identity. Bhabha contests static cultural constructs by showing how national identity is constantly being "narrated" through the cultural texts of the people. In the case of U.S. Latina/o or other ethnic literatures, the publication of new texts along with the recuperation of earlier excluded works similarly generates a continually evolving vision of a diverse ethnic community.[24] Thus ethnicity is to some degree a construct of ethnic literature. This postulation in effect reverses the sequence ETHNIC GROUP IDENTITY → ETHNIC TEXT that has been an assumption of much scholarship on this literature. Literary critics need to consistently acknowledge the ongoing transformation of U.S. Latina/o culture to avoid perpetuating the notion that a Latina/o "essence" exists.

The counternarratives generated by Latinas, gay and lesbian writers, and others impel formulation of a model of culture and cultural identity that can accommodate minority voices *within* Latina/o communities. Bhabha's observations on minority discourse and cultural identity in postcolonial societies afford insights into this process. His argument—that minority discourse reveals the performativity of national culture—has applications for ethnic groups as well, for similar power structures exist in both contexts.[25] Bhabha asserts that minority discourse

contests genealogies of "origin" that lead to claims for cultural supremacy and historical priority. Minority discourse acknowledges the status of national culture—and the people—as a contentious performative space. (157)

Significantly, in his theory of the "location of culture" Bhabha does not claim that cultural identity is solely performative, like a show or an act with no historical or social foundation. On the contrary, he postulates that the narra-

tives that construct the nation are characterized by tension between the historical, nationalist myths of origin and the contemporary, everyday performances
of the people's daily lives.[26]
    Ethnicity is thus located in the contested territory where past, present, and
future converge. Sollors's postulation of "the invention of ethnicity" can serve
as a suggestive metaphor for the relationship between cultural identity and
literary works. He indicates that the expression is intended

> not to evoke a conspiratorial interpretation of a manipulative inventor
> who single-handedly makes ethnics out of unsuspecting subjects, but to
> suggest widely shared, though intensely debated, collective fictions that
> are continually reinvented. (1989, xi)

Within ethnic communities, these "collective fictions" may take the form of
nationalist models of cultural identity and authenticity. Collective fictions are
neither intrinsically positive nor negative. However, through the workings of
power relations in a given community, a nationalist paradigm can operate as a
normative/regulatory discourse that censures dissenting voices and perpetuates the illusion of cultural essence.
    In short, defining U.S. Latina/o identity, and its relationship to literature, is
a complex task. Literary texts make visible the tension between the everyday
"performances" of Latinos — ongoing activities, practices, and identifications — and the historical authority of cultural tradition. Many of these performances comment on or directly challenge static, nationalistic paradigms of La-
tina/o identity: negotiation with American "dominant culture";[27] exploration
of unconventional gender roles; "non-Latino" cultural expression; and so on.
United States Latina/o cultural identity cannot be homogenized or totalized,
and Latina/o literature both documents and participates in its transformation.

CULTURAL PERFORMANCE, EXCESS, AND DRAG

My project on U.S. Latina/o fiction focuses on the *performative* aspects of
identity, the "practices of everyday life," in Michel de Certeau's words,[28] that
continuously transform culture. At the same time, I examine the ways in which
performances marked as "Latina/o" (both by the dominant culture and within
Latina/o communities) have served to reinforce the notion that a definable
Latina/o cultural essence exists. I propose a way of reading U.S. Latina/o
fiction that takes into account commonalities and connections among the texts

on one hand, and the ongoing process of cultural change on the other. This reading strategy acknowledges the temporality and performativity of culture without denying the significance of cultural tradition and collective fictions.[29]

The array of subject positions articulated in the nine novels I discuss requires a theoretical approach that can accommodate diversity and change. I have found feminist critic Judith Butler's groundbreaking work on performance and performativity to complement Bhabha's theorization of cultural identity. Butler has been engaged in a project whose purpose is to challenge the exclusivity of gender categories. Through interrogation of psychoanalytical theories of gender identity formation and sexuality, Butler proposes that gender is performative: "There is no gender identity behind the expressions of gender; . . . identity is performatively constituted by the very 'expressions' that are said to be its results" (1990, 25). Although Butler's work is devoted to gender and feminist theory, the questions she raises have broad implications in the domains of racial and ethnic identity as well.

Butler asserts that cultural performances of male and female identity are "acts, gestures, enactments [that] are *performative* in the sense that the essence or identity that they otherwise purport to express are *fabrications*" (1990, 136). She claims that identity categories are in fact effects created by normative and/or regulatory discourses (1990, ix).[30] Gender identity is thus performance — a spectacle requiring an audience for interpretation — and performative, having no original referent. Butler argues that identity must be understood as a process, an ongoing discursive practice that produces the appearance of substance and the illusion of origins (1990, 33).

In similar fashion, cultural markers such as language, familial structure, material culture, and religious practices may be read as expressions of essential, unchanging ethnic identity. Hence the images of the Chicano migrant worker and *barrio* dweller, the Latin Lover à la Ricky Ricardo, the self-sacrificing Latina, and an everyday reality that is magical and/or mystical have become symbols of Latina/o "essence" in the American popular imagination. Furthermore, the novels that I discuss allude to collective fictions — paradigms of "authentic" *chicanismo*, Puerto Ricanness, and *cubanidad* — that circulate within U.S. Latina/o communities. Yet the tremendous diversity found within a single ethnic group necessitates revision of limiting, conventional models of ethnicity. My readings of Latina/o fiction suggest that cultural identity is not static or naturalized but involves a certain degree of cross-dressing, of drag, in a metaphoric sense. Indeed, a central postulation of this study is that both cultural identity and gender resemble drag shows that parody the notion of essentialized identity categories. I use the drag analogy to emphasize both performance and its implications: identity, as drag, is both spectacle and process.

Butler argues that drag undermines the concept of a feminine essence that is the exclusive property of females, or a masculine essence that is the domain of males. She asserts that drag destabilizes gender "by calling into question the claims of normativity and originality by which gender and sexual oppression sometimes operate" (1993, 128). Likewise, in my discussions of nine Latina/o novels I show how *ethnic* performances that appear to reflect a priori Chicana/o, Puerto Rican, or Cuban identity can be read as parody, calling into question the concept of cultural essence. The narrator of Judith Ortiz Cofer's *The Line of the Sun* interprets her immigrant community's replication of the *patria* in their New Jersey tenement in this way, as a parody of Puerto Ricanness. In other novels, narrative performances of gender or ethnicity are repeated to such excess that writing itself becomes a medium for the production of a drag spectacle, as in Cecile Pineda's *The Love Queen of the Amazon* and Ana Castillo's *So Far from God*.

The danger intrinsic to this view of identity as drag, as ongoing performance and impersonation, is its implication that ethnic difference has no social or historical foundation. United States Cuban cultural critic Coco Fusco justifiably criticizes postmodern approaches to minority identity for this very reason. In *English is Broken Here,* Fusco argues that interpreting identity as pure process, as infinitely transformable and performative, ignores the political forces that influence subjectivity, such as racism and "the determining force of collective historical experience" (27). A primary objective of my project, then, is to acknowledge both these sociohistorical forces and the performative aspects of U.S. Latina/o culture and identity. Ethnic difference has not ceased to exist in the 1990s. But it must be articulated in terms that allow for heterogeneity, for multiple and shifting subject positions, within the ethnic groups that generate texts. The eruption of voices that contest the paradigms of cultural nationalism and unified ethnic discourse undermines the notion of Latina/o "essence," to the point that the categories "ethnic" and "American" can no longer be viewed as easily distinguishable entities.[31]

My close readings of the U.S. Latina/o novels in this study support Hall's argument that ethnicity "has not lost hold of the place and the ground from which we can speak, yet it is no longer contained within that place as an essence" (1989, 20). In these novels, characters' performances and their shifting among subject positions suggest limitations of both essentialist and constructionist models of ethnicity. Rechy's and Ortiz Taylor's gay and lesbian characters champion perpetual movement between identifications and communities as the means to achieve full expression of the multifaceted self. In a similar way, the immigrant narrators of *The Line of the Sun* and Julia Alvarez's *How the García Girls Lost Their Accents* experience ethnicity as an ongoing series of performances and negotiations involving their ancestral culture and American dominant culture. My focus on performativity acknowledges the indistinct boundaries of all identity categories by taking into account ever-changing social and political circumstances.

Underlying my readings of these novels is the assumption that ethnic "performances" can be readily identified. Some of them are readable as Latina/o because they are based on well-known Latina/o collective fictions and cultural mythologies (references to Aztlán, the Virgin of Guadalupe, Cuba's Varadero Beach, traditional foods, and so on). In addition, the interpretation of cultural practices, language use, and physical appearance as indicators of ethnic difference implies that there is a norm or standard against which these indicators are measured. This marking of difference can be best understood by examining the power relations through which particular acts are designated as performances of ethnicity, gender, sexuality, or race in American society.

In all cultures and societies, the presence of marginalized or dissident identities is made evident through performances of difference that mark these identities as extraneous elements — as "excess" — in relation to a dominant ideology. In "The Psychological Structure of Fascism," Georges Bataille proposes that forces emanating from marginalized groups can only enter into play when a society's fundamental homogeneity has begun to dissociate (156). Such dissociation becomes possible when the social system's internal contradictions begin to be apparent to readers of the social text. In the United States, the civil rights struggles of the 1960s revealed that the prevailing notion of homogeneous American culture and history had been constructed through the exclusion of racial, ethnic, and sexual difference. The discrediting of the "melting pot" vision of American society was the result of a change in the way history began to be recorded. The principal agents in the various civil rights and New Ethnicity movements were minority political activists, artists, and intellectuals. They were representatives of oppressed communities who instigated subversion by valorizing the very "excesses" that American society censured.

The opposition of these marginalized sectors to dominant cultural norms brings them visibility. In spite of rapid population growth of Latinos, Asian-Americans, and other people of color in the United States, the norm around which American culture is organized arguably continues to be white, middle-class heterosexuality.[32] I propose that those identities/subject positions that fall outside this standard — racial and ethnic minority groups, gays and lesbians — are identified by their excesses. Ethnic cultural production critiques the power relations in American society that operate to mark non-Anglo skin color, physical features, language, and customs as "ethnic excess." In Elías

Miguel Muñoz's *The Greatest Performance,* the U.S. Cuban lesbian protago-nist discovers that the "melodramatic" Latino music and the rich Cuban foods that she cherishes are perceived as excessive by her Anglo lover. Likewise, performative acts ascribed to gay and lesbian sexualities contest the normative nature of heterosexuality and in so doing mandate revision of gender con-structs that fail to allow for homosexuality. Foucault observes that since the nineteenth century Western society has treated "transgressive" sexualities as excess that must be regulated (1978, 146–49). The Cuban émigré commu-nity's exclusion of the gay and lesbian protagonists in Muñoz's trailblazing novel intimates that a similar view circulates in racial and ethnic minority cultures as well.

My emphasis on the role of "excess" in the construction of ethnic identity may appear to contradict the notion of difference as lack — as an indicator of inferiority or inadequacy in relation to a dominant group. Yet the works that I study suggest that excess and lack are closely associated in the context of ethnicity. In fact, certain episodes in the novels indicate that it is possible to interpret the same ethnic performance as both excess *and* lack. Latina/o char-acters' use of Spanish or accented English may be read as the lack of adequate language skills, or as the excess of a superfluous language and a foreign accent in an English-dominant country (see chapter 4). Furthermore, in spite of the excessive visibility that results from ethnic characters' appearance and be-haviors, they are simultaneously *invisible* — unseen as individuals and subjects of history. William Boelhower asserts that even apparently invisible "assimi-lated ethnics" have the power to make visible the ethnic signs that circulate throughout American culture. He points out that these ethnic subjects under-mine homogeneous American national identity by "[floating] about in the dominant culture as exegete or interpreter of the ethnic traces inscribed every-where (but nowhere) in the American topology" (109). The protagonist of Sheila Ortiz Taylor's engaging novels *Faultline* and *Southbound* represents just such an "interpreter of ethnic traces" as she unearths her family's pain-stakingly erased Chicano background.

This notion that ethnic excess and lack coexist in a dynamic relationship further underscores the role of performance in cultural identity. Moreover, the wide array of subject positions of ethnic "performers" (writers, artists, actors, musicians) generates performances that may reflect solidarity with an ethnic cultural heritage (e.g., nationalist ideology) or work to critique it. From this perspective, ethnic writing — a site of ethnic subjectivity — is not limited to overt expressions of resistance to the dominant culture. Significant commen-tary on ethnic identity may be found in a text's apparent endorsement of the dominant ideology; works that project such a stance provide telling commentary on the hegemony of whiteness, heterosexuality, and middle-class values in American society.

In many immigrant novels, this hegemony is reflected in the immigrant characters' strong faith in assimilation and the American Dream. These novels, like African-American narratives of "passing," are infused with the desire of those marked as different to be invisible, to pass as "average Americans." Ironically, achieving this invisibility implies gaining the visibility conferred upon members of the dominant group. Works by minority writers that "pass" as mainstream American literature do so through their apparent assimilation of dominant ideology and their lack of resistance; they may appear to represent the ultimate betrayal of minority culture. But this is an oversimplification that fails to consider the significance of the strategies employed in performing as an (Anglo-) American.[33] These strategies reveal that invisibility is only attained through suppression of that which is identified as excess in relation to societal norms: a foreign accent, non-Anglo social customs, "inappropriate" clothing, music, or food.

U.S. Latina/o identity is thus perpetually being transformed through the enactment and interpretation of ethnic performances that appear in literary texts and at other sites of artistic production. The novels of marginalized sexualities, immigrant assimilation narratives, and "magical realist" stories that I discuss participate in the destabilization of the various national identity categories contained within the rubric of "U.S. Latina/o." The macho protagonist of Oscar Hijuelos's *The Mambo Kings Play Songs of Love* emulates an ideal of Cuban masculinity that circulates in this novel as well as in *The Greatest Performance*, yet this ideal is revealed to be an oppressive fabrication. In many of the other works as well, even performances that appear to affirm norms and traditions of the characters' ancestral culture can be shown to subvert the notion of essential ethnic identity.

READING AGAINST ESSENCE

In this introductory chapter, I have highlighted critical/reading approaches that promote an anti-essentialist view of Latina/o culture and identity. My project responds to the necessity of developing critical methodologies for U.S. Latina/o literature that involve neither totalization nor judgment based on a work's "authenticity." In a deliberate move against static, homogenizing definitions of ethnicity and ethnic literature, this book explores the ways Latina/o voices call into question collective fictions that regulate performances of gender, sexuality, and cultural identity. I offer readings of nine U.S. Latina/o novels, focusing on key identity issues: gay and lesbian sensibilities in works by Chicana/o writers; the rejection of exile mentality and development of a U.S. Cuban ethnic voice; the emergence of an ethnic consciousness in Puerto Rican and Dominican immigrant novels; and the relationship between stylistic imitation ("magical realism") and Latina/o culture. I show how these novels support the notion that cultural identity is located in the tension between tradition and collective fictions, and the performativity of everyday life. My readings indicate that what has been viewed as Chicana/o, Puerto Rican, Cuban, or Latina/o cultural "essence," both from within the ethnic communities and from without, is in fact a construct.

Chapter 2 highlights the Chicano/a gay/lesbian problematic in novels by John Rechy and Sheila Ortiz Taylor. In Rechy's *City of Night* (1963) and Ortiz Taylor's *Faultline* (1982) and *Southbound* (1990), gay and lesbian characters transgress cultural norms of both American dominant society and the Chicana/o community. As Chicana lesbian critics have observed, because homosexuality subverts patriarchal family structure and binary gender constructs, it is perceived as a threat to the unity of the Chicana/o community.[34] Moreover, there is considerable evidence that Anglocentric gay communities tend to interpret ethnic difference as excess.[35] These thought-provoking novels suggest that Chicano/a gay and lesbian identities are constituted through performances that reflect shifting identifications with a variety of communities. The characters' constant negotiation among subject positions challenges the exclusivity of oppositions such as masculine/feminine, exile/ethnic, and homosexual/heterosexual. Although these works emphasize gay and lesbian issues, ultimately the novels deconstruct the very notions of gender and cultural essence. Rechy's and Ortiz Taylor's fiction proposes that identity cannot be articulated in terms of stable, definable parameters but must be viewed instead as a continuous series of performances.

Chapter 3 shows the close correlation between gender and cultural identity in two U.S. Cuban novels, Oscar Hijuelos's *The Mambo Kings Play Songs of Love* (1989) and Elías Miguel Muñoz's *The Greatest Performance* (1991). These works portray prescribed performances of gender excess (hypermasculinity and hyperfemininity) as intrinsic to middle-class U.S. Cuban cultural tradition. In *The Greatest Performance*, Cuban authenticity is predicated on adherence to strictly defined gender roles. The novel's gay and lesbian protagonists challenge the émigré community's paradigm of cultural identity by subverting these constructs of masculinity and femininity. In Hijuelos's paean to machismo, the immigrant protagonist's near-obsessive acting out of the "Latin Lover" role points to the inaccessibility of essential masculinity and Cubanness. At the end of *The Greatest Performance*, the two characters incorporate their Cuban cultural heritage into a subversive drag fantasy. This fantasy, and the endlessly repeated phallocentric performances by the protagonist of *Mambo Kings*, support a reading of "authentic" Cubanness as a drag show that parodies the notion of essentialized identities.

Chapter 4 focuses on two finely crafted novels by Latina (im)migrant writers Judith Ortiz Cofer (*The Line of the Sun*, 1989) and Julia Alvarez (*How the García Girls Lost Their Accents*, 1991). These works deal with assimilation and the immigrant generation's adoption of dominant cultural values; performances of identity are influenced by the relative importance of "passing" as American. The novels highlight the performativity of both Puerto Rican/Dominican cultural identity and ethnic American identity, neither of which is depicted as fixed. The dominant norms mentioned above are the standard against which the characters' ethnic excess is measured. Their total assimilation is impeded by the persistence of cultural markers: flamboyant or unfashionable clothing; loud, boisterous *salsa* music; inability to speak standard, unaccented English; non-white physical features; preservation of an idealized, mythical notion of the homeland and originary cultural identity.

Both Ortiz Cofer's and Alvarez's novels are narrated by immigrant daughters, which produces an interesting generational dynamic. These narrators represent their parents as wholehearted, unquestioning advocates of complete assimilation, while emphasizing their own struggle to negotiate between cultures and languages. In spite of the parents' efforts to eliminate telltale signs of ethnic excess, their performances ultimately mark them as outsiders. The daughters' experiences of assimilation and the cultural issues it generates move them to explore identity through writing. Their awareness of the writing process in turn leads them to a deeper understanding of the ongoing invention of ethnic identity and culture.

The fifth and final chapter illustrates how "magical realism" and other stylistic codes, like the gender and cultural performances discussed in the previous chapters, can be read as indicators of Latina/o essence. This chapter focuses on two novels by Chicanas: Cecile Pineda's *The Love Queen of the Amazon* (1992), and Ana Castillo's *So Far from God* (1993). I contextualize these works by exploring the recent proliferation of media attention on magical realism in U.S. Latina/o fiction, a phenomenon that I argue has been influenced by the essentializing tendencies of mainstream publishers and reviewers. In large part because of the widespread popularity of Latin American Boom fiction, magical realism has come to be viewed as emblematic of Latina/o culture. Thus the mystical and miraculous occurrences that appear in numerous U.S. Latina/o texts reinforce the connection between U.S. Latina/o and Latin American literatures.

Such a connection is at best tenuous, and at worst nonexistent. Close readings of these two novels confirm that their imitation of aesthetic codes associated with Latin American literature does not reflect an underlying Latina/o essence. On the contrary, both *The Love Queen of the Amazon* and *So Far from God* resemble textual drag shows: Writing is the medium for repetitive performances that are ostensibly manifestations of originary Latina/o cultural identity. As Butler asserts, drag purports to perform femininity yet ultimately points to the inaccessibility of feminine essence. These novels, likewise, appear to reaffirm their essential "Latino-ness" ad infinitum—through the proliferation of magical realist episodes and Latin American historical figures in *Love Queen*, through the accumulation of markers of *chicanismo* in *So Far from God*. The necessity of endlessly repeated performances, of excess, reveals that cultural essence is elusive. In *Love Queen*, the Peruvian narrator attempts to capture the totality of Latin American culture in a written text—and fails resoundingly. *So Far from God* can be read as an anti-essentialist project as well, even though the Chicana narrator's primary concern is to rescue her community's endangered cultural tradition from oblivion. Her critique of the community's collective fictions, along with her pastichelike incorporation of signs of Chicano/Latino culture, articulate a challenge to binary paradigms of ethnic identity and resistance.

Clearly the U.S. Latina/o novels included in this project deal with diverse themes, which are developed by means of a variety of narrative techniques. My objective is to show both the similarities in the works' approaches to the problematic of Latina/o culture and identity, and the unique contributions each one makes. I recognize that grouping the novels according to their writers' ancestry—Puerto Rican, Dominican, Chicana/o, Cuban—risks the same kind of essentialism that I try to challenge throughout this study. I believe, nevertheless, that the identification of commonalities, of connections among works, writers, and literatures, need not result in static, homogenizing definitions. My intention in this study is not to divide U.S. Latina/o fiction into rigid, artificial categories. Rather, my organizational strategy acknowledges the pervasiveness of the cultural identity constructs that have been read as Chicana/o or Cuban-American or Puerto Rican essence. By recognizing and questioning these constructs, I support my view of U.S. Latina/o identity as an ongoing process of invention involving cultural heritage, gender roles, and dynamic interaction with American dominant culture. The value of this model lies in its flexibility, for it neither ghettoizes Latina/o culture nor treats the concept of ethnic difference as obsolete. My hope is that this approach to U.S. Latina/o fiction and identity enriches the texts and stimulates the careful reading by an attentive audience that these fine works deserve.

TWO

INVISIBLE CHICANOS

*Gay and Lesbian Identities in the Fiction
of Sheila Ortiz Taylor and John Rechy*

In the world through which I travel,
I am endlessly creating myself.
— FRANTZ FANON,
Black Skin, White Masks

In the previous chapter, I discussed the potentially significant relationship between paradigms of cultural identity and ethnic literary criticism. In the case of Chicana/o literature, this relationship has become more visible as critics have acknowledged "dissenting" voices that challenge dominant narratives of Chicana/o culture and identity.[1] Gay and lesbian Chicano/a writers and their texts, for example, articulate subject positions that operate as counternarratives to essentialist gender norms. In so doing, these gay and lesbian voices point to the ongoing process of negotiation — the endless creation of self, to paraphrase Fanon — that is intrinsic to cultural identity.

The formulation and projection of a unified collective identity as a strategy for gaining political power was an integral part of the civil rights movements of the 1960s. Unfortunately, these identity politics created hierarchies of oppression within the groups themselves. The cultural nationalism that was the Chicano Movement's most visible ideological position tended to promote a static view of culture and uncritical affirmation of family and gender roles (Yarbro-Bejarano 1986, 390). Although the Movement achieved the important goals of giving a unified voice to an oppressed minority and bringing attention to Chicano culture and experience, Chicanas frequently found themselves excluded from decision-making processes. As the Chicanas attending a special women's workshop at the 1970 Mexican American National Issues Conference declared, "The effort of Chicana/

Mexican women in the Chicano movement is generally obscured because women are not accepted as community leaders" (Vidal 133). Angie Chabrám-Dernersesian describes these women who destroyed the illusory harmony of Chicano identity:

> These were the Chicanas who replaced the discourses of compadres and carnalismo with the discourses of comadres (sisters) and feminismo (feminists), macho with hembra, and fiercely combated male domination in the leadership of the Chicano Movement and the political life of the community (84).

In the ensuing years Chicanas have only gradually gained access to power structures and modes of cultural production.[2]

The resistance encountered by Chicanas, and by U.S. Latinas in general, to their participation in the political and cultural spheres of their communities has its foundation in the challenge to patriarchal family structure and traditional gender roles that these women's work represents. In the introduction to *Chicana Lesbians: The Girls Our Mothers Warned Us About,* Carla Trujillo remarks that "as Chicanas, we grow up defined, and subsequently confined, in a male context: daddy's girl, some guy's sister, girlfriend, wife, or mother" (ix). As Chicana feminists have pointed out, Chicanas who articulate a subject position not based on male-centered definitions of female identity have been judged traitors, *vendidas,* or *malinchistas* who have allied themselves with the dominant culture. In a 1971 article, Francisca Flores forcefully critiqued what she called the "Chicano philosophy," which holds that the role of women is as mother to a large family: "Women who do not accept this philosophy are charged with betrayal of 'our culture and heritage.' OUR CULTURE HELL!" (Vidal 137). Thus writing by Chicanas challenges androcentric identity politics that make Chicana subjectivity "culturally unintelligible."[3]

By arguing that gender cannot be excised from ethnicity, Latina feminists call for the revision of monolithic views of Latina/o identity. Chicano/a gay and lesbian subjectivities subvert (hetero)sexist cultural norms even more radically; literary critics and popular opinion alike have denied the very existence of these identities. Gloria Anzaldúa eloquently describes this erasure, declaring that "[t]he lesbian of color is not only invisible, she doesn't even exist. Our speech, too, is inaudible. We speak in tongues like the outcast and the insane" (Moraga and Anzaldúa 165). The Latino male supposedly enjoys greater sexual freedom than his female counterpart. Evidence gathered by sociologist Tomás Almaguer shows, however, that gay Latinos must reconcile their sexual identity with their primary socialization into "a Latino culture that does not recognize such a construction: there is no cultural equivalent to the modern 'gay man' in the Mexican/Latin-American sexual system" (75).[4] Clearly the intersection of Latina/o subjectivity with sexuality is a space of shifting allegiances and of invisibility. I will briefly discuss attempts that have been made to theorize Chicano/a gay/lesbian identity before examining these subjectivities in fictional works.

THE "INVISIBILITY" OF CHICANA LESBIANS AND GAY CHICANOS

The writings of Anzaldúa, Almaguer, Cherríe Moraga, and other cultural critics offer provocative theories about the factors that make Chicano/a gay and lesbian identities unintelligible according to cultural norms. In their battle against sexual oppression in their communities, Latina feminists have challenged a cultural tradition that fails to validate or even recognize female sexuality. Ana Castillo asserts in "La Macha: Toward a Beautiful Whole Self" that Latinas indoctrinated with traditional Catholic mandates learn to associate their sexuality with evil. Thus acknowledging female desire of any kind would imply sinfulness and decadence:

A sexual woman was a woman begging rape, begging vulnerability to society. . . . [I]f one admitted to her sexuality, she was uncovering the disguise that she alone knew she had worn as the "decent" woman, the "good girl." (26)

For Chicana lesbians, then, the repression of female sexuality dictated by Catholic convention is tantamount to negation of their identity.

Likewise, Cherríe Moraga writes in *Loving in the War Years* of the difficulty encountered by Chicanas in general in developing an autonomous sense of self and of female sexuality in particular. Moraga observes that the Chicana lesbian is left in a quandary, for her upbringing works to erase her very identity (103). Moraga concurs with Castillo in concluding that considering the pressure from religious doctrine and cultural tradition, "[i]t is no wonder that Chicanas often divorce ourselves from conscious recognition of our own sexuality" (119).[5] Norma Alarcón reaches a similar conclusion in her exploration of the influence of La Malinche iconography on Chicanas. Alarcón argues that through the continued portrayal of La Malinche as having betrayed her people through sex, Chicanas may come to believe that their sexuality condemns them to enslavement and self-hatred (1983, 183).

In addition to the repression of female sexuality described by these feminists, the powerful influence of family in many U.S. Latina/o communities makes lesbianism an unacceptable subject position. The patriarchal order that is portrayed and critiqued in much Latina cultural production constructs the identity of Latinas in relation to men: as daughters, *novias,* wives, mothers. The Chicana lesbian, Trujillo asserts, is to some extent an extreme Chicana feminist: "By being lesbians, we refuse to *need* a man to form our own identities as women. This constitutes a 'rebellion' many Chicanas/os cannot handle" (ix). It should be noted that the repression described by Moraga, Castillo, and Trujillo is not unique to Chicana/o culture. Lesbian sexuality is generally viewed as excessive in patriarchal societies, for it represents a threat to the male-dominated heterosexual order.[6]

Latina lesbians' opposition to these roles threatens to destroy the balance of power upon which the family unit depends. By rejecting conventional family structure, Latino/a gays and lesbians may be seen as undermining a significant source of cultural unity and resistance to Anglo oppression. Almaguer comments that

> any deviation from the sacred link binding husband, wife, and child not only threatens the very existence of *la familia* but also potentially undermines the mainstay of resistance to Anglo racism and class exploitation (90).

In other words, the Chicana/o family can only present a unified front against Anglo domination if traditional gender roles are maintained. Numerous Chicanas have recounted experiences that indicate that lesbianism and solidarity with Chicana/o culture are viewed as mutually exclusive political positions. Moraga claims, for example, that a Chicana's sexual commitment to Chicano men is regarded as proof of her loyalty to her people (105), while Castillo has encountered negative reactions by many Chicanos to homoerotic content in her writing. Such readers, Castillo surmises, are unable to reconcile lesbianism with commitment to the culture; heterosexual Chicanas in particular have accused her of "copping out" from "the struggle with the family or the illusion of male/female love" ("La Macha" 118).

Chicana lesbians are caught in the crossfire of a battle between sexual and cultural identity, for these women can never be "just lesbians" or "just Chicanas." Instead, factors such as skin color, class, life experiences, and their own "performances" influence the configuration that their identity assumes.

In her poem "Trying to be Dyke and Chicana," Natashia López describes this struggle with vivid sensory images:

Dyk-ana
Dyk-icana
what do i call myself
people want a name
a label a product
what's the first ingredient
the dominant ingredient
can you taste Chicana
or smell Dyke . . . (Trujillo 84)

In the poem's final line, López proclaims a new identity through the neologism "Chyk-ana," revealing how Chicana lesbian subjectivity is forged through writing.

The silence shrouding the issue of Chicano/Latino gay identity is currently far greater than that surrounding the problematic of Chicana lesbians. There has been published as yet no theoretical work on gay Chicano/Latino identity that offers the kind of insights that the writings of Moraga, Anzaldúa, Castillo, and other Latinas have afforded. Almaguer endeavors to begin unpacking the complex factors involved in the articulation of Chicano gay identity in his article "Chicano Men: A Cartography of Homosexual Identity and Behavior." Almaguer attributes the apparent absence of a parallel to the Anglo-American gay man in Chicano/Latino culture to the powerful influence of prevailing Latin American paradigms of gender and sexuality. Almaguer's research on homosexuality in Latin America seems to indicate that for Latino men sexual identity is assigned on the basis of sexual aim, not object choice (77). Thus a man may be *activo* — the anal penetrator, who is not stigmatized because his behavior is considered part of "normal" male sexuality — or *pasivo* — the anal-passive individual, who is viewed as subservient and feminized (78).[7] Almaguer observes that "[u]nlike in the North American context, 'one drop of homosexuality' does not, ipso facto, make a Mexican male a *joto* or a *maricón*" (84).

The fact that Almaguer's postulations are based on ethnographic studies of homosexuality in Latin America makes his theorization of *Chicano* gay identity problematic. Nevertheless, the treatment of Latino homosexuality in a variety of novels suggests that the perceptions that Almaguer highlights circulate among Latinos in the United States as well.[8] Moraga's observations support Almaguer's theory. She claims that among Chicanos, the predominant attitude toward the feminized *loca*/queen is contempt for his transgression of patriarchal cultural standards; he is seen as having consciously chosen "a role his culture tells him to despise. That of a woman" (111). Expressly gay Chicano identity in any other form is thus as culturally unintelligible according to traditional Latina/o gender constructs as Chicana lesbian identity. As the character Eduviges in Arturo Islas's *Migrant Souls* declares, upon being told that her brother Felix was killed by a young man he had tried to seduce, "I don't believe a word of it. There are no homosexuals" (121).

By living in the United States, gay Latino males are ostensibly offered a wider range of options with regard to sexual identity. The negotiation between concurrent membership in two minority groups nonetheless presents unique problems. Almaguer points out that gays who are members of ethnic minorities often must distance themselves from the traditional support systems of family and religion in order to integrate into predominantly white, middle-class American gay communities. Marginalization of Latino/a, black, and Asian-American gays and lesbians in American gay communities shows that racial difference cannot be so easily effaced (see chapter 1, note 35). At the same time, the prevailing Latina/o norms of gender and sexual identity discussed earlier — closely associated with cultural loyalty — entangle gay Chicanos in a perplexing web of conflicting forces and untenable options.

Based on the previous observations, it is evident that the existence of gay and lesbian Chicanos creates a knotty problem for monolithic models of identity. On one hand, gay/lesbian subject positions challenge the heterosexism of Chicano nationalism; on the other, Chicano/a subjectivity destabilizes Anglocentric gay/lesbian identity constructs. The effects of these competing subjectivities are visible in cultural production, where identity is constantly being performed and transformed. In the Chicana/o cultural sphere, numerous literary works allude to the intersections of ethnicity, gender, and sexuality in ways that have yet to be thoroughly examined and theorized.[9] Through my readings of Sheila Ortiz Taylor's and John Rechy's novels, I will show how gay and lesbian voices call attention to the performative aspect of Chicana/o identity.

The postulation that gay and lesbian subjectivity has implications for Chicana/o cultural identity finds a parallel in Judith Butler's work in feminist theory. Butler argues that, in general, gay/lesbian identities undermine the coherence of gender identity categories and reveal the performative nature of gender. Her model, an alternative to ethnic identity paradigms that cannot accommodate diversity, treats identity as process rather than as stable essence. This allows for diversity and change within the overarching category, in this case, Chicana/o identity.[10] Viewing identity as constituted through an ongoing series of performative acts acknowledges both changing historical conditions and shifting subject positions of ethnic group members. The notion of identity as performance should not conjure up the image of a faceless, amorphous being, bereft of identity, going to the closet and selecting and donning identity accoutrements according to his/her/its whim of the moment. As George Lipsitz has observed, in ethnic communities "[s]ubject positions may be fluid, multiple, and open, but they are not infinitely fluid, multiple, or open. At every turn they are constrained by past and present power relations."[11]

In my use of the concept of performance, I take these power relations into account by considering the significance of dominant cultural norms. As I pointed out in chapter 1, dress, traditions, behaviors, and language associated with Latina/o cultural heritage operate as performative acts that the dominant culture has identified as signs of ethnic excess. More subtly, skin color and other physical features in which agency is not involved become performances of racial excess in relation to the dominant "norm" of whiteness. For the Anglo-American majority — the dominant "audience" — racial and linguistic difference are as much performances of ethnic excess as is the practice of ethnic traditions.

Michel Foucault's theory of subject formation suggests societal implications of these performances of excess. Foucault argues that institutions and power structures are not established in response to the need to contain preexisting transgressive subjects, but rather that these systems of power in fact constitute the subjects they come to represent.[12] In American society, the dominant group judges the performative acts emanating from minority groups to be "excessive" in relation to arbitrary societal norms. These performances in turn produce the illusion of a preexisting, essential subjectivity (Chicana/o, black, gay/lesbian, and so on). Throughout this book, I argue that this view of cultural identity as static and monolithic should be questioned. Although ethnic identity is not simply free-wheeling performance, it does involve perpetual reinvention and modification.

The relative invisibility of Chicano/a gay and lesbian voices hints at the threat to culturally inflected gender constructs that these identities represent. A variety of Chicana/o writers have shattered the silence by representing homosexuality, what Cindy Patton calls the "unrepresentable," "the unspeakable, the perceived but best not said" (34). The fictional works of Chicanos Sheila Ortiz Taylor and John Rechy boldly explore this dangerous territory at the intersection of Chicano/a and gay/lesbian subjectivities. The gay and lesbian performances in Ortiz Taylor's *Faultline* and *Southbound* and Rechy's *City of Night* highlight the multifaceted and ever-changing character of identity.

SHEILA ORTIZ TAYLOR: "COMING OUT"
AS CHICANA AND THE ETHNIC CLOSET

You insult me
When you say I'm
Schizophrenic.
My divisions are
Infinite.
— BERNICE ZAMORA, "So Not To Be Mottled"

Sheila Ortiz Taylor is a self-identified lesbian writer of Chicana background who has published three engaging novels, a book of memoirs, and a collection of poetry.[13] Critics of Chicana/o literature generally have not included her works in their studies, in part because her writing foregrounds lesbian identity while traditional signs of Chicana/o cultural identity are less prominent. Ortiz Taylor mentions her Mexican-American background in the introduction to her first novel, and Chicana/o culture plays a significant role in her third. Overall, however, her writing does not appear to express substantive identification with a Chicana/o community/problematic and could be categorized as "lesbian" fiction. Ortiz Taylor is thus a controversial figure in Chicana/o literature, a "late-blooming Chicana"[14] who has recently made ethnic identity a focus of her work.

Gay and lesbian ethnic writers like Sheila Ortiz Taylor present a problem for those critics who rely on identity classifications that disregard intersections between categories. Ortiz Taylor's works suggest that identity cannot be so cleanly split into mutually exclusive fragments but rather involves constant negotiation and movement among various subject positions. In her first novel, *Faultline* (1982), protagonist Arden Benbow is a divorced lesbian mother of six who is struggling to win custody of her children. The text comprises a series of narratives about Arden by her friends, family, and acquaintances, interspersed with Arden's own commentary. The story of Arden's youth, marriage, and subsequent relationship with the wife of her husband's best friend unfolds through the reports of these "character witnesses." Her ex-husband, the man who supplies her with feed for her 300 rabbits, her live-in nanny (a black drag queen), an elderly former showgirl who owns a trailer park in Mexico, the social worker sent to investigate Arden's suitability as a mother, and a variety of other characters all provide first-person testimonial accounts.

Faultline is in many ways a typical lesbian coming-out novel, for it focuses on the protagonist's trajectory from a traditional heterosexual marriage to her first lesbian relationship. The very concept of "coming out," which implies a simultaneous theatrical entrance and confessional act through which homosexuality is made visible, supports a performative model of Anglo-American homosexual identity. In *Epistemology of the Closet*, Eve Sedgwick explores this notion of coming out as performance and the role of coming out in the constitution of homosexual subjectivity ("the relations of the known and the unknown, the explicit and the inexplicit around homo/heterosexual definition" [3]). In Ortiz Taylor's novels, there is constant play between "the known and the unknown, the explicit and the inexplicit" of both sexuality and ethnic identity. Near the beginning of *Faultline*, Arden offers a testimonial in which she describes the process through which she came to acknowledge that she was a lesbian. "I did not spring from my mother's loins a lesbian," she declares, "though I have met in the past year or two several promising young women who believe they did" (3). Arden was able to perform as a lesbian only after breaking free of the powerful influence of compulsory heterosexuality, to which she had assumed there was no alternative. This prevailing societal norm manifests itself in the subconscious of properly conditioned women of Arden's generation in the form of an "unattractive person in . . . white gloves, dressed like an Avon lady, [who] exists in any woman who did not spring from her mother's loins as a fully constituted lesbian" (4). Thanks to the policing of this white-gloved model of convention, Arden dutifully accepts the role of wife and mother and continues to perform as a heterosexual until she recognizes and acts upon her desire for Alice.

In *Southbound*, the hilarious 1990 sequel to *Faultline*, Arden Benbow has made a home with her unconventional family—her lover Alice, six children, nanny Topaz Wilson, and three hundred rabbits. This household continues the legacy of the "pioneer family" that Ortiz Taylor proposed in her 1985 novel *Spring Forward/Fall Back*. This pioneer family (a lesbian couple, a single mother and her daughter in *Spring Forward/Fall Back*) is a utopian, multigenerational, nonheterosexist community of people joined together for mutual support and nurturance. As described by one of the characters in *Spring Forward,* such a family "doesn't need to be exclusive. Or even stable, for that matter" (96). In *Southbound*, Arden's pioneer family must respond to the challenge of change when the protagonist reluctantly begins seeking a teaching position and faces the prospect of leaving Los Angeles. Arden survives a series of calamities on the way to interview at the Modern Language Convention and is offered a teaching position at a college in Florida. After she accepts the job, she sets out for Florida with Topaz to find a house for the family, and the comical adventures of "Operation Southbound" begin.

In *Southbound*, Arden no longer attempts to impersonate a heterosexual, but she is frequently reminded that performing as a lesbian is still unacceptable within some circles. After losing her luggage en route to the convention, she half-seriously threatens to wear a friend's grass-stained baseball pants to her job interview the following day:

> "They'll think you're a lesbian," said Alice.
> "I *am* a lesbian," I said.
> "You won't want them to think so just yet, dear. It's not politic. Not if you're serious about getting a job." (124)

Alice's comment alludes to the popular notion of a lesbian essence that manifests itself through the identifiable look of the stereotypical, softball-playing butch. The necessity of "cross-dressing" as a heterosexual in order to gain access to employment (i.e., economic power) requires Arden to temporarily efface any signs by which the dominant culture could read her as a lesbian.

In addition to *Southbound*'s focus on the struggles of Arden and Alice's unusual family, the novel might also be considered to some extent Ortiz Taylor's "Chicana coming out story."[15] As mentioned earlier, the author introduces *Faultline* with a brief autobiography in which she comments, "The family I knew in Los Angeles was my mother's family, thirteen children presided over by my Mexican-American grandmother, who made flour tortillas so thin you could read a book through them." In *Southbound*, Arden's impending move from Los Angeles — her birthplace and the heart of her family history — prompts a series of recollections that bring her own Chicana heritage into focus. In the chapter titled "Dropping By," Arden and her teenage daughter Jamie pay a brief visit to the house where Arden's mother and twelve brothers and sisters grew up. Arden reminisces about her own childhood visits to the house; in retrospect she is able to identify ethnic performances that distinguished her Chicana/o relatives from the Anglo-American mainstream. She recalls her great aunts, "speaking Spanish so fast it sang around my head like a thousand swooping birds, while they patted thin the flour tortillas as big as my head, or rolled up masa inside corn husks" (41).

The end of this passage hints at Arden's experience as an assimilated Chicana, performing ethnic difference through acts of memory in spite of earlier generations' attempts to erase the past. "Never look back," the favorite phrase of Arden's uncle Ukie, encapsulates the ideology of assimilation that Arden rejects by telling the family history:

> Never look back . . . the family philosophy. For six generations they had wandered through Southern California on their Spanish land grant . . . never recording, never claiming, until finally they had finished here in this small house, unsure even to whom it now belonged. (42)

This incident highlights the tension between the historical component of cultural identity—in this case, Arden's family roots—and the temporality of culture, for which the relatives' wandering is a fitting metaphor.

Outwardly Arden appears to have assimilated completely, yet her mother is a constant reminder of the fragility of any claim to fixed cultural identity. Arden's mother has worked hard to become Americanized and believes that through language she can establish her identity once and for all. She has no interest whatsoever in speaking Spanish with Arden's father:

> He liked to sit in her mother's kitchen and practice his Spanish. . . . But as a young woman my mother was simply not willing to sit in her mother's kitchen and learn Spanish after having assiduously not learned it for twenty-five years. (51)

Even more telling is Arden's mother's insistence on manipulating identity labels in order to disclaim her ancestry: " 'We are not Mexicans,' she would say. 'We are not Indians. We are Early Californians' " (51). By denying her ethnicity, the mother subscribes to the assimilationist ideology that promotes erasure of one's "foreign" cultural heritage. In spite of her mother's desire to "never look back" to the family's Chicana/o past, Arden finds it important to know who these mysterious aunts and uncles were, where they came from, why they spoke Spanish. Although Arden's primary identification appears to be as an "Anglocized" lesbian, by seeking out and telling the story of the family's assimilation she performs ethnicity indirectly. Just as Arden's search for her family history produces a series of performances of Chicana/o identity, Ortiz Taylor "comes out" as a Chicana through the writing of these two novels.

In *Southbound*, Arden also establishes connections with her ethnic past by learning to prepare traditional foods, a ritual that is one of the most widely practiced means of affirming ethnic identity. William Boelhower maintains that for the ethnic subject, this type of apprenticeship has significance beyond the simple acquisition of a skill, for it involves "a representative symbolic perspective of food, a common store of ethnic wisdom, maxims, and folklore, [and] a shared cultural passion" (115). Arden's grandmother teaches her how to make special enchiladas, built up in layers like "archaeological levels in an ancient dig" (68). This assessment is particularly apt, for through the enchilada-making Arden ensures the survival of an ethnic tradition for another generation while simultaneously carrying out her own archaeological investigation of her ethnic heritage. Later, during an afternoon spent learning to make tamales from her mother, she recalls her grandmother and great-aunts "[turning] out tamales like they were on an assembly line" and telling stories in such rapid Spanish that Arden "could only pick out a word here and there" (145).

Ostensibly Arden wants to learn to make tamales so that she can prepare them herself after she moves to Florida. On an unconscious level, she may be responding to the impending loss of the last tenuous connections to her ancestral culture, a loss that exile from her family home represents. It is also significant that this exile will take Arden to a university English department. Until recently, these departments were notorious antiethnicity enclaves where upholding the Anglo-American canon resulted in almost total disregard for the literatures of minority writers. Arden will thus face a struggle for acceptance by colleagues who view as superfluous — as excess — the ethnic difference that she has come to celebrate.

Arden's tracing of her ethnic roots does not seem to be an attempt to recapture a mythical Chicana/o past or origin, for she cannot impede the historical transformations of which she is a product. Instead, Arden will live ethnicity in the present in a new configuration, negotiating between her Chicana/o cultural heritage and the dominant Anglo-American culture. Each Thanksgiving she introduces diversity into the customary American feast by preparing enchiladas, which she refers to as "our family history" (68). When a dinner guest asks her what they are, she explains that her family always ate enchiladas at Thanksgiving "because we're Chicanos on my mother's side." Alluding to her experience of becoming aware of ethnic difference, she adds, "I didn't realize until I married that other people didn't eat them too" (69). Had Arden's enchiladas been just one part of a traditional Chicana/o feast, the event would serve to build ethnic solidarity, as Boelhower comments: "The feast generically functions as an act of historical synthesis in which each participant feels integrated into the semiotic space of his ethnic culture" (116). The enchiladas, on the other hand, are a foreign element added to an otherwise conventional American menu. As a kind of performance viewed as "exotic" from the dominant (Anglo) perspective, the enchiladas call attention to Arden's ethnicity.

MAKING AND BREAKING CONNECTIONS: THE ILLUSION OF IDENTITY

Faultline and *Southbound* are problematic as ethnic Latina texts because they foreground lesbian subjectivity, while their ethnic signs and performances are less apparent. Both novels repeatedly hint that appearances are deceptive, that one's identity has more to do with performative acts than with biological essence. In *Spring Forward/Fall Back,* a character comments about homosexuals that "[y]ou could be standing right next to one and never know it" (191). Both *Faultline* and *Southbound* suggest that there is truth beyond the obvious homophobia in this statement. If sexual orientation and other identity markers — race and ethnicity in particular — cannot consistently be recognized, then categories like "white" and "heterosexual" can no longer be considered exclusive. The phenomenon of passing and historical debate on race designations offer a clear indication of the instability of these categories. Gays and lesbians passing as straight, as well as members of racial and ethnic minority groups passing as Anglo-American, make the composition of all such groups indeterminate at any given moment.[16]

The move to "deassimilate" that is articulated in *Southbound* may be read as Arden's attempt to recuperate a sense of Chicana/o heritage diminished through years of passing as a "nonethnic" American. For in spite of the access to social privilege that passing confers, those who can and do pass inhabit a space which Michelle Cliff describes as "the penumbra of the eclipse . . . the half-darkness" (45). Mirtha Quintanales, a light-skinned Cuban-American lesbian, expresses the alienation that can accompany passing:

But is [passing] really a privilege when it always means having to become invisible, ghost-like, identity-less, community-less, totally alienated? . . . It should be easy enough at least for *lesbians* to understand the meaning of being and yet not being, of "merging" and yet remaining utterly alone and in the margins of our society. (Moraga and Anzaldúa 154)

This correspondence between passing and invisibility is also an important focus of Peggy Phelan's essays in *Unmarked: The Politics of Performance.* Phelan asserts that the "normative" and unmarked nature of heterosexual identity is affirmed by the efforts of many gays and lesbians to pass as straight. She adds that

[i]t is easy to pass as heterosexual because heterosexuality is assumed. . . . The one who passes then does not 'erase' the mark of difference, rather the passer highlights the invisibility of the mark of the Same. (96)

Likewise, assimilation by ethnic group members (i.e., passing as white/"nonethnic" Americans) highlights the invisibility that disappearing into the dominant culture offers. Arden, on the other hand, reverses the traditional immigrant trajectory, thereby giving herself ethnic visibility. Like her protagonist, Ortiz Taylor reclaims Chicana identity through the writing of *Faultline* and

Southbound; these novels in turn broaden the visible spectrum of Chicana/o experience.

In addition to the constant play between ethnic visibility and the invisibility of assimilation in the novels, the characters' sexual orientation is often ambiguous. A variety of supposedly heterosexual characters acknowledge and act upon their attractions for people of the same sex. In *Faultline,* a former rest home orderly and a private investigator (neither of whom has previously shown gay inclinations) are brought together by a series of events involving Arden. Maurio and Michael soon find that they have fallen in love, and they make an announcement to that effect at a dinner party with Arden and friends:

[Michael] wanted us to know that improbable as it seemed he and Maurio were silly in love and very happy, wanting us to share their silliness, their happiness, and not to think it was odd or against nature or criminal or reprehensible or ungrateful. (76)

In *Southbound,* likewise, the fianceé of Arden's ex-husband Malthus suddenly breaks their engagement and decides to join a community of lesbian potters. Slippage between identity categories is a pervasive motif in both *Faultline* and *Southbound* and is presented as a positive force that allows full expression of the multiple facets of one's identity.

Ortiz Taylor's novels propose that the construction of subjectivity always involves shifting identifications that are made visible through performative acts. This movement, in turn, reveals the fallacy in treating "gay," "lesbian," "Chicana/o," and other identities as static and/or monolithic. In both *Faultline* and *Southbound,* identity is constituted through a continuous process of formation and fragmentation of diverse communities (of Chicanos, academics, lesbians, Tupperware ladies, and so forth). Arden's search for her roots does not lead her to believe in the accessibility of a mythical Chicana/o cultural essence; on the contrary, she finds that she is perpetually defining herself through the making and breaking of connections with a variety of communities.

The view of identity developed and articulated in these novels is not wholly anti-essentialist, for Arden acknowledges that communities are often defined according to standards of cultural authenticity. Feeling uprooted and alone on her trip to Florida, for example, she seeks comfort through a "fix" of Mexican food: "Now this soup spoke to me . . . the opaque crescents of simmered celery floating docilely near a bed of fresh cilantro suggested authenticity. . . . I plunged my big spoon into that healing soup" (189).

Yet Arden's gastronomical bonding with her ancestral culture, which she achieves by consuming a bowl of *albóndiga* soup, reflects only one facet of her identity. In *Faultline,* the multiple narrative voices all participate in the fabrication of "Arden Benbow" by providing a variety of perspectives on her character. Each narrator has observed particular performances that have created for him/her an image of who Arden is. The fact that none of these narrators, including even Arden herself, can capture the totality of the protagonist's "true" persona underscores the inaccessibility of "essence."

The novel's motif of the faultline and the shifting associated with it are symbolic of this process of evolution. Movement along a faultline (the San Andreas fault) indirectly catalyzes Arden's and Alice's relationship; while providing mutual support for each other following an earthquake the two women finally acknowledge that they have fallen in love. As Alice reflects, "Things would have gone on in this quietly disappointing way as long as there was no slip, no shock to fling us out of the ways of custom and into the ways of innovation and creation" (98). In both geological and emotional terms, the earth moves, precipitating a visible shift in sexual orientation for both Arden and Alice. The two women begin "performing" as lesbians; it is impossible to determine if they simply became lesbians at this point or if they were always lesbians.

Southbound likewise emphasizes this kind of mutability; as Arden muses,

Doors were beginnings and endings. Through them the same person could not pass — come to think of it — twice. Because the person would be different on the return trip. Even the door would be different, having sloughed off or rearranged some of its molecules and door atoms. (108–9)

The numerous mishaps and incidents of mistaken identity that Arden experiences on the way to the Modern Language Convention confirm that for those who can "pass," the self is an ongoing series of performances. Her friend Allison Honey summarizes Arden's identity crisis:

"First, she's Arden Benbow. Right? But she arrives wearing her mother's suit, a scarf belonging to somebody named Tom, carrying Aunt Vi's cane, and Alice's purse. The luggage of a party named Ruth has gone on to Seattle without her. Now phone calls from people named Muffie for somebody named Teddie, who is really Arden." I stared. She was right. My identity had taken on the texture and substance of Play Doh (121).

This situation is a comical illustration of the process whereby the same individual occupies a variety of subject positions and performs accordingly. Arden's experience demonstrates the shifting between communities, the Play Doh-like malleability, that characterizes identity.[17]

Later in *Southbound,* Arden's recollection of a favorite Hollywood classic film offers yet another apt metaphor for the self. The scene from *Flying Down to Rio* that she recalls involves biplanes, circling above a hotel on opening night, with showgirls tap dancing on the wings. Suddenly it occurs to Arden that perhaps each individual is "the sum total of all the tap dancers perched on the biplane of self" (174). This whimsical image of performance, movement, and risk hints at the limitless possible configurations that identity may assume if it is regarded as a journey, as a process of discovery, as "the creation of a personal significance" (*Southbound* 174).

The primary problem that this model presents for critics of ethnic literature is that it negates the possibility of parameters that would enable ethnic identity to be clearly defined. Yet seeking a "correct" or "authentic" ideological stance or expression of minority subjectivity is to immunize it from the play of history and the effects of constantly evolving power relations. Chicana/o culture encompasses a broad array of ideologies and performances, some of which have been made visible through the cultural production of Chicana/o artists. A recurring topic of debate among critics is the type of connection to Chicana/o tradition that a writer must retain in order for his/her identity to remain culturally intelligible as Chicano/a.

My postulation is that an explicit connection may not be immediately evident in a literary work; what *can* often be discerned through reading is a stance in relation to both Chicana/o and dominant cultures. This position may reveal solidarity with ethnic cultural tradition as perceived by the writer, or a stance that is critical of that tradition. In either case, the power relations influencing minority identity formation are implicit in the writing, and these are inscribed in even the most proassimilation ethnic texts. It could be argued that the assimilationist political agenda that informs Richard Rodríguez's *Hunger of Memory* is blatantly anti-Chicana/o; yet his autobiography is widely read as emblematic of one facet of the minority experience in America. Ortiz Taylor's writing, on the other hand, works to *reaffirm* Chicana/o identity by reconstructing a part of family history that was nearly erased through assimilation.

"Traditional Chicana/o culture" is itself a construct, a collective fiction that is influenced by variables such as gender, class, generation, and geographical location. Insofar as this cultural construct fails to accommodate lesbian sexuality, writers like Sheila Ortiz Taylor, Cherríe Moraga, and Gloria Anzaldúa lend visibility to a marginalized sector of the Chicana/o community. Ortiz Taylor's novels are testimonials to the performativity of Chicano/a and lesbian identity. As such, they serve as reminders to critics of U.S. Latina/o literature that the models of cultural identity implicit in our theoretical approaches must be carefully developed. Inclusion of texts like *Faultline* and *Southbound* in the Chicana/o canon is a step toward acknowledging the diverse ideologies, sexual orientations, and degrees of identification with a specific community that Chicana/o identity encompasses.

JOHN RECHY'S RENEGADES AND THE ENDLESS PURSUIT OF SELF

I want no
memory

rather to embrace
every instant
to a frenzy . . .

I want to set
my body on fire
— FRANCISCO X. ALARCÓN, "Body in Flames"

John Rechy's first novel, *City of Night* (1963), brought him international acclaim for both its outstanding writing and its stunning portrayal of the underworld of gay hustlers in urban America. In the ensuing years, the El Paso–born Chicano writer has published nine additional novels and the nonfiction "documentary" *The Sexual Outlaw*. Rechy has also earned a reputation as an outspoken champion of gay rights and critic of the pervasive homophobia of dominant American culture. Like Sheila Ortiz Taylor, Rechy's foregrounding of gay issues and identity resulted in the exclusion of his works from many discussions of Chicana/o fiction.[18] Yet in his writing there exists an unmistakable gay Latino subjectivity that is first established in the opening pages of *City of Night*. This novel was thus a trailblazer: It was a gay treatise published years before Stonewall that alluded to a Chicano problematic before national attention had been focused on Chicana/o identity. In Rechy's later works, *This Day's Death* and *The Miraculous Day of Amalia Gómez,* in particular, the gay Chicano subjectivity hinted at in his early novels is developed even further.

Rechy's novels, like Ortiz Taylor's, support a reading of identity as performance, both as spectacle and as constituted through performative acts. The performances of Rechy's characters—the unrestricted pursuit of sexual pleasure through homosexual encounters, cross-dressing, sadomasochism—are judged as excess in relation to middle-class American codes regulating the expression of sexuality and gender. These characters are thus constructed as sexual/social "outlaws" through the dominant culture's condemnation of their supposed transgressions.[19] The protagonists, in turn, persistently question the authority of these regulatory structures over sexuality.

The Professor, a character in *City of Night,* proclaims the worldview that Rechy's works reflect: "The only immorality is 'morality' — which has restricted us, shoved into the dark the most beautiful things that should glow in the light. . . . Why is what I do Immoral, when it hurts no one?" (70). In *The Sexual Outlaw* Rechy offers a possible response from the perspective of the heterosexual majority. In a section entitled "The Gay Threat," Rechy suggests that straight society fears that the acceptance of homosexuality would lead to an eventual undermining of monogamy and traditional family structure (205). By their very existence homosexuals defy the biblical injunction to "be fruitful, and multiply," as Harold Beaver notes; homosexuality "transgresses against breeding."[20] The gay subculture of Rechy's novels is thus identified by its deviation from the norms of American heterosexual propriety and, like racial and ethnic minorities, is subjected to oppression.

In *City of Night,* sexual identity is constituted through performative acts that Rechy's protagonists repeat endlessly in the sexual underground they inhabit. In the sexual "theaters" of the sixties gay scene — bars, hotel rooms, parties, bathhouses, alleys, parks — these characters assume a variety of roles that dispel any notion of monolithic gay identity. The narrator of *City of Night* quickly learns to distinguish between the recurring "types" he will encounter in his explorations: the queens with their "superficial gayety — giggling males acting like teenage girls;" the scores, "men who paid other men sexmoney"; the "unpaid, mutually desiring males — the easy pickups"; and the hustlers, whose roles include "youngmanoutofajob butlooking; dontgiveadamnyoungman drifting; perennialhustler easytomakeout; youngmanlostinthebigcity pleasehelpmesir" (31–32).[21] The narrator, scarred by a destructive relationship with his abusive, tormented father, chooses to make it as a hustler in part because the role requires a facade of toughness, of apparent insensitivity. "I would wear that mask," he declares (33), tacitly agreeing to perform according to an already-written "script" each time he hits the streets.

After countless scores in New York, El Paso, Los Angeles, San Francisco, and Chicago, the narrator/protagonist makes his way to New Orleans for Mardi Gras, where he reflects that "I had acted out a role for them — as I had acted it out for how many, many others?" (341). In New Orleans, one of his scores sees through the narrator's impassive veneer, pointing out that he acts in order to fulfill the hustler image that society has invented: "Like all other legends, it's already there, made by the world, waiting for him to fit it. And he tries to live up to what he's supposed to be" (360).

At this point the narrator acknowledges that he has been performing a part written by others, for the hustler image is one facet of the gay identity construct that circulates in American society. In *The Sexual Outlaw*, Rechy examines this Foucauldian notion that official/institutional discourses on homosexuality produce transgressive subjects and then subjugate them:

> The law tells us we're criminals, and so we've become defiant outlaws. Psychiatrists demand we be sick, and so we've become obsessed with physical beauty. Religion insists we're sinners, and so we've become soulful sensualists. (193–94)[22]

City of Night's narrator similarly expresses a sudden feeling "of having been in someone else's dream. And how many other dreams? How many of all the people I had known had ever begun to know me?" (360). The novel offers evidence of the impossibility of definitively establishing identity beyond a given performance. In this sense, the never-ending sexhunt of Rechy's protagonists — the perpetual repetition of performative acts — functions as a metaphor for identity in general.

These characters are driven by an insatiable need, beyond physical desire, for the fleeting affirmation that their sexual encounters provide. The characters are also difficult to pin down, for their life-styles and their own perceptions of themselves do not necessarily coincide. The narrator of *City of Night* refuses to admit that he might be attracted to his partners. He claims that in his sexual encounters, which he insists are merely performances with no motivation beyond the economic, desire is only directed toward him. He summarizes the sensation these contacts produce: "I will feel hugely excited and momentarily surfeited, to be, oneway, the object of their desire — but surfeited, again, only for those few moments" (182). A fellow hustler outlines the rules that he claims define identity on the streets:

> "Whatever a guy does with other guys, if he does it for money, that dont make him queer. Youre still straight. It's when you start doing it for free, with other young guys, that you start growing wings." (40)[23]

In other words, as long as sex remains a commodity that is sold for economic gain, the hustlers can continue to assert their masculinity by claiming that they experience no homosexual desire.[24]

City of Night's narrator evidently shares this philosophy; the driving force behind his endless sexhunt is his need to be desired without desiring in return: "To reciprocate in any way for the money would have violated the craving for the manifestation of desire toward me. . . . The money which I got in exchange for sex was a token indication of one-way desire" (54). At the same time, it is difficult to distinguish between the allure of the streets with their easy money, and what may be Rechy's protagonists' own forbidden longings. These characters' denial of reciprocal desire may be a genuine representation of their sexual orientation or a product of internalized homophobia. In either case, this insistence on unidirectional desire produces a perplexing situation with regard to gay subjectivity. Within the American cultural space in which the protagonists' same-sex encounters are carried out and described, the men would be categorized as homosexuals.[25] Ironically, then, even as they disavow their own sexual agency — that is, by maintaining that they only perform as passive sexual *objects* — they articulate a subjectivity that dominant cultural standards identify as gay.

These situations reveal the power relations involved in the hegemony of heterosexuality in American society. In Anglo-American culture, men are generally categorized as homosexuals based on the prevailing "one-drop rule" mentioned by Almaguer. Thus the characters' homoerotic acts are not within the realm of straight male sexuality. Regardless of the self-conception that Rechy's protagonists maintain, they are subject to the normative standards that have defined homosexuality in the United States.

Whereas gay identity and performance are foregrounded in all of Rechy's novels, Chicano/Latino subjectivity is articulated in more subtle ways. When *City of Night* is read in its original version, without the introduction that Rechy added to the 1984 edition, the overt Chicana/o signs can be easily overlooked. In the novel's first section, in which the narrator recalls his turbulent childhood in El Paso, he mentions his mother, "a beautiful Mexican woman who loves me fiercely," her Virgin of Guadalupe figurines, the traditional Mexican Nativity scene that the family assembled each year (14). Later, in New York, the rain and the endlessly running showers of the YMCA evoke the memory of a song from the narrator's childhood, "a Mexican kid song: 'Let it rain, let it rain, Virgin of the Cave' " (25).[26] When Rechy's first novel is read as a *bildungsroman*, it is not surprising that the narrator's "search for self" involves rejection of his ethnicity. He leaves his troubled family life in El Paso in the hope of remaking himself; this process involves erasure of his past, including his cultural heritage. Moreover, the narrator's sexuality conveys an implicit rejection of the rigid familial gender roles discussed by Almaguer and Moraga. By circulating in a space inhabited primarily by men whose objective is the untrammeled pursuit of sexual pleasure, this protagonist refuses to perform as the paternal link in the ethnic family unit.

The narrator associates his Mexican mother with suffocating love and stifled independence, so his detachment from his ethnic past results in part from his rejection of his mother. The "ethnic mother" is thus a key figure in both Rechy's and Ortiz Taylor's works. The relationship of Arden Benbow to her Chicana mother is vastly different from that of Rechy's narrator to his mother, however. In *Faultline* and *Southbound,* Arden seeks to connect with her Chicana/o heritage. In the process she discovers that her mother, in adhering to the family's "never look back" philosophy, has made a conscious effort to erase visible signs of her ethnicity through assimilation. In *City of Night,* the narrator's mother represents a cultural heritage that is clearly coded as Mexican, and he has no apparent interest in interrogating his ethnicity.

When one considers the sociohistorical context from which *City of Night* emerged, the narrator's lack of ethnic identification is perhaps to be expected. In the early 1960s, neither "Chicano" nor "gay" political identities existed. In addition, Almaguer's description of the traditional Chicano/Latino sexual system indicates that to simultaneously perform as a Chicano and as a gay male is to perform without a cultural script. Nevertheless, in the thirty-plus years since *City of Night* was first published, Rechy's writing has made gay Chicano identity more visible. Most of his novels have at least one protagonist who is both Chicano and gay; *This Day's Death* (1969) focuses on the conflict between the obsessive love of the protagonist's Mexican mother and his need to break away and explore his sexuality.[27] In 1984 Rechy added an introduction to *City of Night* that calls attention to his own ethnicity. He describes his mother as "Mexican, a beloved, beautiful woman," and mentions that he spoke only Spanish until he entered school. In his teens, Rechy recalls, he began writing an autobiographical novel whose narrator was "doubly exiled in many ways: by his 'mixed blood' (especially significant in Texas)" (x). He finished writing *City of Night* at his mother's home in El Paso, translating passages for her into Spanish (xiii). Rechy's foregrounding of his ethnic background, taken in the context of his self-identification as gay, allows this fascinating novel to be read as a treatise on being young, gay, and "Chicano" in 1960s American society.[28]

IDENTITY FALLACIES AND THE CONTRADICTORY POLITICS OF EXCLUSION

The apparent conclusion to be drawn from such a reading of *City of Night* is that neither gay nor Chicana/o cultural space can accommodate the simultaneous performance of gay and Chicano identity. Instead, in Rechy's works (as in Ortiz Taylor's writing) gay Latino subjectivity is constructed through constant movement between subject positions and the blurring of distinctions between categories. The utopia that Rechy's characters pursue, which is to be achieved through the "street revolution," offers the freedom "[t]o enact fantasies —. . . Merely dreamt by others . . . —thus to cancel identities" (*Sexual Outlaw* 287). As I indicated previously about Ortiz Taylor's works, Rechy's novels call into question the meaning of "heterosexual" and "homosexual" by revealing the difficulty of defining either term. Homosexual panic — the fear of sameness, the acknowledgement of one's own potential for homosexuality, of the fine line involving desire and performance that separates straight from gay — is a recurring motif in *City of Night*. This panic, according to Sedgwick, is a result of the inherent contradiction in Western societies that condemn male homosexuality even as their social systems are structured around an intricate web of male homosocial bonds. She points out that

> such compulsory relationships as male friendship, mentorship, admiring identification, bureaucratic subordination, and heterosexual rivalry all involve forms of investment that force men into the arbitrarily mapped, self-contradictory, and anathema-riddled quicksands of the middle distance of male homosocial desire (186).

The only men who are truly immune to homosexual panic, Sedgwick asserts, are consciously gay men; all others risk, to varying degrees, being perceived as having slipped too far along the homosocial-homosexual continuum. A character in *City of Night* who is struggling with his sexuality expresses this fear of being unmasked:

> "Gay people . . . seem to cancel out so much that could be. . . . The effeminate ones . . . they frighten me. They seem sometimes to know so much. With a look, they can make you feel — so — well — so — . . . Like youre trapped." (229–230)

In Rechy's writing, this notion that causes panic in straight men — that homosexuality is always lurking, ready to erupt, at all levels of society — is championed as potentially liberating. By suggesting that the boundary between the supposedly mutually exclusive categories of gay and straight is indeterminate, Rechy's works reveal the role that dominant cultural discourses have played in establishing heterosexuality as norm.

The characters who most thoroughly challenge the binaries of gender and sexuality are the drag queens that populate Rechy's novels. Although their flamboyant dress, makeup, and posturing make their appearances theatrical spectacles that could easily be judged simple gender parody, closer reading of their performances reveals a more nuanced subversive potential. As one character in *City of Night* indignantly declares, " 'Dressing up . . . does not mean wearing costumes!' " (248). In fact, the costumes worn by Rechy's drag queens are only one part of a complex cultural phenomenon that ultimately calls attention to the instability of gender identity categories. As Esther Newton observes in *Mother Camp: Female Impersonators in America,*

[a]t its most complex, [drag] is a double inversion that says, "appearance is an illusion." Drag says "my 'outside' appearance is feminine, but my essence 'inside' is masculine." At the same time it symbolizes the opposite inversion; "my appearance 'outside' is masculine but my essence 'inside' is feminine." (103)[29]

This double inversion reveals that femininity and masculinity are performative, not inextricably linked to sex and gender. Consequently, the exaggerated "femininity" of the queens has no real referent, for it is a parody of an attribute that is itself a social construction.

Drag is not, however, merely the imitation of femininity; it is ostensibly the imitation of a supposed original feminine gender identity. Judith Butler nonetheless argues that the notion that feminine "properly" belongs to the female sex (or that masculine is the rightful property of the male sex) is the effect of a normative and regulatory system that prevails in Western society. This system, which Adrienne Rich has called "compulsory heterosexuality," assumes a clear-cut relationship between gender and performances of sexuality. Drag queens call this relationship into question. Although biologically male, they engage in performative acts (physical appearance, mannerisms, behavior, sexuality) that the mandates of compulsory heterosexuality code as female. Rechy's drag queens offer evidence of the insufficiency of the binary model of gender, which fails to account for their particular combination of sex and gender performance. When the performance of drag—the imitation of a feminine "essence," which is itself an imitation—is considered along with the queens' sex, the gender that is constituted is neither male nor female. Drag queens thus defy the basic tenet of compulsory heterosexuality, that there are "true," naturalized male and female gender identities, even more dramatically than other gays and lesbians.

Within the gay subculture that Rechy's novels portray, characters constantly subvert the dominant constructs of femininity and masculinity that have enabled the definition of gender identities. In *City of Night,* the narrator's commentary on both the queens' performances of femininity and the butch gay men's exaggerated yet fragile masculinity points to the interdependence of the two supposed opposites. For the drag queens in this text, Mardi Gras is liberation, the one time and place in which they are free to perform without fear of societal retribution: "The golden image of at last being Women — for that one glorious day! — of not possibly hassling getting busted . . . is a fulfilled daydream" (284). The media encourage the drag spectacle for the entertainment of the same American public that condemns the queens for their "deviance." On this day, the queens' hyperfemininity, their gender excess, is projected for consumption by a heterosexist mass public:

Hips siren curved, wrists lily-delicately broken, they will stare in defiant demureness from theater screens and home screens all over the country; and those painted malefaces will challenge — and, Maybe, for an instant, be acknowledged by — the despising, arrogant, apathetic world that produced them and exiled them. (284)

City of Night implies that this arrogance toward the drag queens arises in part from heterosexual society's smug sense of security in regard to gender identity. Yet it is a false security; in order to maintain its status, the dominant culture must identify its Others (homosexuals, ethnic and racial minorities) and denounce them for the excesses that make them visible. The very existence of drag queens such as those in Rechy's works reveals that the fabricated gender binary that Western society upholds does not coincide with empirical reality.

At the opposite end of the femininity-masculinity spectrum from the queens are Rechy's "butch" hustler characters. These figures likewise play an important role in undermining the artificial correlation of sex, desire, and gender identity, through repeated insinuations about the illusory nature of these characters' masculinity. Unlike the drag queens, the hustlers devote their energies to erasing all traces of anything that might be construed as femininity. They are constantly performing in order to fulfill a preconceived role within the gay subculture. Tantamount to successful performance is a specific combination of costume, stance, and refusal to express desire that has come to represent masculinity within this homoerotic space. Black leather is obligatory, as it symbolizes the "masculine" attributes of power and domination that the butch hustlers strive to project. In a San Francisco leather bar, the narrator of *City of Night* comments on the artificiality of the butch drag performances he observes:

And the hustler emphasizes his masculinity in one of various poses—one leg propped against the wall; cigarette held between thumb and finger— . . . the rehearsed, inviting Tough Look. (151)

Just as the queens become a parody of femininity, many in this leathered group are parodies of masculinity: posing stiffly; mirror-practiced looks of disdain nevertheless soliciting those they seek to attract. (241)

Nicknames, too, are an integral part of the charade; the hustlers go by names like Tiger and Chuck, names that are "as obviously emphatically masculine as the queens' are emphatically obviously feminine and for the same reason: to emphasize the roles they will play" (102).

The performances of both the hustlers and the queens are based on the notion that the masculinity and femininity that they emulate have real referents in heterosexual society. To make their show more credible, the hustlers strive to affirm their straightness by rejecting the possibility that they may experience desire toward other men. Although the space of Rechy's novels is clearly outside mainstream society, the dominant notion that heterosexual males are the true possessors of masculinity persists. Consequently, the hustlers work to maintain their butch facade even though their sexual contacts are primarily or solely with men. *City of Night*'s narrator analyzes the complex sexual dynamics that allow the hustlers to perpetuate their masculine (i.e., straight) image:

[T]he queens [are] technically men but no one thinks of them that way— always "she"—their "husbands" being the masculine vagrants—fleetingly and often out of convenience sharing the queens' pads—never considering theyre involved with another man (the queen), and as long as the hustler goes only with queens—and with other men only for scoring . . . he is himself not considered "queer" (97).

The narrator is nevertheless skeptical of the permanence of this masculinity, for he has observed indications of a hidden "feminine self" in even the most outwardly masculine members of the community. By underscoring the necessity of repetitive performances and constant vigilance, Rechy's works suggest that both masculinity and femininity are constructs.[30]

The distinctions that hold the artificial binaries of gender and sexuality in place also facilitate prioritization of one term (male, heterosexual) and subjugation of the other. A similar hierarchy exists between Anglo-Americans and members of racial and ethnic minorities; in *City of Night,* the infrequent appearance of racial difference calls attention to the gay subculture's Anglo-centric orientation. An incident involving a black drag queen and two of her white "sisters" reveals the subtle racism that results in certain identities — homosexuals of color, for example — being culturally unintelligible. The black queen tells of having dressed up recently as the Queen of Sheba; one of the white queens expresses skepticism, arguing that the Queen of Sheba was white. As a final insult she exclaims condescendingly, " 'Why! whoevuh heard of a nigguh *Queen?*' " (48). The racial and sexual subtexts of this exchange reveal the superior status accorded whiteness in American popular culture. While the Queen of Sheba may not have been black, the white queen fails to realize that this historical figure most certainly was not white either. By suggesting that the concept of a "nigguh Queen" is incomprehensible, this character inadvertently alludes to the homophobia implicit in the traditional identity constructs of a number of minority groups.[31]

The foregoing conversation offers some insight into the invisibility of the narrator's own ethnicity as he circulates through various gay communities during the course of the novel. The pervasive racism of 1960s American society, including the gay subculture whose acceptance this character requires for economic survival, discourages the expression of ethnic difference. To some extent, the gay subculture is a microcosm of American society, for in both spaces the holders of power are those who can claim to be white and heterosexual. A deconstructive reading of *City of Night* reveals that the boundaries of both these identity categories are far from clearly defined. I have already examined the phenomenon of passing that allows the undetected "contamination" of white cultural space by people of color, and of heterosexual space by gays and lesbians. Rechy's Chicano narrator infiltrates the Anglo-centric gay community and avoids discrimination by passing as a nonethnic white. Within the gay community, he achieves the hustler's position of power by denying his desire for other men — by passing as straight.

Paradoxically, sexuality is the site of simultaneous rejection and expression of ethnicity for many of Rechy's Chicano characters. The narrator of *City of Night* is driven by a need to break free from the stifling, unconditional love of his (ethnic) mother, escaping into a radical life-style that rejects the traditional gender roles of his ethnic heritage. He disappears into the gay subculture by disavowing his ethnicity; nevertheless the behavior of several of the hustlers in Rechy's novels can be interpreted as ethnic. Many of these protagonists resemble the Latino figure of the *bugarrón* (the *activo* in Almaguer's terms) by acting as the penetrator in same-sex encounters, their heterosexuality never questioned. It would be difficult to substantiate a claim that the phenomenon of the *bugarrón* is specific to Latino cultures. Yet in Anglo-American culture, same-sex erotic activity is not generally associated with "normal" (i.e., straight) male sexuality. Rechy's hustlers' insistence on their own heterosexuality would thus be more credible in a conservative Chicana/o community than in American society at large. Their identity could conceivably be viewed as heterosexual by an ethnic audience, while Anglo-American readers would perceive their performances as constitutive of gay identity. *City of Night* creates a stage upon which Latino and Anglo codes of sexuality intersect.

The ethnic heritage of the narrator of *City of Night* is thus implicated in his process of "finding himself," which includes the exploration of his sexuality. He does not visibly perform his ethnic identity, although he maintains a tenuous connection to his Chicano past through his memories of his mother and his El Paso childhood. The narrator's ethnic subjectivity is also implicit in his critique of dominant American culture, even though his outsider perspective is ostensibly the result of being gay. By circulating through the anonymous spaces of urban America yet refusing to embrace the values of dominant society, he becomes what Boelhower calls an "intersubject," a member of an ethnic group

who may choose to identify positively with his ethnic cultural system or simply express it as the unknown difference that allows him to criticize the dominant culture to which he undeniably belongs. (111)

The narrator's criticism focuses on societal condemnation of "transgressive" sexuality, and the resulting marginalization of homosexuals and other supposed transgressors. Yet the oppression that he observes and experiences as a member of the American gay subculture in the 1960s cannot differ substantially from that inflicted upon him as a Latino. His assessment of "the arbitrary stamp of 'differentness' imposed on [the gay community] by the world that creates it and then rejects it" (223) aptly describes the status of ethnic and racial minority groups as well. The white, heterosexual American majority identifies all these communities as "other" and then persecutes them for the threat to social order that their otherness represents. Rechy again coincides with Foucault in claiming that the dominant culture has invented the "crime" of homosexuality in order to castigate gays through "[w]idespread entrapment — creating the 'crime' it insists it wants to curb" (*Sexual Outlaw* 29). Rechy's writing persistently emphasizes the role that societal institutions play in designating acts as performances that are excessive or subversive, and therefore censurable. In so doing, his works question the power structures that produce oppression of diverse U.S. minority groups and push these groups to define themselves.

In this way, Rechy's works hint at a Latino/ethnic problematic, obliquely portraying the racism of American society while focusing on gay male identity. In his "Imaginary Speech to Heterosexuals" in *The Sexual Outlaw*, Rechy attacks as particularly retrograde the oppression of gays by straight men of color. He criticizes homophobic members of racial minorities for their failure to acknowledge the parallel between their own oppression and that suffered by homosexuals in American society, asking "Why do so many of you — who should know so well what it's like — oppose us while you wallow in transparent machismo? The evil that pursues us is the same evil that pursues you" (*Sexual Outlaw* 233). What is unclear is whether Rechy's subject position here is that of a gay Chicano or simply as a "deracialized" gay man. Regardless, his criticism is aimed at members of diverse minority groups who refuse to recognize that their communities share many of the same political concerns (not to mention group members). This commentary resonates with Tomás Almaguer's conclusion that the gay Chicano is a culturally unintelligible figure for both gay and Chicana/o communities.

City of Night provides an incisive critique of the tendency of American society to regard *all* difference — racial, ethnic, or sexual — as excess that must be censured.[32] Rechy alludes to this allegorical move in *Sexual Outlaw* by telling straight blacks and Chicanos, "We [homosexuals] provide a barometer for tomorrow's general repression. We're first — but you're next" (233). Rechy's protagonists argue relentlessly that this condemnation of homosexuality is a defensive attempt to bolster a binary model of sexual orientation that can never be more than a heterosexist illusion. Butler concurs that heterosexuality is perpetually at risk;

it "knows" its own possibility of becoming undone. . . . That it can never eradicate that risk attests to its profound dependency upon the homosexuality that it seeks fully to eradicate and never can or that it seeks to make second, but which is always already there as a prior possibility. (1991, 23)

In less overt fashion, Rechy's novels insinuate that defining the boundaries between "American" and "ethnic" is equally problematic. That is, American culture can no more claim to be free of ethnic traces than heterosexuality can assert its independence from homosexual "contamination."

Rechy's texts avoid making conclusive determinations about identity; his protagonists' sexual encounters invariably provide an illusion of closure that quickly dissipates. His writing continually emphasizes the radical refusal of resolution or commitment that characterizes the life-style of the gay subculture of the 1960s and 1970s, declaring that joy is found in the "hunt that goes on endlessly like the infinitely burgeoning sum of a geometric progression" (*Sexual Outlaw* 286). This description of nonprocreative eroticism — endless and nonutilitarian — echoes poststructuralist theory's critique of the possibility of conclusive meaning.[33] As Harold Beaver observes, gay sexuality lacks the legitimation historically accorded heterosexual couplings, remaining "vacant of all ultimate meaning (no Virgin, no Christ Child), revealing in a dazzling succession only a further vista of signs behind signs behind signs" (117). The dominant (heterosexual) culture thus regards gay sexuality as it does racial or ethnic difference: as excess that is simultaneously superfluous (it produces no progeny) and dangerously destabilizing.

A related motif of never-ending search infuses many of Rechy's novels. The purpose of the protagonists' search is always the same: to attain knowledge of self and to find meaning that will lend order to life's chaos. *City of Night*'s narrator acknowledges that he is "hunting Someone, urgently — that someone unfound in the dim past, in the parks, the moviebalconies, the bars, the streets, the sexrooms" (316–17). He is unable to define more clearly the object of his search; he knows only that "beyond that window and this churning world, out of all, all this, something [is] to be found: some undiscovered country within the heart itself" (340). He also gradually realizes that there is value in the seeking itself and that the search must continue indefinitely, for "[i]f I relented now in that journey through this submerged world, whatever meaning I might have found would evade me forever" (244).

What the narrator finds is that the meaning he seeks will indeed forever elude him, that "[l]ife reveals itself, if at all, slowly — and often through patterns discovered in retrospect" (160). By suggesting that identity is a process without conclusive answers or definitions, Rechy's writing allows for the constant slippage between identities that makes gay Latino subjectivity readable. For the narrator of *City of Night* and various other Rechy protagonists, identity is constantly being transformed through repeated performances: sexual encounters with men, but also with women; the strategic simulation of desire; incidents that hint at the characters' ethnic background or their relationship to American dominant culture. Rechy's works continually assert that these performative acts that constitute identity are not intrinsically subversive, condemnable, or excessive; American society only judges them to be so in relation to a specific (and, he argues, arbitrary) set of norms.

Rechy's nonfiction writing supports this view that individual identity can never be distilled into simple terms. In *The Sexual Outlaw* he argues that liberation from constraining labels and from the need for resolution is to be celebrated, for "within the hunt is the core of the mystery. The search for what is *not* to be found. The search is the end. Not the answer — the riddle. . . . Everything is found in nothing" (300). Perpetually moving among subject positions, outlaws who avoid capture by never staying in one place, the protagonists of Rechy's novels blur distinctions between the poles of supposed binary oppositions — gay/straight, male/female, ethnic/mainstream.

In *Faultline* and *Southbound,* as well as in *City of Night,* characters establish associations with a variety of communities through their responses to ethnic cultural heritage, their expression or concealment of desire, and so on. The novels show that these associations are far from immutable: ethnic, gay, and lesbian communities continually evolve. Their transformation is made visible by the "nontotalizable" minority voices within the communities themselves. Viewing identity as performance avoids the imposition of a monolithic model that fails to reflect changing social and political reality. The narrator of *City of Night* observes that "[f]rom face to face, from room to room, from bed to bed, the shape of the world I had chosen emerged — clearly but without definable meaning. Each morning . . . the endless resurrection of each new day began" (120). This image of movement and "endless resurrection" is an eloquent metaphor for the performativity of culture and identity, to which Chicano/a gay and lesbian voices give compelling testimony.

THREE

IDENTITY AS DRAG

Performing Gender and Cubanidad
in The Mambo Kings Play Songs of Love
and The Greatest Performance

I stand astride many frontiers, belonging fully
to none of my communities yet . . . deeply and
irrevocably connected to all of them.

— FLAVIO RISECH

This chapter's epigraph encapsulates the key identity issues that I have been exploring: negotiation between communities, the powerful influence of cultural heritage, and the tension that these generate for the ethnic subject. The essay from which the quote is drawn, "Political and Cultural Cross-Dressing: Negotiating a Second Generation Cuban-American Identity," supports the notion of drag as a metaphor for cultural identity. Risech describes the array of "identity garments" that he has worn, as a gay, politically progressive Cuban-American, in different circumstances. He mentions the "intricately tailored suit" that is read as heterosexuality, the political drag that he has developed in order to survive visits to Miami, the non-Latino "dress" that is fashionable in North American gay communities. Risech also identifies the danger that accompanies some of these performances, the "high costs associated with presenting oneself in certain kinds of 'garb'" (527). He observes that to exhibit leftism as a Cuban-American in Miami, or queerness in Havana, can result in ostracism or more violent repercussions.

These varied performances attest to the dynamic nature of U.S. Cuban[1] culture and the multiple possibilities that this identity category encompasses. At the same time, the need for perpetual "cross-dressing" by some U.S. Cubans indicates that restrictive identity paradigms continue to operate. The collective fiction of authentic *cubanidad* that circulates in the Miami Cuban community, for example, condemns both homosexuality and leftist political inclinations.[2] In this chapter, I show how recent U.S. Cuban fiction makes readable the tension generated between such static cultural mythologies and the everyday performances that challenge them.

Most critics take the 1959 Cuban Revolution as their point of reference for discussion of U.S. Cuban literature as a discernible literary corpus. Cuban émigrés have been living and writing in the United States since the late eighteenth century, but not until large numbers of Cuban exiles began arriving during the 1960s did a sizable body of so-called Cuban-American or U.S. Cuban literary works become accessible.[3] Consequently, the emergence of U.S. Cuban literature is a relatively recent phenomenon in the development of U.S. Latina/o literature. Particularly in the past fifteen years, the increase in the number of Cuban immigrants and their descendants residing in this country has been accompanied by the publication of numerous literary works by writers of Cuban descent. Rather than coalescing around common thematics or ideology, this literature is noteworthy for its diversity.[4]

Debate continues among critics as to the classification of writers of Cuban descent in the U.S. as exiles, immigrants, or ethnics. Gustavo Pérez-Firmat describes exile sensibility as being retrospective, with a powerful fixation on the culture of origin (1987, 3). He argues that exile literature is generally written in the native language, since the use of English is viewed as "an intolerable symptom of cultural dissociation" (1987, 4). Eliana Rivero similarly asserts that exile writers, who were often writers before being immigrants, tend to re-create social, political, and personal "landscapes" of their native land in their nostalgia-tinged works ("From Immigrants" 191). Both critics view U.S. Cuban *ethnic* writing, on the other hand, as more likely to engage questions of biculturalism and cultural transformation.

In "Hispanic Exile in the United States," Juan Armando Epple suggests an alternative paradigm that distinguishes three generations of Cuban exile writing. The discourse that Epple associates with the first generation of postrevolution Cuban exiles, like the writing described by Pérez-Firmat and Rivero, is characterized by "nostalgic hyper-valuation" of the homeland's beauty (336) and an attitude of "affront—many times rhetorical and propagandistic—toward the Revolution" (347). Epple attributes a second register of exile writing to authors who emigrated from Cuba as children and grew up in the United States. He asserts that works of this generation reflect a critical stance toward assimilation but also cast a skeptical eye toward the historical-cultural paradigm of the previous generation, particularly its idealization of the homeland (347). Finally, Epple proposes a potential third generation whose works likewise engage issues of ethnic representation and acculturation, but which present exile and displacement as generalized phenomena that are emblematic of the era of globalization (349). Epple's model is provocative in that it offers more fluid definitions of "exile" and "ethnic" writing and does not treat the two categories as mutually exclusive.

A growing number of U.S. Cuban writers are indeed producing literature that involves a complex engagement of their Cuban cultural heritage that is neither nostalgic nor assimilationist. This shift is due in part to the increasingly "ethnic" and ideologically heterogeneous character of U.S. Cuban émigré communities.[5] Many of these authors came to the United States as children or adolescents, while others were born here. Critic Carolina Hospital calls these U.S. Cubans who do not identify exclusively with either a Latin American or a North American cultural tradition "los atrevidos" ("the daring ones"). Their writing, like other hybrid literatures (Chicana/o, Asian-American, and so on) "mingles and intertwines different cultural legacies" (Hospital 18).

This literature has begun to establish a visible cultural space, as the recent commercial success of Cristina García's *Dreaming in Cuban* indicates. Unlike exile-oriented writing, with its nostalgic, static view of Cuban culture, these works are testimonials to the performativity of cultural identity. The exile perspective tends to be highly nationalistic, downplaying or ignoring the ongoing transformation of culture. Much recent U.S. Cuban literature, on the other hand, can be read as a challenge to the fossilized notion of *cubanidad* (ca. 1959) that first-generation exile literature promotes. These U.S. Cuban works are situated between the two cultural forces that Pérez-Firmat terms "traditional" and "translational" (1994, 3). That is, they reflect constant tension between the cultural encyclopedia and the everyday adjustments of bicultural existence, between what Homi Bhabha calls the pedagogical and the performative aspects of culture (145).

In this chapter, I continue to explore the relation of performance to culture and identity and to develop the concept of identity as drag. I focus on how gender and cultural identity are constituted in Oscar Hijuelos's clever *The Mambo Kings Play Songs of Love* (1989) and Elías Miguel Muñoz's moving novel *The Greatest Performance* (1991). Although their Cuban immigrant protagonists are diametric opposites—a womanizing macho musician in *Mambo Kings*, a lesbian teacher and a gay artist in *The Greatest Performance*—both novels offer insight into the construction of identity. Through its stereotypical characters, *Mambo Kings* appears to promote a notion of essential masculinity, femininity, and Cuban culture, while *The Greatest Performance* critiques the restrictive gender constructs associated with *cubanidad*. In both novels, exclusionary identity paradigms (the macho, the hyperfeminine woman, the nationalistic "authentic" Cuban) are ultimately revealed to be illusions produced through repetition of performative acts. In *Mambo Kings*, the very performances of gender and ethnicity whereby the characters ostensibly assert their identity in fact operate as "drag" that parodies the notion of originary masculine/feminine/Cuban essences. The representation of gay and lesbian subjectivities in *The Greatest Performance* further undermines the static, essentialist standards of Cuban authenticity that work to regulate performances of gender and sexuality within the émigré community.

THE CONSTRUCTION OF THE ETHNIC MASK: DEFINING *LA CUBANIDAD*

The Mambo Kings Play Songs of Love is the second and most popular of Oscar Hijuelos's four novels. His first, *Our House in the Last World*, was published in 1983, and his most recent works are *The Fourteen Sisters of Emilio Móntez O'Brien* (1993) and *Mr. Ives' Christmas* (1995).[6] *Mambo Kings* tells the story of two Cuban brothers, Cesar and Nestor Castillo. They are musicians who journey from their hometown to New York in 1949 to pursue their dream of becoming successful performers. In spite of a period of professional achievement in the United States, the brothers' lives are marked by tragedy: Nestor dies in an automobile accident, and Cesar drinks himself to death in a seedy hotel room.

The Greatest Performance is Elías Miguel Muñoz's third novel, preceded by *Los viajes de Orlando Cachumbambé* (1984) and *Crazy Love* (1988).[7] The text is composed of a dialogue between two narrative voices, that of Rosa, a U.S. Cuban lesbian, and Mario, a gay U.S. Cuban man. Mario and Rosa first meet as young adults in California but invent a past in which they were friends — soulmates — growing up in Cuba. Through the memories and confessions that the two friends share, they construct a space in which they can explore identity as gay/lesbian Latinos, without fear of punishment or repression.

The main body of *Mambo Kings'* narrative is presented as an extended reminiscence woven by Cesar Castillo; these memoirs are framed by a prologue and an epilogue narrated by Nestor's son Eugenio. Eugenio's intervention at the beginning and end of the novel, and the verbatim repetition of one passage in both the body of the text and the epilogue, imply that he controls the narration. Yet the protagonist of *Mambo Kings* is unequivocally Cesar, and the text is organized around the concerns and struggles of his intensely lived existence. Cesar's memoirs contain no commentary that would reflect Eugenio's first-generation ethnic perspective. The narrator of the memoirs, who appends various carefully researched footnotes to the main text, writes with an omniscient narrator's intimate knowledge of Cesar and considerable insight into his character.

In an essay on *Mambo Kings*, Pérez-Firmat offers an insightful reading of this problematic narrator by postulating that Eugenio is Cesar's "translator." He stops short of attributing the entire narration to Eugenio by arguing that Eugenio occupies a position somewhere between the narrating "I" and the narrated "he" (1994, 148). Pérez-Firmat proposes that the nephew *underwrites* Cesar's memoirs; while Eugenio may not be responsible for the specific "verbal shape" of Cesar's recollections, "he is at least generally responsible for the memoirs as a whole" (147). The presence of this enigmatic narrative voice precludes reading the text as either (auto)biographical "truth" or entirely Eugenio's invention.

As if to underscore the questionable veracity of the memoirs, an important motif in the novel is an actual episode of the *I Love Lucy* show, with the two original guest characters replaced by Cesar and Nestor Castillo. Both the prologue and the epilogue include Eugenio's description of this episode that he has viewed countless times, one in which Cesar and Nestor supposedly appeared at the invitation of Desi Arnaz. This blurring of the distinction between reality and fiction is paralleled by Ricky Ricardo's rapid evolution into a symbol of Cubanness for millions of American viewers. The television character's transformation by American dominant culture into an ethnic icon provides a glimpse of the process whereby Latina/o identity becomes essentialized. Cesar himself seems convinced that Desi Arnaz is the quintessential Cuban as well as the embodiment of the American dream realized. Arnaz had come to the United States in the 1930s and "had parlayed his conga drum, singing voice, and quaint Cuban accent into fame" (33). As Ricky Ricardo, Arnaz won the hearts of the American public not only through his music, according to *Mambo Kings*, but also through a certain Cuban mystique that translated into sex appeal. He fit the popular stereotype of the Latin Lover perfectly.[8]

By association, being Cuban works to Cesar's advantage when he inquires about a job advertised by his Irish landlady: "A tingle went through her body, because when Cesar said 'job' he pronounced it 'yob,' just like that Ricky Ricardo fellow" (230). Cesar describes himself as "a white Cuban bolero singer like Desi Arnaz . . . a Latin-lover type, dark-haired and dark-featured . . . Swarthy to Americans, but light-skinned when compared to many of his friends" (27). Both Arnaz and Cesar benefited from the fact that they were "white." The American public accustomed to the Ricky Ricardo-Cesar Romero image read Cubans as racially white; thus the notion of a black Cuban seemed to be a contradiction. At one dance hall where Cesar's mambo band was scheduled to perform, the owner refused to allow the black band members to enter the premises ("He wanted Desi Arnaz, not these ebony-black Cubans" [165]). The irony of this racist view of Cuban culture is that the principal Cuban music-makers of the period were black: Cachao, Celia Cruz, Beny Moré, and Pérez Prado, among others.

The fact that mainstream audiences saw Arnaz as the personification of Cubanness attests to the widespread recognition of his television character, Ricky Ricardo. The tremendous popularity of this media invention is evidence of the commodification of the exotic, of the ethnic Other, that allowed Latin performers to eke out a living during the 1950s and 1960s. Cesar recalls the numerous Latin musicians he would meet riding the subway to late-night jobs: the flamenco guitarist, the tango accordionist who performed in a gaucho hat, the aging *zarzuela* singers. The Mexicans in particular seemed to respond to the market's appetite for ethnic excess, which their clothing proclaimed: The men wore big sombreros, pants decorated with bells, and elaborately tooled cowboy boots, while the woman's costume was a dress made of Aztec-looking fabric and a mantilla. Their instruments formed part of the pastiche spectacle as well,

their oversized guitars, trumpets, and an accordion that resembled an altar, its fingerboard shiny with hammer-flattened religious medals of the Holy Mother, Christ, and the Apostles, bloody with wounds, hobbling on crutches, and pierced through with arrows to the heart (257).

Cesar becomes skilled at tailoring his ethnic performances to be acceptable to the often conservative Anglo audiences, selecting a mixture of American and Latin American favorites. He performs English versions of some Spanish tunes, like the famous "Peanut Vendor" song. His heavy Cuban accent allows him to play a linguistic joke on his unwitting English-speaking public, for they fail to detect the humor as he croons, "Oh, why don't you try my peanuts, you'll never find peanuts as tasty as mine" (156–57).

All these performances—the Latin musicians' hyperbolic costuming, Cesar limiting the foreignness of his songs to make them accessible to Anglo specta-tors, Desi Arnaz taking advantage of the exotic appeal of his flamboyant "Cuban" mannerisms and accent—present an image of Latin identity that is attractive to American consumers. Dominant culture's demand for these eth-nic performances does not reflect tolerance of cultural diversity, however. The popularity of these Latin artists underscores society's prevailing Anglocentrism whereby ethnics are identified as "Other" by their excesses (albeit appealing ones): their deviance from middle-class Anglo-American norms of "proper" appearance, behavior, and language.

In *The Greatest Performance,* Rosa and Mario experience a slightly different form of this racism in their interactions with American gay and lesbian communities. They discover that gaining acceptance into these Anglocentric communities requires a sort of cultural whitewashing, which they achieve by downplaying or concealing their Latina/o roots. The "Anglo" performances that Rosa and Mario employ in order to be culturally intelligible to their lovers resemble assimilationist moves by the protagonists in *The Line of the Sun* and *How the García Girls Lost Their Accents* (see chapter 4). Rosa and Mario learn that they cannot expect to find tolerance of racial and/or cultural difference in the gay/lesbian community. Mario acknowledges that he is lucky to be fair-skinned, for he is convinced that what makes him attractive to other men is that he is a "sexy babe . . . who looked more Gringo than Cuban" (122). By all appearances, his Cuban cultural background is erased completely in his "performances" with numerous lovers. Mario perceives their expectations of him and strives to fulfill these by immersing himself in 1970s white gay culture. One lover is tall and blonde, with "fine white fingers," and lives in an apartment filled with plants, wicker, posters of Fleetwood Mac, and incense (68). For an older French lover Mario plays the part of the man's "little American *ami*," with "tight white pants, his hair bleached by the summer sunlight" (68). Another lover is a business executive who is the proud owner of an autographed photo of Richard Nixon. He introduces Mario to Shirley Bassey's song, "The Greatest Performance of My Life"; after the affair Mario wearily observes that he is "[t]ired of performing" (69–70).

As these incidents indicate, Mario engages in acts — roles created for him by others — that allow him to be comprehensible as a gay man in American society. He is frequently reminded that in order to project this "non-Latino" gay identity he has eliminated most traces of his family background and his Cuban past. At a gay bar in Laguna Beach one New Year's Eve he recalls an earlier December: "The time I broke away. Low winter clouds, a regatta . . . Merry Christmas! *Feliz Navidad* at home with pork roast and black beans. How long ago was it?" (72). Embracing American gay culture liberates Mario from the pain and oppression of his past, but this freedom is gained by suppressing outward signs of his cultural heritage. By erasing visible evidence of his *cubanidad* — and by performing whiteness — he avoids the rejection that can accompany being identified as ethnic Other.

Like Mario, who discovers the benefits of perpetuating the illusion that he is non-Latino, Rosa realizes she must disavow much of her cultural heritage to be accepted as a lesbian in the United States. By the time she meets her Anglo lover Joan, she says, "I had already stopped fighting my 'deviance.' I had said to myself, Niña, your native island is Lesbos, not Cuba" (92). By rejecting Cuba and choosing Lesbos as *patria*, Rosa implicitly supports the notion that Cuban and lesbian identities are irreconcilable, that to be a Cuban lesbian is to be a contradiction in terms. In spite of her apparent acceptance of this incompatibility, Rosa is dismayed by the degree of cultural deprogramming that her relationship with Joan seems to require. Joan finds various aspects of her lover's life-style to be objectionable if not downright hazardous to her health: Rosa's penchant for "unbearably delicious but totally unhealthy" Cuban cuisine; her "boisterous, melodramatic and 'dishonest' Spanish music" (114). In her attempts to make "a meat-and-potatoes kind of gal" out of Rosa, Joan introduces her to the wonders of Emmylou Harris, a high-fiber, cholesterol-free diet, and camping (which Rosa sardonically terms "the discomfort of the outdoors").

In effect, Joan is trying to erase Rosa's ethnic difference, to make her Anglo, by censuring her ethnic "excesses" (rich food, bombastic music). Seduced by the material abundance of the life she shares with Joan and their intense sexual relationship, Rosa acts out her assigned Gringa role in spite of the sacrifices it demands:

Meanwhile I was having to play my music in the car, or at home only when Joan wasn't around, or very low, so that she wouldn't hear it if she happened to be around and I just couldn't resist the urge for some Raphael or Manzanero. My only cherished traces of the past, I thought . . . remnants that I felt forced to hide as if they were a terrible and shameful drug addiction. . . . Trashy memories of underdevelopment. (116)[9]

The dominant culture, represented by Joan, views Rosa's "cherished traces of the past" as blatantly excessive in relation to white, middle-class norms of propriety. In order to be culturally intelligible as an American lesbian — according to Joan's racist standards — Rosa must suppress the indicators that mark her as underdeveloped Other.[10]

Both the commodification of ethnic performances seen in *Mambo Kings,* and Rosa's and Mario's perception that *cubanidad* is fundamentally incompatible with American gay/lesbian identity, are manifestations of ethnic essentialism. Both phenomena reflect a prevailing societal belief in clearly definable identity categories and in the related notion of ethnic "authenticity." Yet as

Judith Butler points out with respect to gender, these essentialized identities are illusions generated by the repetition of the very performative acts that are presumed to be evidence of originary identity.[11] In *Mambo Kings,* a radio interviewer expresses skepticism about Desi Arnaz's public persona to Cesar, declaring that "no one has ever considered him very authentic or original." However, Cesar judges Arnaz's character and his repertoire of Cuban musical classics to be proof of his Cubanness, responding that "[f]or me, he was very Cuban, and the music he played . . . was good and Cuban enough for me" (339).

The notion of a Cuban essence, of an invariable cultural identity shared by all Cubans, is a thread that runs through the entire narrative of *Mambo Kings.* Cesar frequently refers to incidents from the *I Love Lucy* show as exemplary of the Cuban character; the program is presented as an accurate representation of immigrant life even though it is fictional. Cesar recalls life in New York shortly after World War II, when numerous Cuban performers immigrated to the United States in search of opportunity. He describes how the apartments were filled with Cubans, "just the way it always happened on the *I Love Lucy* show when Cubans came to visit Ricky in New York," with castanet players, flamenco dancers, jugglers, animal trainers, singers, "the men of moderate height with wide-open expressions, the women buxom and small" (36).

Cesar's recollections often resemble episodes of the television show so closely as to suggest that he no longer can (or chooses to) distinguish between the stereotypical, media-fabricated *cubanidad* of Ricky Ricardo and the complexity of his own day-to-day experiences. He portrays Cubans with broad brushstrokes, as gregarious people who are constantly getting together to consume endless plates of pork steaks, rice, beans, *plátano verde, yuca.* They share a common character, in Cesar's naive view: "Cubans then (and Cubans now) didn't know about psychological problems. Cubans who felt bad went to their friends, ate and drank and went out dancing" (114). Supposedly a Cuban will even react to bad news in predictable fashion, his face contorting "like a mask of pathos" (188).[12]

This essentialized Cubanness, illusory as it may be, nevertheless holds powerful appeal for non-Latinos like the Castillos' Jewish friend Bernard(ito) Mandelbaum. After befriending Cesar and immersing himself in the mambo scene, Bernardito falls in love with a Cuban "hot tomato" and through a series of Cuban "performances" gradually transforms himself:

Bernardito not only learned a Latin life-style, speaking a good slangy Cuban Spanish and dancing the mambo and the cha-cha-cha with the best of them, but he also slowly turned his and Fifi's apartment into a cross between a mambo museum and the parlor of a Havana mansion of the 1920s. . . . Lately he had started to look as if he had stepped out of that age, parting his hair in the middle, wearing wire-rim glasses and a thin mustache, baggy, suspendered *pantalones,* bow ties, and flat, black-brimmed straw hats. (274)

In the tradition of the "white Negros" of the 1950s, "urban adventurers who drifted out at night looking for action with a black man's code to fit their facts,"[13] Bernardito stylizes himself as a Latino. The irony of Bernardito's self-fashioning is that while he follows the traditional immigrant trajectory of remaking himself, he does not assimilate but rather replaces his Russian Jewish ethnicity with another that he finds more attractive.

In both novels, the 1960s and 1970s are a time of intensive efforts to affirm Cuban identity and unity within the Cuban immigrant community, for the exiles perceive the revolution as a siege on the *patria* of their memory. Desi Arnaz adds a note to a Christmas card to Cesar in the early 1960s that reads, " 'We Cubans should stick together in these troubled times' " (259). The response of the Southern California Cuban community in *Greatest Performance* to the "troubled times" that caused their exile is to form the "Cuban Club José Martí," a place where they can gather to revel in the collective fictions of their shared *cubanidad.*[14]

Rosa's sarcastic description of the Cuban Club makes clear her skepticism about the members' attempts to re-create the essence of their homeland. At the club the older men play dominoes, the young people court each other, and the older women observe approvingly and gossip about potential couples. In fact, the Cuban Club is a gold mine of performances of "authentic" Cubanness; Rosa's brother Pedro is the archetypal "Cuban stud," the perfect match for

the beautiful and untouchable-before-marriage *Cubanitas,* his typical medallion with the Virgin of Charity hanging from his neck. . . . Pedro, who rapidly lost the Castilian accent he picked up in Spain and who now sounded more Cuban than Ricky Ricardo, if that were possible. Pedro who still talked without pauses, long strings of sentences in which the ghastly phrase *oye, chico* was patriotically interpolated every two words. (117)

Pedro's Cuban performances—his Virgin of Charity medallion, his recently acquired Cuban accent and "patriotic" speech patterns—work to reaffirm his ties to the *patria.* Yet Rosa's comparison of her brother with Ricky Ricardo points to the illusory nature of the identity those performances appear to express.

In *Mambo Kings,* Cesar discovers Cuban exile solidarity in the bars of Union City "where in the early sixties many of the feverish Cubans had settled" (262). Here all conversations center on the disastrous changes for which Castro's Communist government is responsible. Cesar also reads the anti-Castro pamphlets his friends give him, fiery treatises that condemn the Cuban government and depict an idealized prerevolution Cuba in glowing, essentialist terms. One of these publications refers to "the sincere, happy spirit of Cubans" and the "gaiety of everyday Cuban life and commerce with its rum and good cigars and its bounty of sugar and all that springs from sugar" (264). The propaganda conveniently ignores both cultural diversity and the severe economic stratification that the rum, cigar, and sugar industries had generated.[15]

In *The Greatest Performance,* Mario and Rosa are subjected to standards of "authentic" *cubanidad* resulting from this same homogenization of Cuban national identity. The two protagonists find that if they wish to be regarded as bona fide members of the émigré community, they must perform in ways that reflect solidarity with their heritage. As an adult, Mario has broken away from his family, while Rosa still has frequent contact with hers. Settled in their Orange County home, her family has become a parody of middle-class Cuban society. On a typical Friday night, they eat black beans, rice, fried plantains, *picadillo,* ham croquettes, meatballs, *flan, mercocha,* and other Cuban specialties and drink Cuba Libres and sweet Cuban coffee while lamenting the condition of the Cuban economy and lambasting communism.[16] They reminisce about the good old days in Guantánamo, laud Rosa's brother for his success in real estate and the "lovely and domesticated and patriotic Cuban girl" he is dating, and remind Rosa that she needs to get busy and find a good man so that she can start producing grandchildren (133). Thus within Rosa's family, preservation of Cuban culture is closely allied to perpetuation of the rigid gender roles of 1960s Cuban society.

In *The Greatest Performance,* the immigrant family is portrayed as being staunchly conservative with respect to traditions and values of the culture of origin. As such, the family functions as a bastion against the encroaching dominant culture. Consequently, Rosa's dreams of going away to college are dismissed because "you just don't do that kind of thing in a Cuban home, right? The kids don't go off and study somewhere far from the family. . . . I would only leave the house . . . by the hand of my lawful-wedded husband" (87). Against her parents' will, she manages to move out while she is still in college, later becoming a teacher and buying a condo with Joan. Although Rosa is certain that her family is suspicious of the women's relationship, she maintains the charade through a series of Cuban performances intended to divert attention from her "deviant" life-style:

When Papi, Mami and Abuela visit me once in a blue moon, I make them *cafecito*. If they ask about my so-called "roommate," I tell them she's fine, that I hardly ever see her because we have such different schedules. Then we talk about the smog, the traffic, or the latest hearsay about the Cuban condition. And thus the illusion endures. (94)

The Greatest Performance thus suggests that within the microcosmos of the U.S. Cuban community, the performative acts that perpetuate the illusion of authentic *cubanidad* cannot accommodate transgressive (i.e., gay and lesbian) sexualities.

THE MACHO AND *LA MUJER:* PERFORMANCES OF MASCULINITY AND FEMININITY

Rigid, limiting gender constructs are a key component of Cuban identity as it is constituted both through Cesar Castillo's memories and through Rosa's and Mario's dialogue. Significantly, these constructs are predicated on the notion of essential, definable masculinity and femininity. Cesar's observation that Desi Arnaz "was Cuban and knew how to present the proper image of a man" (138) alludes to this integral relationship between gender and cultural identity. Cesar first learned about masculinity from his father, whose overpowering manliness permeated the household "with a scent of meat, tobacco, and home-made rum" (214). He describes his father, from whom Cesar received constant physical and verbal abuse: "No softness in Pedro's face, no kindness, no compassion. Pedro was a real man. He worked hard, had his women on the side, showed his strength to his sons" (214).

For Cesar, the essence of a Cuban man is his maleness, which centers around his penis (his "big thing," his *pinga*) and achieving sexual satisfaction, regardless of the cost. Over the course of his life he dedicates himself to seducing countless women, which does not prevent him from pursuing a long-term relationship with an Anglo woman named Vanna Vane. His first sexual encounter with Vanna sets the tone for numerous later trysts; he plays the role of the powerful macho, proudly showing off the instrument of his masculine prowess and making violent love to her. He recalls that she "liked him, liked it, liked his manliness and his arrogance" (17), and Vanna is further seduced by the exotic sound of the sweet Spanish nothings with which Cesar woos her:

"Tell me that phrase again in Spanish. I like to hear it."

"*Te quiero.*"

"Oh, it's so beautiful, say it again."

"*Te quiero*, baby, baby."

"And I '*te quiero*,' too." (18)

This interchange establishes a close association between ethnicity (represented by the Spanish words) and gender as constituted through Cesar's performances of masculinity, that is, his sexual conquests. From Vanna's perspective, Cesar's sexuality is inseparable from his Latino identity — his fulfillment of the stereotypical "Latin lover" role — and through language this intersection of identities is made visible.

From this point on in *Mambo Kings*, Cesar Castillo's discourse on masculinity unfolds in straightforward fashion. Periodically he pontificates on the meaning of being a man: " 'A man's got to do as he likes, or else he's not a man' " (67). His wife commits the grave error of taking his philandering as a personal affront, to which Cesar responds, "So I was led around by my penis, so what? What did a few laughs, a few fucks with women I'd never see again, have to do with anything, especially our love?" (53). He insists that his wife's accusations of cruelty are unjust, for he "was just being a man and doing as [he] saw fit" (53). For Cesar, manliness is synonymous with power and domination; the construct that he views as masculine essence is built upon a foundation of sexual conquests. The female body is the foil that is necessary for the male performances to succeed, so Cesar offers his brother the following advice on how to establish his authority: "[T]reat her good sometimes, but don't let her get too used to it. Let her know that you are the man. A little abuse never hurt a romance. Women like to know who's the boss" (103).

Cesar believes that being the "boss" gives him the right to impose his will on his women, particularly since he believes that he knows just what to say and do to appeal to their "essential" feminine needs. He justifies forcing himself on a young lady who has been saving herself for marriage, speculating that "he might have been a little rash in his impetuosity, but hell, he was just being a man" (299). He is astonished to find that afterward she is inconsolable, for he had assumed that he would be able to placate her with his usual strategies — "he'd treat her well, touch her hair, call her pretty, make everything all right with compliments" (299).

Only toward the end of his life does Cesar begin to express doubts about the codes of appropriate masculine conduct that he has always accepted and followed without question. Lonely and unfulfilled, his physical attractiveness waning, he muses that

[h]e'd always thought his big *pinga* would take care of things, that he could get what he wanted by staring into a woman's eyes with his pretty-boy looks, press home his manhood by treating his ladies like shit, with arrogance, as if they were worthless. (346)

Cesar is troubled to think that the sexual performances that he had always considered natural expressions of his gender identity, manifestations of his masculinity, may have contributed to his sense that he has nothing to show "for all his years in the world" (346).

Femininity is likewise essentialized in *Mambo Kings*, for the female characters seem to share a common identity that is defined solely in relation to men.[17] These characters, whether Latinas or Euro-Americans, are depicted as little more than objects of male desire whose lives are devoted to attracting and serving men. In a passage that takes place in New York's Imperial Ballroom, where the Mambo Kings are performing in 1950, an anonymous narrative voice appends a footnote describing the elaborate procedures that women go through "to enhance their loveliness so that they could find themselves a good man for life . . . so that each could tremble in a man's arms and find a man to take care of her" (82). This expert voice claims that the time-consuming, painstaking process of dressing and putting on makeup is worthwhile because it enables women to snare and keep the men of their dreams. This "good man" is one who will dominate his partner (his power makes her tremble) and will relieve her of any responsibility for taking care of herself. In spite of her efforts, a woman must be prepared for the inevitable — competition from others who are more desirable — and accept the fact that there is little she can do "when she's been losing those precious looks that hooked him up in the first place" (83).

The male characters in *Mambo Kings*, as well as the anonymous narrator mentioned above, view appearance as a means of performing femininity. The female characters' behavior, especially toward men, is likewise a performative act that produces the illusion of essential femininity. With very few exceptions these pathetic characters are constructed as accommodating, uncomplaining servants for their husbands, lovers, fathers, and other male relatives. Cesar describes his ex-wife as "thin, pensive Luisa who was there for his pleasure and who never expected anything from him" (53). Similarly, the wife of the Castillos' cousin Pablo is depicted as a practical and kindhearted woman "for whom marriage and childbearing were the great events in her life. She lived to take care of the men in that house" (35).

Nestor's wife Delores is one of the few women in the novel who has a voice and who questions the suffocating rigidity and inescapability of the female role. By age twenty-seven she is already weary of waiting on the Castillos and

their musician friends; a photograph of Delores with five of these men reveals
"a woman of intelligence and beauty literally trapped inside a crush of men. . . .
In the crush of machos, she seems to be waiting with annoyance to be lifted out
of there" (170). She asks herself why she willingly acts like a slave, and encour-
aged by her success in night school courses she dreams of enrolling in college.

The only other Latina character who asserts her autonomy and refuses to
accept a subjugated status is one of Cesar's many lovers, a Cuban woman
named Celia. One night a drunken Cesar demands that they go out on the
town in spite of Celia's insistence that it is much too late. Rather than allow
Cesar to go out alone, Celia ties him to an easy chair, saying that he needs to
learn the lesson that " 'when you have an engagement with someone, as you do
with me, that's it. . . . You may have been able to do what you wanted with
these other *fulanas*, but forget about that with me' " (301). Cesar, of course, is
furious and responds by ending his relationship with Celia the next day. He
justifies his decision by telling her that no woman can be allowed to treat a
man that way: " 'You have humiliated and dishonored me. You have tried to
reduce me in my stature. This act is something I cannot tolerate or forgive!
Ever' " (301–2). In short, Celia's "performance" of empowerment blatantly
opposes the standards of female conduct that Cesar has always demanded.

The paradigm of prescribed femininity offers Latinas like Delores no escape
from their oppression, for failure to perform appropriately evokes condemnation by the men upon whom their livelihood depends. American women are
far too independent and demanding to be acceptable wives according to Cuban standards, if Ricky Ricardo's exasperation with Lucy is any indication. In
the episode of the *I Love Lucy* show in which the Castillos appear, Ricky
launches into a long tirade in Spanish about American women that concludes
with "debía haberme casado con esa chica bonita de Cuba que nunca me puso
problemas, que sabía quién le endulzaba el pan . . . ella me dejaba tranquilo"
(141).[18] The mythical perfect woman is thus physically attractive, grateful for
her husband's support, and knows better than to question his behavior. Yet in
spite of the seemingly tireless efforts by *Mambo Kings*' female characters to
please their men, their performances never quite measure up to the men's
feminine ideal. As Cesar remarks to his nephew, " 'Women, boy, will ruin you
if you're not careful. You offer them love, and what do you get in return?
Emasculation. Orders. Heartbreak' " (223).[19]

A similar notion of ideals of masculinity and femininity is central to the
construction of identity in *The Greatest Performance*. Whereas Cesar's
memoirs in *Mambo Kings* celebrate the supposedly irrefutable differences
between men and women, Rosa and Mario provide a convincing critique of
such essentialism. The restrictive gender identities and roles that the two char-

acters were conditioned to accept as the norm exclude Rosa and Mario because they deviate from these standards. They have been haunted by fear since childhood, for they were both raised in traditional, middle-class Cuban families in which gender roles were sharply defined and homosexuality was condemned. Thus in *The Greatest Performance* masculinity and femininity are defined more obliquely than in *Mambo Kings*. Through the representation of gay and lesbian identities that are culturally unintelligible as male and female, the novel challenges the exclusionary gender binary that *Mambo Kings* appears to reinscribe.

Mario recalls that in 1960s Cuba the prevailing standards of masculinity required a "real man" to have (or to claim to have) "big balls and a huge dick, *un pingón*, [to be] a man who fucks women" (36).[20] As a child, Mario had failed to exhibit appropriate behavior for a future Cuban macho; he was a weak and sensitive child who was more interested in painting with watercolors than in playing baseball. The local pedophile Hernando picked up on this: "He knew I was a *pájaro*, a queer, from the very moment he laid eyes on me. . . . He says he knows I am in need of a man. Kids like me need special protection, we're delicate and fragile like girls" (36). Hernando's twisted idea of "protection" involved repeated visits by Mario during which the boy was coerced into engaging in oral sex and sodomized. In effect, Hernando's actions served to reinforce the masculinity/femininity binary; he asserted his maleness by exercising his power over a feminized male, that is, a boy that he had positioned as female.

At the same time, Mario began to feel attracted to other boys in a way that he didn't associate with sex. His classmate Antonio beat him up and called him a faggot even though Mario claimed to only want his friendship, longing to hold his hand, to touch his hair, his neck (41). As Mario grew more aware of his sexuality, he began to seek homoerotic encounters. He tells Rosa about his experiences with the other boys at summer work camp:

> "They're waiting in line for me, Rosi."
> "Who? Who's waiting in line?"
> "The boys at the barracks. . . . They're all waiting their turn . . . in front of my cot."
> "What are they waiting their turn for?"
> "You know . . . "
> "And do you want them to do it?"
> "I'd love it . . . "
> "Okay. Let the boys fuck you, then."

"They promise they'll never tell on me. Tattletales are punished by stoning. . . . This will be our secret." (140–41)

In a cultural context in which supreme value is placed on traditional masculinity, Mario defies the prevailing Cuban gender norms by assuming the *pasivo* role.[21] The motifs of secrecy and crime are further developed as Mario recalls the terror his encounters with Hernando caused him, for he lived in constant fear that his father might find out. He describes the emotional turmoil the relationship produced: "Blackmailed into committing a crime against my body. Eager and reluctant; threatened and forced, curious; feeling sinful, self-conscious and spiteful; embittered, impassioned" (121). As he grows up, Mario's sense of self is heavily influenced by official discourses that operate to criminalize his desire and to render him invisible, cloaked in a shroud of secrecy.

In Mario's brief relationship with a Nuyorican lover, he discovers that the man's perception of himself is heavily influenced by the *activo/pasivo* binary as well. The lover continually asserts his own masculinity; he refers to a previous partner as *un tipo* because, in Mario's words, "he's too macho to admit that he had an *amante*" (101). Reading his lover's discourse and actions, Mario finds the Nuyorican's claims of maleness to be unconvincing. As his lover listens to the "macho laughter" of the loud Caribbean men in his neighborhood, Mario observes, "he will quiver with fearful lust and curiosity, thinking himself one of those real men. Man of the house. Hair on his chest, a gold medallion" (100). The sexual relationship between the two men reflects this culturally coded *activo/pasivo* hierarchy. Mario notes his lover's insistence on occupying a position of power and domination during their erotic encounters: "He kisses me reluctantly, but he will let me run my tongue down his arms, his neck; down the ecstasy line that passes through his belly button" (102). Thus the Nuyorican is able to maintain his masculinity insofar as his lover submits to him; Mario becomes "unintelligible" as male.

Like Mario, Rosa had already felt the full weight of societal expectations with respect to her gender role during childhood. While her family was still living in Cuba, her mother had tried in vain to convince Rosa to conform to the rigid constraints of appropriate feminine conduct:

Was [Mami] worried, perhaps, about my Tomboy look, my disdain for domestic activities, my total apathy toward the opposite sex? She was determined, I could tell, to drive out of me all traces of masculinity, to force me to be fragile, tender, womanly. (18)

Rosa's mother maintained that being feminine required "calmer" behavior: speaking softly, playing with dolls (not hunting birds, climbing trees, or playing war games, Rosa's favorite pastimes), staying home more, and wearing a skirt. Nevertheless, at some point her mother apparently gave up trying to turn Rosa into a model of Cuban femininity. The only family sermons on women's responsibilities to which Rosa is subjected as an adult come from her grandmother, who insists that Rosa needs to get married to ensure that she will have someone to take care of her.

The grandmother is the voice of Cuban tradition, blaming Rosa's rejection of marriage and family on the corrupting effects of American society. But Rosa had first become aware of her desire for other females when she was a child. In fact, Rosa responds to her grandmother's entreaties, " 'I would've felt the same way if I'd stayed in Cuba, Abuela. It's not the country, it's me' " (93). She reminisces about playing doctor with a neighbor girl ("She'd hug me and I'd touch her 'sick' tummy and she'd touch the 'bebé' I had between my legs and it felt so good"), and about being the husband when they played house (17). She often fantasized about being a handsome knight, a tough militia man, a virile and feared lieutenant who drove a jeep; in her fantasies, Rosa always managed to get the lady of her dreams. On a symbolic level, Rosa's appropriation of a male persona allows her sexuality to remain within the parameters of both compulsory heterosexuality and Latina/o gender norms. Through her performances of masculine roles, her sexual object choice (women) is legitimized. In addition, as a "male" she is entitled to act as a sexual subject, a privilege that the traditional Latino sexual system denies her as a woman.[22]

As an adolescent, Rosa was intensely attracted to her beautiful and intelligent classmate Maritza. Her "romance" with Maritza turns out to be a lesbian rewriting of the timeless narrative of doomed, unconsummated love. It is a tale that Rosa knew well, having learned all of Armando Manzanero's *boleros* and love ballads — songs about "forsaken lovers and adoring lovers and forever-ever-lovers" (25) — by heart. The girls' relationship never went beyond hand-holding, a few kisses, and Rosa's passionate, lovelorn serenades for Maritza. In Rosa's final private concert for her sweetheart, the popular songs take on the added significance lent them by the forbidden nature of Rosa's desire. Her words, "we feel this love, sublime and profound . . . This love that makes us proud . . . This love so weary of goodbyes" (25) can be read as a testimonial reflecting the tragedy of the so-called love that dares not speak its name.

The principal punishments Rosa suffered for her sexual orientation were her mother's constant harangues and her own self-condemnation that led her to pray frantically to be "cured":

I begged God to help me. Damn how I prayed! I'd kneel during Mass
and I'd tell Jesus Christ and the Virgin of Charity: Look, here, please, you
guys, pretty please, you've got to save my body from temptation and my
soul from eternal damnation. . . . I'll look at the statue of Christ on the
cross and — Wham! — Rosita Rodríguez has been cured! . . .
   But there were no miracles for me. (17–18)

Mario's unmanly conduct, on the other hand, brought harsher consequences.
His father's shouts of "No son of mine is gonna be a faggot!" and "I won't have
a faggot for a son! I'll kill him first!" (67) were typical of the widespread
homophobia of Cuban society. Mario remembers countless instances of physical abuse inflicted by his father, who beat him because he was caught sitting
under a tamarind tree kissing the palms of a neighbor kid's hands; because he
liked to draw pictures of "naked toy-brothers"; because he supposedly looked
and acted like a girl (135). Rosa recalls that most Cubans viewed gay males
with scorn:

Pájaro. Bird. One of the words Cubans used in those days (still today?) to
denigrate a gay man. What were some of the other ones? Ah yes, Duck,
Butterfly, Inverted One, Sick One, Broken One, Little Mary, Addict, Per-
vert. (16).

The far more virulent societal condemnation of male homosexuals in comparison to lesbians hints at the threat that the figure of the *maricón* represents.
The gay male's adoption of the passive "feminine" role is regarded as the
supreme betrayal of the patriarchal order. In effect, he willingly surrenders the
power and authority that are his right in male-dominated society.[23]
   The association of homosexual behavior with bourgeois decadence and
counterrevolutionary activity led to institutionalized oppression of Cuban
homosexuals during the decade. Mario alludes to this period when gays were
rounded up, along with traitors to the revolution, and subjected to "treatment" in work camps, "a magical site where sick men and women turn normal
and the deserters pay their dues" (43). Rosa, too, recalls these "raids" on long-
haired men, prostitutes, gays and lesbians whose justification was that "[t]hose
people are sick. . . . And their sickness is contagious" (17).[24] During childhood,
then, Rosa's and Mario's attitudes toward their own desires were heavily
influenced by the official discourses of medicine, the law, and the Catholic
church that conflated homosexuality with sickness, criminal activity, and sin.
Before leaving Cuba, the two protagonists had been potential targets of both

family condemnation and official censure even before their own sexuality had fully developed.

Rosa's and Mario's immigration as teenagers to southern California creates a new set of challenges to their identity, even though in the United States homosexuality is tolerated to a greater extent than in Cuban society. As gay Latinos in a system dominated by a heterosexual Anglo majority, they find themselves marginalized because of both their sexual and their cultural identity. When the characters are with their families or other members of the Cuban immigrant community who cling steadfastly to their Cuban cultural heritage, they are pressured to act "straight." Lourdes Argüelles and B. Ruby Rich examine this pervasive sexual conservatism in their study on homosexuality and homophobia in twentieth-century Cuba and in postrevolution Cuban émigré communities. The authors assert that in prerevolutionary Cuba, "discrete lesbian or gay male identities in the modern sense — identities that are based on self-definition and involve emotional as well as physical aspects of same sex relations — were rare" (688). Even after the revolution, no organized gay countercritique or resistance to the official discourse on homosexuality developed. Argüelles and Rich comment that in 1960s Cuba as in other Latin American countries, homosexuality continued to be seen as a clandestine activity with solely sexual implications (691).

This homophobia has flourished in many U.S. Cuban enclaves, where an increase in cultural conservatism has reified the patriarchal dominance and rigid gender definitions mandated by traditional Cuban sexual ideology. David Rieff's observations about the simulacrum of "the Cuba of yesterday" fashioned by the Miami Cuban community corroborate this claim. Rieff points out that much of the artistic richness and cultural diversity of prerevolution Cuban culture is absent from this simulacrum, even though "Cuban Miami remained almost as gay a place as Havana had been, but no one admitted to the fact" (126). The homophobia that Mario and Rosa encounter within their own community, then, is in part the result of the exiles' efforts to claim a unified Cuban identity. This nationalistic view of Cuban culture is based on a vision of prerevolutionary Cuban society that ignores the complexity and contradictions of that society. The dominant discourse of the émigré community fails to acknowledge that all cultures are continuously being transformed.

In *The Greatest Performance*, dominant (i.e., homophobic) U.S. Cuban codes of moral conduct assume a regulatory role to promote this camouflaging of contradictions within the exile community. For Rosa, the Cuban Club represents not only the pastiche of Cuban culture that the exile community has become, but also a fortress of prescribed gender performance. At the club she is a prime target for what she calls the "unavoidable Cuban Cow Club Questions," thinly disguised warnings that her apparent disinterest in any of the eligible young Cuban bachelors is jeopardizing her right to call herself Cuban:

> "OYE, CHICA, ROSITA, WHEN ARE WE GOING TO MEET YOUR BOY-
> FRIEND?" . . .
> "AREN'T YOU WORRIED THAT YOU'RE GETTING TOO OLD FOR MAR-
> RIAGE?" . . .
> "OYE, CHICA, ROSITA, HOW COME YOU HARDLY EVER COME TO THE
> CLUB?"
> "AREN'T YOU BECOMING TOO MUCH OF A GRINGA, ROSITA?" (117–18).

Rosa's perspective as a lesbian — she refuses to perform as a "normal" Cuban woman — allows her to contest the exclusionary notion of Cuban identity that is celebrated by the Cuban Club members. Thus a powerful collective fiction of the Cuban émigré community parodied in the novel is that *cubanidad* and heterosexuality are inextricably linked.

REPETITION, EXCESS, AND THE DRAG ILLUSION

The articulation of gay and lesbian Cuban subjectivities in *The Greatest Performance* operates to de-essentialize both cultural and gender identity, particularly as these are portrayed in *Mambo Kings*. Yet even when the novels are considered independently of one another, each text supports a notion of identity as process rather than as product. *Mambo Kings* presents a stereotypical vision of gender that reinscribes the historical hierarchy of male as oppressor/ female as oppressed. The text appears not to critically examine in any substantive way either the behavior of Cesar Castillo's strutting Cuban macho or that of the numerous sexually insatiable yet subservient women. Because of Eugenio's ambiguous role in the narration of the text, the novel's gender stereotypes could conceivably be interpreted as hyperbolic creations of the nephew's (phallocentric) imagination. At the very least, the caricature of masculine and feminine figures in the novel suggests that they be read as parodies of gender identity categories.

The hypermasculinity and hyperfemininity of these characters (their excess) makes them resemble drag performers whose objective is to produce convincing gender illusions. The seemingly interminable repetition of their performative acts implies, in addition, that identity can never be permanently established. I pointed out in chapter 2 how the futility of such repetition can be seen in the never-ending sexhunt of John Rechy's hustler characters and the overwhelming emptiness that they experience between encounters. As Butler asserts, power works to produce the illusion of a seamless, uniform heterosexual identity through both repetitive performances and the exclusion of potentially disruptive homosexual subjectivities (1990, 140). Yet the very necessity of repetition indicates that this heterosexual identity is neither permanent nor uniform. In *Mambo Kings*, the endless, baroque proliferation of feminine and masculine signs can never fully constitute the respective gender identities.

Cesar's recollection of "the way the ladies dressed for those nights of love" is an example of this type of repetition whose purpose is to confirm their femininity. He recalls the women's array of hats, earrings, necklaces; their "[f]rilly slips, step-ins, girdles and garters, brassieres, lacy-fringed and transparent at the nipples;" and above all, the panties: "[f]lower-crotched flame panties, black-seamed white panties, panties with felt-covered buttons, fluffy ball panties . . . black sable panties, fake leopard-skin panties, butterfly-wing panties" (20). Cesar comments that "if these ladies didn't wear the right kinds of little things underneath, he would head into the lingerie department of stores like Macy's and Gimbels" to select appropriate costumes for his paramours' future performances (20–21). This notion that there are "right" and "wrong" kinds of intimate apparel offers evidence that in Cesar's worldview merely being female does not definitively establish a woman's femininity, that one has to *perform* femaleness.

Ironically, the sheer repetitiveness of Cesar's own sexual performances—what he would consider proof of his maleness—implies that masculine identity is likewise a tenuous construct. The Mambo King's adult life is a virtually unending series of amorous encounters through which his irresistible appeal for women is affirmed time and again. Aside from his fetish for erotically correct undergarments, he is not particularly choosy about the partners he takes to bed. He enjoys the carnal pleasures of "some girl on Coney Island," a woman with a broken leg in a cast, a woman standing next to him at the Macy's Thanksgiving Day parade ("a massive woman with pendulous breasts, but, *coño*, was she motherly"), a French woman he meets on a harbor tour boat (159–61). To console himself after Nestor's tragic death in a car accident—Nestor was driving as Cesar and Vanna Vane necked in the back seat—Cesar embarks on a period of untrammeled sexual activity:

So for a time his life was a rainfall of frilly panties, bursting girdles, camisoles, slips, brassieres, gartered nylons, thick condoms, baking soda and Coca-Cola douches, curly blond, red, and black pubic hair. He enjoyed the company of pear-bottomed, sweaty-thighed Negresses. . . . He banged Italian beauties ... and spinsters. .... He made it with cigarette and hatcheck girls, hostesses and twenty-five-cents-a-dance girls. ... He made it with three of the musicians who played with Tiny Tina Maracas. (197–198)

In a rare occurrence, Cesar experiences rejection at the hands of his brother's widow Delores. Overcome by desire for her, he tries to convince Delores that he could satisfy her just as he has so many other women. His justification for his actions is his concern that Nestor's death has left Delores without a man and therefore lacking: "I may have crossed the boundary of good manners, but if I did, that was because I wanted so badly to give to her all that God had chosen to take away" (202). By refusing him, Delores deals a serious blow to Cesar's delusions of omnipotent masculinity: She confounds his assumption that all women's needs are the same and that he is the answer to those needs.

In the final passage of *Mambo Kings*, Cesar is in such a deteriorated state that he is no longer physically able to continue his sexual pursuits. As he languishes in the Hotel Splendour taking inventory of the women in his life, he realizes that his countless romantic encounters have failed to provide him with the affirmation of self — what he would call love — that he was seeking. His male identity came to be defined by sex to the extent that when sexual conquest is impossible he loses the sense of who he is. As Cesar compiles one final compendium of the "loves" of his life, the recurring theme is how love has failed him in spite of his claims to have cared about his women:

And suddenly he remembers all these faces, pretty young female faces that he spent endless energies chasing, some of whom he loved, and some of whom he hardly knew.

And I loved you, Ana ... don't you ever think that memory has left me ... And I loved you, Miriam ... And I loved you, Verónica ... but we were never to be ... And I loved you Vívian. .... [Y]ou told me, "I hope you're the man who will be my husband and to whom I will lose my virginity," but I was stupid and became very angry, thinking "Why wait?" especially because of the state I was in ... and I loved you, Margarita ... I was never Tarzan or Hercules, all I ever wanted was a little comfort, a few kisses ... [I]n my household I had been made to feel like shit ... It was only because of the way some women looked at me that I knew I was worth something more. .... I loved you because you seemed to finally love me. (389–92)

Cesar's insistence that he was not a he-man like the icons of supreme masculinity, Tarzan and Hercules, is not particularly convincing at this point in the narrative. Sex is the performance upon which Cesar's sense of his maleness has depended. On his deathbed he remains as obsessed with his manliness as he was when, as a boy, he proudly displayed his erect penis to one of the family's female servants ("He was at the age when he wanted to flaunt his newfound virility before the world" [211]). The emptiness he feels in his final days is not only because he believes that love has failed him; he is also experiencing firsthand the impossibility of ever definitively establishing his masculinity.

The compulsive repetition and excess in *Mambo Kings* allow the text to be read as a symbolic drag show through which the notion of gender identities is parodied. In *The Greatest Performance,* drag is incorporated in literal form by means of fantasies that Rosa and Mario share and develop together. The drag performances in which the two characters imagine themselves participating enable them to explore uncharted territory of gender and cultural identity. As previous discussion of Mario's and Rosa's childhoods has indicated, early expressions of their sexuality tended to reflect the sexual invert roles — femme *loca* and butch dyke, respectively — associated with the popular conception of homosexuality in Cuba. With their Anglo-American lovers, they learn to mask their Latina/o excess by "cross-dressing" as Anglos.

Mario and Rosa call upon their creativity and begin constructing an ethnic gay/lesbian space: a sort of utopia where homophobia and Anglocentrism — and their normative/regulatory implications — have been abolished. The characters begin by inventing an alternative version of their childhood, exorcising the pain of recriminations and repressed desires with fantasies of a past in which they would be free to perform as they choose. They imagine the show they would have planned for their neighbors in Cuba: a campy musical love story starring Rosita as The Carnival Queen and Marito as her leading man, Amor. As they elaborate their fantasy, they envision themselves cancelling the show because at one rehearsal Mario confesses that he wants to be the Carnival Queen. Rosa imagines what the moment would have been like:

You shared your secret with me that evening. And I shared mine with you. You told me that you didn't like playing the handsome Amor, that who you really wanted to play was the Carnival Queen. I told you that . . . deep down inside I didn't want to be her, that who I really wanted to be was Amor. And so you said . . . "Why can't we do the show for ourselves, being the person that we want to be?" And we performed for each other, didn't we? And we fulfilled our wish (23).

This provocative passage is particularly significant when its intersecting performances of cultural identity and sexuality are examined. I would argue, in fact, that cross-dressing allows the two characters to perform ethnicity and sexuality simultaneously. Rosa's reminiscence/fantasy of a Latina/o drag show demonstrates how subverting the heterosexist masculine/feminine binary does not diminish ones Cubanness. The hypermasculinity and hyperfemininity of the figures of the virile, dashing Amor and the ultrafemme Carnival Queen, respectively, make traditional Latino/a gender norms visible. Rosa's and Mario's homosexuality, which is unintelligible according to these norms, is incorporated into the spectacle when they articulate their desire to reverse gender roles. In their fantasy, the two characters challenge Cuban tradition through their sexuality yet retain their claim to Latina/o identity. Later, the ravages of AIDS leave Mario emaciated, and one day Rosa tells him that thanks to his "sexier cheek bones" he is finally turning into Rosita Fornés (138). Here a "gay disease" allows Mario to perform as female, indeed, as an icon of *Cuban* femininity. Again, gender subversion and sexual transgression are intricately linked to *cubanidad*. Cuban identity, embodied by Fornés's highly recognizable facial features, is inscribed on the body of a *gay male;* this intriguing intersection of identities undermines the heterosexism of Cuban culture.

The drag motif as developed in *The Greatest Performance* serves to highlight the performative dimension of identity. As discussed above, the draglike performances of Cesar and the female characters in *Mambo Kings* reinforce the postulation that drag parodies the notion of originary gender identities. Rosa's and Mario's version of drag further underscores the constructedness of the supposedly essential masculine and feminine identities portrayed in *Mambo Kings*. Ultimately Cesar is no more a carrier of masculine essence than is Amor, as played by either Mario or Rosa. Likewise, neither the femininity of the female characters in *Mambo Kings* nor that of the Carnival Queen is ever definitively established. The drag narrative in *The Greatest Performance* directly questions gender roles and compulsory heterosexuality, while the theoretical implications of drag for *Mambo Kings'* male and female characters make reassessment of identity categories necessary. Mario and Rosa never actually performed their Latina/o drag show as children, but its narration in *The Greatest Performance* calls attention to the need to acknowledge diversity within U.S. Cuban culture. Reading the two novels together produces a powerful challenge to essentialized Cubanness that is organized around prescribed performances of masculinity, femininity, and sexuality.

MEMORY AND THE INVENTION OF IDENTITY

While issues of gender and cultural identity are foregrounded in *The Mambo Kings Play Songs of Love* and *The Greatest Performance,* both novels portray identity in general as transitory. The recurring motif of the Castillo brothers' appearance on the *I Love Lucy* show lends visible form to this notion of identity as performance and as fleeting image. For Nestor's son Eugenio, each time the episode is screened his dead father is reincarnated as he appears "again and again at Desi Arnaz's door" (366). Through the media-reproduced simulacrum of the images of Cesar and Nestor, the brothers are revived endlessly, year after year, in countless households. Eugenio reflects that the experience of watching yet another repeat of the episode is "like watching something momentous, say the Resurrection . . . my father was now newly alive" (4). Evidently viewing this particular show is something of a ritual for both Eugenio and his uncle Cesar, whom he struggles to wake from a drunken stupor with "Uncle, get up! Please get up! You're on television again" (5). Eugenio considers seeing his father again, if only for brief moments, to be an occurrence of almost spiritual significance. When the brothers are no longer visible on the screen, when they have once again ceased to exist, Eugenio reflects that "the miracle had passed, the resurrection of a man" (8). Like the sacrament of Communion, watching the program is a ritual based on the symbolic consumption of an absent signified, Nestor Castillo.

After each "resurrection," all that remains are memories, traces like those left by Cesar's demonstrations of his masculinity. In his later years, Cesar begins to realize that he has nothing lasting to show for his life of hedonism, and remembering becomes his obsession. During one of the Mambo King's reflective moments in the Hotel Splendour, he contemplates the sheer repetitiveness of daily life:

> How many thousands of cigarettes had he smoked? How many leaks had he taken? Belches? Fucks, ejaculations? . . .
> He did more figuring. Bottles of rum and whiskey, enough to fill a warehouse, all turned into piss. He'd consumed enough food and left the world enough shit to fill Fort Knox. . . .
> Endless numbers of cigarettes.
> A million smiles, pinches on nice female bottoms, tears. (381–82)

Cesar realizes that what drove all his excesses was his desire "to be someone significant" (382). The endless food, drinks, cigarettes, and sexual conquests were escapes through which he avoided confronting the emptiness of his life, his lack of a sense of self.[25]

Cesar concludes his tally of excesses with a despairing "And for what?" (382), finally acknowledging that outside of memory there is no tangible evidence of his existence. He laments that "it seemed that all he had were memories, that where his pleasures resided now was in the past" (268). He has destroyed his health, his musical career has ended, and he has succeeded in driving away every woman who ever loved him. Cesar has no health insurance, no security, "no little house in the Pennsylvania countryside"; he possesses only "[a] few letters from Cuba, a wall filled with autographed pictures, a headful of memories, sometimes scrambled like eggs" (308).

Cesar's reminiscence and self-searching at the Hotel Splendour reveal the persistence of Cuba in his memory and its impact on his sense of who he is. As an immigrant who has enjoyed considerable success in the United States, he does not experience acute nostalgia or debilitating longing for the homeland like the impoverished Puerto Rican characters in *The Line of the Sun* (see chapter 4). Even so, his Cuban cultural heritage provides the inspiration for many of the songs he writes, "songs written to take listeners back to the plazas of small towns in Cuba, to Havana, to past moments of courtship and love, passion, and a way of life that was fading from existence" (39). His music, with its focus on a place that can be revisited only through nostalgia, reinforces some of the collective fictions of Cuban culture that the émigrés hold dear. Fully immersed in his pursuit of the American dream, Cesar forges commercial success out of both his fellow immigrants' emotional attachment to their *patria*, and the exoticness, for mainstream America, of the culture that his songs portray. This simultaneous engagement of traditional *cubanidad* and American consumerism illustrates the negotiation that is integral to the invention of ethnic culture.

Cesar's own connection to Cuba grows more powerful with the passage of time. During his first years in New York, he had fantasized about a triumphant, immigrant-makes-good return to his village of Las Piñas: "[I]n emulation of the Hollywood movies, he would drive into Las Piñas in a fancy automobile, laden with nice gifts from the States, pockets filled with money" (207–8). Only after Nestor's death does Cesar actually make the trip back to Cuba, and he does so seeking emotional healing more than admiration. Selectively recalling the positive aspects of home — its beauty and tranquility, happy childhood moments with Nestor, his mother's unconditional love — he arrives in Havana in 1958 in the midst of the revolution. The capital is still much as he remembered it, and he describes the street where his ex-wife and daughter live as "a beautiful calm street, sunny and quiet — the other Havana of his dreams" (204). After a couple of Tres Medallas brandies and an espresso, he begins to experience the desired soothing effect that being home produces: "Cuba was making him feel better already" (205).

Cesar's 1958 visit to his homeland reaffirms his belief that he has a permanent emotional center in Cuba. He revels in the joy of returning to his mother's comforting embrace:

> He was happy to be home. His mother's affection was so strong that for one brief moment he had an insight into love: pure unity. That's all she became in those moments, the will to love, the principle of love, the protectiveness of love, the grandeur of love. (209)

Home, for Cesar, *is* his mother; he has managed to erase most of the memories of his tormented relationship with his abusive father ("Cesar had the worst trouble thinking about his father; even remembering his appearance was difficult" [212]). Thus the notion of the *madre patria* has almost literal significance for Cesar: A return to Cuba is a return to his mother.

With the death of Cesar's mother a few years after the triumph of the revolution, home as he had known it ceases to exist. Likewise, because of the changes wrought by the revolution, the Cuba of the past is no longer accessible to the Cuban immigrants living in the United States. Cesar observes that numerous Cuban musicians are fleeing the island and arriving in Miami, many of them feeling bitter and disenchanted "because [their] Cuba no longer existed" (259). Travel from the United States to Cuba becomes impossible; Cesar often finds himself daydreaming about Cuba and notes that "[i]t made a big difference to him that he just couldn't get on an airplane and fly down to Havana to see his daughter or to visit the family in Las Piñas" (258–59). On a more symbolic level, Cuban immigrants are transformed into exiles, and in the Cuban characters' nostalgia their homeland acquires the aura of a lost paradise. Rosa's family in *The Greatest Performance* typifies this exile mentality with their endless talk about "how happy they would be . . . if they could all go back to Guantánamo some day" (133).

In Cesar's final years, Cuba serves as his metaphor for the past. He perceives both Cuba and the past to be ephemeral and irretrievable, as a conversation with his girlfriend Lydia indicates:

> "See, the worst part of it is that things don't exist anymore."
> "What things?"
> "Cuba." (353)

While his nostalgia for Cuba is focused more on his mother than on an abstract concept of the country, he expresses an exile's painful sense of loss as he sits in the Hotel Splendour and ponders, "What happened to his Cuba? His memories?" (334). Ironically, Cesar's possessive reference to *his* Cuba highlights the fragility rather than the strength of his connection to the homeland.

In *Mambo Kings*, this juxtaposition of the image of prerevolution Cuba and Cesar's memories underscores the role of imagination and illusion in the reconstitution of both. The novel affirms that all memory relies heavily on invention, as indicated by Cesar's and Desi Arnaz's efforts to determine if they might have met in Cuba: "And then in the way that Cubans get really friendly, Arnaz and Cesar reinvented their pasts so that, in fact, they had probably been good friends" (127).[26] Cesar's project, as "underwritten" by Eugenio, is the invention of his own history by gathering diverse memories and fabricating as needed to fill in the gaps. Cesar's reminiscences seem to be motivated by a desire not only to relive his history but also to fix it permanently; Eugenio's longing to resurrect his dead father hints that this is his desire as well. In contrast, for Rosa and Mario in *The Greatest Performance* the pain of their past makes memory more a burden than a source of pleasure. Yet they refuse to allow themselves to be tormented by the things they recall; their liberation begins as they rewrite the past and reinvent their memories. They achieve this by weaving together dialogue, descriptions of photographs, invented recollections, and fantasies to produce an intriguing unconventional narrative.

The fantasy that Rosa and Mario were childhood confidantes is inspired by a photo in Rosa's old album. She points out a picture of her special "buddy" from the neighborhood and declares, "In my childhood story you have become that kid, Marito. Or rather, he has become you" (16). Next is a series of flashbacks in which the two characters recount key events from the past: Mario's abuse-filled childhood, Rosa's year in Spain before being reunited with her family in the United States, Mario's period of self-discovery in the California gay community, Rosa's integration into American life and her sexual liberation. This "history" provides the foundation and the motivation for the more elaborate fantasies that follow. In one fantasy Mario wreaks revenge on the pedophile Hernando, and in another he possesses God in human form by assuming the form of a vampire. He returns to the sites of painful memories, sharing his images with Rosa; in their final fantasy together, she helps him forgive his father. For Rosa and Mario, memory is a creative endeavor in which they intervene freely. They discover that they have the power to transform the past as well as to influence the present and the future.

Cesar primarily uses memory to nostalgically revisit long-lost people and places from his history. Rosa and Mario experience little of this kind of nostalgia, for living in the United States offers them freedom from the sexual oppression of their ancestral culture. Yet their unavoidable contact with the U.S. Cuban community reminds them that because of their sexual orientation they are, in Edward Said's words, "exiled by exiles" (361).[27] In their daily life they must project an illusion created by acceptable performances, or be ostracized by family and community. Joseph Beam, a gay African-American, eloquently describes this kind of exclusion when he declares, "I am most often rendered invisible, perceived as a threat to the family, or am tolerated if I am silent and inconspicuous. I cannot go home as who I am and that hurts me deeply" (231).

The final passage of *The Greatest Performance* is a moving account of the alienation experienced by individuals who are excluded from the communities to which they supposedly belong. Rosa and Mario respond to this double exile by constructing their own home; as Rosa reflects at the end of the novel,

[a]fter searching Heaven and Earth for a true love, for a generous homeland, for a family who wouldn't abuse us or condemn us, for a body who wouldn't betray our truest secrets, we found each other: a refuge, a song, a story to share (149).

In this refuge, the two characters are no longer subject to repression resulting from the normative influence of the U.S. Cuban community's dominant ideology, of compulsory heterosexuality, of essentialized gender categories.[28] At the same time, they discover that they need not renounce their heritage altogether. During the week they are awaiting the results of Mario's AIDS test, the two friends revel in the comforting familiarity of their shared cultural past. They listen to old records (Los Memes, Los Bravos, Armando Manzanero, Raphael); they watch videos of Latin American classic films and eat their favorite Cuban foods (127). Rosa and Mario discover that their friendship offers them a haven where neither their sexuality nor their cultural background must be disguised. This episode offers textual evidence of the transformation of culture through everyday performative acts. As gay and lesbian characters who are also undeniably Latinos, Mario and Rosa simultaneously affirm the importance of their cultural encyclopedia and add a subversive new chapter to it.

The protagonists' most important invention, then, is the ethnic gay/lesbian space that they forge together, a place where they defy normative definitions of gender, Cuban, and gay/lesbian identities. Mario declares that they are "a unique breed of *Cubanos*," or more accurately, "Cuban hyphen Americans" according to Rosa (107). For the two characters, this new category is necessitated by their refusal to conform to either Cuban or Anglo-American stereotypes of gender or cultural identity. Nevertheless, while the dismantling of anachronistic roles is a progressive move, the alternative — no rules, just improvisation — is a challenge to negotiate. In a key scene, Rosa is assessing her current emotional status as she cooks in the kitchen of the condo she shares with Joan. Rosa has concluded that by the time she arrived in the United States, she was "too old to become a true Gringa, too young to embody the Guantanamera myth" (116). She feels she became truly free when she "broke out of her Cuban closet and invaded the Night of American Pleasures," and she revels in the absence of telltale signs of Cuban excess in her condo: "no maps of the Crocodile-Island, no flags, no black beans no *picadillo* no *yuca* and no *mercocha*. No one screams *coño* in this house. No one longs for a return to the way things used to be" (116–17).

Rosa's apparent rejection of all things Cuban began while she was still in high school, when she "began to see nostalgia as [her] enemy" (84). Concluding that to succeed in America she had to stop "living off memories" the way her parents did, she did everything in her power to assimilate: hiding all her mementos of Cuba, going to American movies, eating hamburgers, and dying her hair blonde (84). Now Rosa celebrates her mobility as a "liberated thirty-something human being with no ties and no roots anywhere" who teaches Spanish language and literature but reads soft-core lesbian porno novels at home (118). That is, like the protagonist in Sheila Ortiz Taylor's *Southbound*, Rosa moves between communities, performing the identity mandated in each space. At the university, her performance is that expected of a generic (i.e., heterosexual) Latina; at home, she assumes the role of (Anglo-)American lesbian. Rosa believes that she has at last freed her lesbian self by rejecting the Cuban conventions that negate the possibility of lesbian identity. Even so, a tone of irony infuses her repeated claims that she is happy as part of the "booming, advanced universe" of middle-class Anglo-American culture.

Rosa knows the satisfaction that comes from successfully acting as if she were at home wherever she happens to be. But she and Mario also share the exile's knowledge that this dissimulation is stressful and often exhausting. The relationship between the two characters frees them from the need for such negotiation. In the space of the story they tell, they no longer perform as assimilated Anglo-Americans nor as culturally conservative (i.e., nationalistic and homophobic) U.S. Cubans.

Through their fantasies, by revising their history, Rosa and Mario are able to erase some of the injustice and oppression they have suffered. Shortly before Mario's death, Rosa uses a final drag fantasy to help him exorcise his anger toward his father. She envisions Mario making a stunning appearance at the Club Cubano José Martí, dressed in a low-cut, rose-colored evening gown and green veil, "blonde hair pulled back in a chignon; high cheek bones, defying eyes caressed by the penumbra" (141). Rosa observes that the women are talking about him: "One of them says you should see a doctor. Or a priest. But a doctor for sure, because you need help . . . because you look and act too much like a woman" (141–42). The club then assumes the role of a jury that is trying the ultrafemme Mario for killing his father; the accused declares that he is not ashamed of his crime. Through this symbolic act, Rosa empowers Mario to take a defiant, liberating stand against the authoritative discourses that have regulated his performances of gender.

The challenge to power and authority that this fantasy articulates is paralleled in the novel's experimental narrative structure. In the first eight chapters, two distinct voices control the narration, alternating between chapters (chapter 1 is narrated from Rosa's perspective, chapter 2 from Mario's, and so on). In the final two chapters of the novel, these two voices are gradually more difficult to distinguish until, with Mario's death, the two narrators fuse into a single voice. A possible interpretation of this disappearance of one of the narrative voices is that Rosa has controlled the narration from the beginning and the final voice is hers. I find more provocative a reading that takes into consideration the novel's continuous questioning of power structures and discourses of authority. The shifting voices decentralize narrative authority in the text: control of the narration cannot be ascribed to a single, definable source. Both this fusion of narrative voices, and the final narrator's fantasy of a utopian space where gender is fluid and nonhierarchical, involve the decentralization of power: "Be ROSAMARIO, ROSARIO, ROSAMAR, MARITOROSA, MARIROSA. . ." (149).

This final fantasy sequence proposes how life might be for Rosa and Mario if they lived in a society that celebrated difference rather than repressing it. In this utopia, identity has limitless, shifting possibilities:

We were made in test tubes and we were able to choose, as adults, the identity and gender that we fancied. Then we were free . . . to change from man to woman, from woman to man, from tree to flower, from ocean water to ivy. Better yet: we have existed from time immemorial as air. (150)

The apparent contradictions in this vision of identity are ones that cannot be resolved, for as both novels suggest, identity cannot be fixed or defined. Mario realizes this when the doctor who gives him the results of his AIDS test asks Mario to tell him who he is: "And for the life of me, I couldn't respond . . . I was a vacuous form where nothingness lived. How could I tell him who I was. Did I know?" (129). Mario can only describe events in his life and memories that might offer clues to the never-to-be-completed puzzle of his identity.

Mambo Kings corroborates this notion of self as a collection of performances subject to perpetual reinterpretation. As Desi Arnaz says to Eugenio at
the end of the novel, "One day, all this will either be gone or it will last forever"
(403). Although Arnaz is referring to his garden, his comment has interesting
implications for questions of identity. When Nestor leaves his apartment for
the last time before his accident, the narrative voice foreshadows his death
with the observation that "[a]lready he was fading away, . . . his being compro-
mised by memory, like a ghost" (177). This comment reveals the ephemeral
quality of Nestor's existence, which is only as permanent as the traces of his
performances that remain in the memories of those who knew him. Both
novels in fact support this notion that identity is a dynamic merging of past,
present, and future. The literary text, as the space of both memory and fantasy,
makes the reading of all these performances possible. Writing is thus closely
connected to the invention of self, as the narrator acknowledges at the end of
Greatest Performance:

> I will create this place where you can be who you've always wanted to be,
> Marito. Where You and I have become the same person. This moment of
> greatness, I will create it. When the performance ends. And life begins
> (151).

Life, for Rosa and Mario, is liberation from cultural and gender norms that
impose narrow standards of "acceptable" conduct. The greatest performance,
then — the story Mario and Rosa share — is the one produced by the text itself.
The novel, as an act of "coming out," makes U.S. Cuban gay and lesbian
subjectivity visible; it thereby reveals the constructed nature of masculinity,
femininity, and Cuban cultural identity. In *Mambo Kings*, likewise, the possibility that Cesar's memoirs are Eugenio's invention allows the text to be read
not as documentation of authentic *cubanidad* but rather as the representation
of a symbolic drag show. In Hijuelos's novel, the compulsion to repeat cultural
and gender performances to excess is a red flag signaling the fragility of these
identity categories. Thus the dialogue between *The Greatest Performance* and
The Mambo Kings Play Songs of Love offers compelling evidence that identity
is an invention — a show that must go on.

FOUR

INVENTION OF THE ETHNIC SELF
IN LATINA IMMIGRANT FICTION

The Line of the Sun *and* How the García Girls Lost Their Accents

I am not african. Africa is in me,
but I cannot return.
I am not taína. Taíno is in me,
but there is no way back.
I am not european. Europe lives
in me, but I have no home there.
I am new. History made me . . .
— AURORA LEVINS MORALES,
"Child of the Americas"

The tension generated when dissimilar cultures come into contact—
tension between past and present, between family history and daily
life—is particularly visible in literature by immigrant writers.[1] Typically, the characters in American immigrant novels assume an identifiable
stance with respect to both their ancestral culture and the dominant culture.
Some immigrant protagonists, frustrated by the difficulties experienced in adjusting to life in the United States, develop an exilelike mentality. Such characters' rejection of dominant American culture and their intense longing for
home are reflected in nostalgic reveries about the "old country."[2] More common in immigrant literature written in English are characters who advocate
assimilation in response to their desire for socioeconomic advancement and
participation in the American cultural milieu.[3]

Successful assimilation implies the adoption of "American" beliefs and behavior patterns. Assimilation came to be associated with "Anglo-conformity"
in the late nineteenth century, when the prevailing perspective held that such
values and attributes were those directly derived from the earliest English/
Protestant settlers (Fine 25). Assimilation was thus distinct from the concept
of the "melting pot," i.e., the blending and fusing of diverse elements to produce "new Americans." Due in part to the antiforeigner sentiment generated
by World War I, the two concepts have become conflated and are both used to
denote conformity and standardization. In traditional immigrant novels, this

cultural upheaval is reflected in characters' struggles to learn English and to acquire customs and attitudes that allow them to blend into the dominant culture. They accomplish this by discarding (or hiding) those cultural traits — "excesses" — that mark them as foreigners. For many such characters, assimilation is a surrender to homogenization that challenges their definitions of self.

Works by Caribbean-born U.S. Latina/o writers are part of a literary corpus that dates back to narratives by nineteenth-century European immigrants.[4] The protagonists of these works assume the role of unique historical subjects establishing their difference from the dominant culture through a series of adjustments and struggles to adapt to the receiving society. The recurring themes in literature by Puerto Rican migrants to New York are common to all urban immigrant literature: adjustment to a hostile metropolitan setting, the transformation of roles and family structures, and the effects of racist oppression and alienation (Gordils 53).[5] Novels by island-born Puerto Ricans living in New York have addressed the (im)migrant experience since at least the 1940s, when large-scale migrations to the mainland occurred as a result of the United States government's Operation Bootstrap program. Bernardo Vega's *Memorias de Bernardo Vega*, written during that decade, deals with the New York Puerto Rican community from the time of Vega's arrival in 1916. The vignettes in Jesús Colón's *A Puerto Rican in New York and Other Sketches* are similarly set in the first three decades of this century. The literature of the Caribbean immigrant experience has been further expanded by the relatively recent publication of novels written in English by mainland residents of Puerto Rican descent and by immigrants from Cuba and the Dominican Republic.[6]

Critics and teachers of U.S. Latina/o literature are inclined to give at least a passing glance to such immigrant writings because of their thematic material. These works are visibly "Latina/o"; even in proassimilation texts by immigrant writers, cultural tradition figures prominently. For immigrants who relocate permanently in the United States, preservation of their heritage is contested through economic pressure to assimilate; in addition, their cultural origin or ground is accessible only through nostalgia. Many immigrant works nevertheless reflect an ambivalent position toward the culture of origin, which they do not summarily reject. I propose that works by contemporary Latina/o immigrant writers challenge the assimilationist notion of discarding one's "old" identity and assuming a new American persona. Assimilation becomes less a goal to be achieved than a literary framing device that allows commentary on the ancestral culture. Whether the narrator's stance toward his/her ancestral culture is affirmative or critical, the text reflects tension generated by the bicultural context. The dynamic subjectivity articulated in such texts is constituted through performances that reveal constant negotiation between the immigrants' culture of origin and dominant American culture.

Thus U.S. Latina/o immigrant fiction, like works by ethnic gay and lesbian writers, lends visible form to the performativity of cultural identity. In the process, immigrant writing offers additional evidence of the diverse ideologies that Latina/o culture encompasses. In two recent novels by island-born U.S. Latina writers, the possibility of complete assimilation is questioned, while memories of the *patria* fail to satisfy the immigrants' yearning for a home. Judith Ortiz Cofer's *The Line of the Sun* (1989) and Julia Alvarez's *How the García Girls Lost Their Accents* (1991) deal with Latina/o immigrant families living in the New York area.[7] Both of these artful texts have female narrative voices and juxtapose preimmigration family history with present-day life in America. In both works, the "island" continues to exert a powerful influence on the immigrant characters.

In Ortiz Cofer's novel, the narrator Marisol pieces together the events that brought her mother, father, and uncle to the United States from their village in Puerto Rico. Their story of poverty and immigrant illusions lays the groundwork for her narration of the family's struggles to adjust to life in their working-class New Jersey ethnic community. The characters in Alvarez's novel, on the other hand — Dr. Carlos García, his wife and four daughters — are members of an upper-class Dominican family forced to flee their country because of the father's involvement in an aborted political coup. The narration is presented in reverse chronological order by a narrative voice that shifts among the daughters. *García Girls* focuses on the family's attempts to become fully assimilated, middle- (or upper-) class Americans, and the novel addresses issues of race and class to a far lesser degree than does *The Line of the Sun.*

From the dominant Anglo-American perspective, the immigrant characters in these novels possess an essentialized ethnic identity that manifests itself through performances that transgress cultural norms. In response to society's censure of their ethnic excesses, the characters either strive to assimilate — to eliminate the excess — or seek refuge in the familiarity of their ethnic community. However, the narrators' experiences challenge the notion of static cultural paradigms upon which assimilation ideology and immigrant nostalgia rely. In both *The Line of the Sun* and *How the García Girls Lost Their Accents,* the characters' daily life is portrayed as what Gustavo Pérez-Firmat would call a dynamic "cohabitation" of cultures and languages (1987, 5). From this interaction of cultural traditions, a subjectivity emerges that is distinct from both the voice of the assimilated immigrant and the nostalgic voice of the exile. This chapter will focus on the manner in which *ethnic* identity is constituted in these texts through the shifting relationships of their narrators — immigrant children in both novels — to their ancestral culture and to American culture. These narrators discover that as ethnic U.S. Latinas, they will be constantly inventing themselves.

EXCESS AND ETHNIC PERFORMATIVITY

Some of Ortiz Cofer's and Alvarez's immigrant characters visibly demonstrate solidarity with the dominant ideology through their efforts to perform as fully assimilated Americans. Other characters, in their attempts to preserve island culture in the United States, engage in performative acts that transgress dominant American norms. Ethnic communities are the site of many such ethnic performances; they are prominent evidence of the vitality and tenacity of ethnic culture.[8] The physical signs of cultural difference — businesses, restaurants, celebrations, traditional clothing — demarcate a space of resistance to assimilation. Generating blips of transgression on the American cultural radar screen, ethnic communities create eruptions of excess that project an image of community identity to the "nonethnic" majority.

According to Judith Butler's model of gender performance, the illusion of essential, originary gender identities is created through performances that dominant norms have ascribed to a specific identity category. I have proposed that this model can be modified in order to theorize ethnic or racial identity as well. In *The Line of the Sun* and *García Girls,* American society operates under the illusion of essential ethnic identity produced by performative acts. This "preexisting" ethnic subjectivity in turn makes the immigrant characters, like the gay characters in John Rechy's works, identifiable targets for oppressive practices. Insofar as the ethnic performances transgress dominant cultural norms, subjugation of the ethnic group through discrimination can be justified. Regardless of the degree to which the immigrants in Ortiz Cofer's and Alvarez's novels try to assimilate, the "law" — dominant American norms of race, language, and so forth — assigns them an essentialized ethnic identity. This in turn allows the power differential between minority and majority groups to be maintained.

The performances through which ethnic identity is constituted are not necessarily acts of volition. Racial difference, for example, is an inadvertent performance of "excess" that makes complete assimilation impossible for some immigrants. For those immigrants with racial difference visibly inscribed on their bodies, no amount of performing will ever permit them to pass as white Americans. Mary Ann Doane examines psychoanalytical implications of race through her reading of Frantz Fanon's *Black Skin, White Masks*. Fanon argues that in colonial societies (and, I would add, in white-dominated societies like the United States), the nonwhite subject is the victim of a "disabling over-visibility." Skin is thus the most immediately visible marker of racial "excess" (Doane 223).[9]

In both novels, non-Anglo characters express a vague recognition of the danger — the racial hierarchy — that lurks behind Anglo-American whiteness. In *The Line of the Sun,* the narrator's mother Ramona first encounters racial difference in the form of a young, blue-eyed American soldier assigned to the island. Her speculation, "How could anyone who had no depth in his pupils see the world the same as she did with her dark brown eyes?" (160), fore-shadows her firsthand experience of the impenetrability of American culture. Likewise, the Garcías' Haitian servant Chucha perceives a threat in the color-less faces of the American diplomatic personnel that whisk the Garcías away from their home in the Dominican Republic. She describes these men and their compatriots as "[t]oo pale to be the living. The color of zombies, a nation of zombies. I worry about them, the girls, Doña Laura, moving among men the color of the living dead" (221). Although her concern is unfocused, Chucha's own experiences as a black in a society stratified by skin color have undoubt-edly given her ample knowledge of the danger that whiteness represents for people of color. Through her comment she anticipates the racism to which the Garcías will be vulnerable as Latinos in the United States.

Ortiz Cofer also alludes to the "disabling over-visibility" of Latinos through advice given to Marisol's uncle Guzmán when he first arrives in New York City. Guzmán is a fugitive, fleeing from the manager of the migrant camp from which he escaped; a fellow Puerto Rican admonishes him, " 'If I were you I would stay off these streets in daylight for a while. At night all cats and Puerto Ricans look black.' " (200). This passage challenges the popular notion of immigrants disappearing into white America by insinuating that the Afro-Hispanic heritage of many Caribbean immigrants makes invisibility possible only in darkness. At night, at least, Guzmán's physical characteristics allow him to occupy a legitimate position on the white-black binary through which race is constructed in the United States. Ironically, Guzmán can achieve a degree of invisibility in American society by performing as a member of an established racial minority, i.e., as an African-American.

Later Marisol notes that skin color sets her apart even from her immigrant classmates. She becomes aware that she is "the smallest, darkest member of a class full of the strapping offspring of Irish immigrants with a few upstart Italians added to the roll" (218). Theoretically, Marisol and her family have the same opportunity to succeed in American society as members of other immigrant groups. Her observation alludes to the fact that being marked by the "excess" of racial difference creates an additional obstacle for Latina/o immigrants like herself. The Irish and Italian immigrants are visible ethnic minorities who possess significant political and economic power. The racially ambiguous Puerto Ricans, on the other hand, can neither disappear into Anglo America nor pass unnoticed among members of other "authorized" minority groups.

Thus the immigrant characters are inescapably marked as "Other" to the (white) majority; as a result they are subjected to incidents of racism through which their status as unwelcome outsiders is reinforced. The Garcías' encounters with Anglo racial intolerance are similar to Marisol's. Their downstairs neighbor in their first New York apartment, a cantankerous old woman with "a helmet of beauty parlor blue hair" whom they call "La Bruja," complains constantly about the family to the building superintendent. In her opinion, "[t]he Garcías should be evicted. Their food smelled. They spoke too loudly and not in English. The kids sounded like a herd of wild burros." La Bruja's criticism of the Garcías stems from her judgment of their life-style as excessive: Their food is too pungent, and their conversations and children are too loud. The family insists on speaking Spanish even though in La Bruja's mythical monolingual America, English should be sufficient for everyone. The super, himself a Puerto Rican, sympathizes with Mrs. García and advises her that "[i]t is a difficult place this country, before you get used to it. You have to not take things personal" (170). His well-meaning advice in fact attempts to justify racial and ethnic slurs directed at an entire group (in this case, Latinos) whose identity has been essentialized by the Anglo-American majority.

The immigrant children experience racism most acutely at school, a microcosm of American society. Here, too, assimilation is contingent upon acquiring American codes of language and behavior, and ethnic performances invoke the curiosity and/or ridicule of their classmates. The García girls confront prejudice firsthand when they are the target of epithets like "spic" and "greaseball" at school (107). They fall victim to Anglo homogenization of Latinos into a single group whose members are all treated with equal contempt. The girls are particularly disturbed by their encounters with racism because they are oblivious to their status as people of color in the United States. As members of the upper echelon of Dominican society, the lighter-skinned "pigmentocracy," they had never been subjected to the kind of oppression that their black and mulatto servants endured daily.

The girls' campaign to become thoroughly Americanized cannot erase their cultural heritage, for their recent immigration and Dominican background set them apart from the majority of their classmates. As a result, even their less overtly racist peers stereotype them as exotic foreigners. Yolanda García's first college boyfriend tells his parents that he is seeing "a Spanish girl," to which they respond that it should be interesting for him to learn about people from other cultures; Yolanda remarks, "It bothered me that they should treat me like a geography lesson for their son" (98). While Yolanda longs to blend in with her American classmates, the parents' well-intentioned yet patronizing reaction to her cultural heritage reminds her that she is still different, an outsider. She feels like a novelty, a museum artifact for the consumption of the dominant culture, but she lacks the language to explain even to herself what bothers her about the comment (98). That is, although the English language — writing — later becomes Yolanda's vehicle for understanding her identity, at this point her vocabulary for complex emotions and adult situations is still limited.

In *The Line of the Sun*, racism is directed toward something even less tangible than the immigrant community's smelly food or noisy conversation; in Marisol's words, the Puerto Rican immigrants are marked by

la mancha, that sign of the wetback, the stain that has little to do with the color of our skin, because some of us are as "white" as our American neighbors . . . the frightened-rabbit look in our eyes and our unending awe of anything new or foreign that identified us as the newcomers. (170)

In spite of her father's best efforts to promote the family's assimilation, they are frequently reminded that they have not made it into the American mainstream. When Rafael decides that it is time to leave the inner city for the suburbs, the family perceives the veiled racism of real estate agents who show them homes in "the middle-class Italian neighborhoods which they seemed to think were the best compromise" (282). These neighborhoods are a compromise between the Puerto Rican *barrio* and the predominantly Anglo-American areas from which the immigrants continue to be excluded. The agents, observing such performative acts as appearance, name, and accent, identify Marisol's family as "generic" ethnics who should be placed with others of their kind.

The immigrant children's knowledge of American cultural norms in *The Line of the Sun* and *García Girls* enables them to observe and comment on this very process by which they and their families are marked as ethnic. In some instances in the two novels, the performances of ethnic excess that betray the immigrants' incomplete assimilation take the form of visible markers like dress and behavior. In both novels, the parents' use of clothing that is inappropriate according to American fashion standards hinders the family's pursuit of invisibility. When Yolanda García is in college, she becomes acutely aware of how different her parents look in comparison to those of her classmates:

> My own old world parents were still an embarrassment at parents' weekend, my father with his thick mustache and three-piece suit and fedora hat, my mother in one of her outfits she bought especially to visit us at school, everything overly matched. (98)

Marisol is similarly mortified when her mother makes a dramatic appearance at her high school, her wild, loose hair, red coat and black shawl and spike heels proclaiming her defiance (or ignorance) of American norms of tastefulness:

> The kids stared at her as if she were a circus freak, and the nuns looked doubtful, thinking perhaps they should ask the gypsy to leave the school grounds. . . . My gypsy mother embarrassed me with her wild beauty. I wanted her to cut and spray her hair into a sculptured hairdo like the other ladies; I wanted her to wear tailored skirts and jackets, like Jackie Kennedy. (219)

In relation to the controlled propriety of white, middle-class fashion — with Jackie Kennedy as icon — Marisol's mother's appearance broadcasts ethnic excess.[10] While Marisol longs to be the antithesis of her exotic, "un-American" mother, she acknowledges that her mother "was what I would have looked like if I hadn't worn my hair in a tight braid, if I had allowed myself to sway when I walked, and if I had worn loud colors and had spoken only Spanish" (220). In addition to censuring Ramona's "inappropriate" clothing, Marisol judges her mother's embodiment of Latina sexuality to be excessive in relation to the controlled sexual expression of middle-class white America. In effect, Marisol's "identity" as a fully assimilated American teenager is actually a tenuous fabrication created through repeated performances whose objective is to suppress all such ethnic difference.

ASSIMILATION: ERASING THE ETHNIC EXCESSES

The scandal created by the flamboyant appearance of Marisol's mother underscores the sharp division that is maintained between "American" and "ethnic" in the American popular imagination. Many of the immigrant characters in

The Line of the Sun and *How the García Girls Lost Their Accents* seem to believe, likewise, that a clear distinction exists between their identity as island-dwellers and the "new" American identity to which they aspire. These characters, by embracing the ideology of assimilation, adhere to a traditional view of discrete cultures whereby performing as a Puerto Rican or a Dominican is incompatible with being an American. For the immigrants in these novels, the very notion of assimilation is based on their assumption that there is a definable American identity paradigm to which they must conform in order to succeed. They strive to learn which behavior patterns are associated with the "American way" and which have been identified as ethnic excess in relation to dominant cultural norms.

In both novels, assimilation is a strategy the characters employ to achieve both economic stability and invisibility, with the freedom from racist oppression that the latter offers. They work toward these goals by replacing their island-made cultural baggage with a new life-style and new traditions. The assimilation of the García girls begins in earnest after their father makes a trial visit back to the Dominican Republic and determines that there is no hope of the family's safe return there:

> He came back to New York reciting the Pledge of Allegiance, and saying, "I am given up, Mami! It is no hope for the Island. I will become *un dominican-york*." So, Papi raised his right hand and swore to defend the Constitution of the United States, and we were here to stay. (107)

Marking his shift in attitude by proclaiming support for two cornerstones of American patriotism — the Pledge of Allegiance and the Constitution — the father abandons his exile mentality and joins the ranks of immigrants striving for complete assimilation.

Like many of the immigrant characters of his generation, Carlos García envisions assimilation as a goal that is attained at the end of a one-way, linear process. This view assumes that later generations can then enjoy all the benefits of being full-fledged Americans: He croons to his American-born grandson "'You can be president, you were born here'" (27). Both García parents fervently believe that with ambition and perseverance their own potential for achievement in the United States is virtually unlimited. Laura García, the mother, spends her rare free moments inventing gadgets that she is convinced will transform American daily life. Laura's inventions offer her access to the American ideal of the self-made (wo)man, a goal that seems especially desirable since she has realized that her venerated family name is meaningless here. Laura's inventions also symbolize her own transformation as she becomes aware of the relative freedom available to her as a woman in American society: "She did not want to go back to the old country where, de la Torre or not, she was only a wife and a mother. . . . Better an independent nobody than a high-class houseslave" (143–44). On a metaphoric level, the act of invention is a fitting motif for the development of identity portrayed in both novels.

Once the García daughters accept the idea of assimilating, they throw themselves wholeheartedly into the project of discarding the annoying island customs that seem absurdly out of place in the United States. By the time Yolanda reaches college, she considers herself "pretty well Americanized" (87); as early as their teen years, in fact, the girls have rejected much of their island cultural background:

> We began to develop a taste for the American teenage good life, and soon, Island was old hat, man. Island was the hair-and-nails crowd, chaperones, and icky boys with all their macho strutting and unbuttoned shirts and hairy chests with gold chains and teensy gold crucifixes. By the end of a couple of years away from home, we had *more* than adjusted. (108–9)

Here the girls express their disdain for the hyperfemininity and hypermasculinity that characterize gender roles in Dominican society. In the United States, they discover, such performances are judged emblematic of Latina/o gender excess and are thus inconsistent with the project of assimilation.

For the García girls, adjusting to the American way of life involves doing everything in their power to adopt the appearance, speech, and behavioral codes projected by the dominant culture. The narrator notes that the second daughter, Sandi, "could pass as American, with soft blue eyes and fair skin" (181). "American," of course, is assumed to signify *Anglo*-American; in the essentializing immigrant view of American identity, racial and ethnic difference are elided altogether. Not long after the family's arrival in New York, Sandi has already observed the way American children behave toward their parents and is tempted to follow suit one night at a restaurant:

> What did she care if her parents demanded that she eat all of her *pastelón*. She would say, just as an American girl might, "I don't wanna. You can't make me. This is a free country." (184)

Food and eating habits continue to be involved in Sandi's assimilation; later, as a young woman, her desire to fit in by looking "like those twiggy models" ultimately leads to anorexia and hospitalization (51).

For all four of the García girls, the era in which they are struggling to

become Americanized — the late 1960s — is a turbulent one. Young people are
questioning the very worth of the middle-class life-style to which most immigrants aspire: "Those were the days when wearing jeans and hoop earrings,
smoking a little dope, and sleeping with their classmates were considered
political acts against the military-industrial complex" (28). This eruption of
dissenting voices on the American scene in the sixties challenged the illusion of
unitary American identity that had bolstered the melting-pot ideology. Yet the
young peoples' protests do not induce the Garcías to question the desirability
of assimilation, such as their firm belief that immigrants must endeavor to
speak perfect English. The García girls' father sends them to boarding school
in part to ensure that they learn to speak the language flawlessly.[11] Yolanda's
success is affirmed when her college boyfriend's parents compliment her on her
"accentless" English (100). As the novel's title implies, convincing performance as assimilated Americans requires immigrants to homogenize their
speech, thereby ridding it of the "excess" of a telltale accent. In the United
States, use of languages other than English are deemed ethnic performances by
the monolingual English-speaking majority, regardless of the speaker's motivation.[12] The intense campaigns by English-only movements offer clear evidence that foreign language use in minority communities in the U.S is considered a form of ethnic excess that is both unnecessary and threatening.

In *The Line of the Sun,* the drive toward assimilation is likewise represented
through the efforts of Marisol's family to perform in ways that they associate
with an American life-style. Even before Marisol is born, while her parents are
still in Puerto Rico her father tells his wife that they will choose a name for the
baby which could be easily pronounced in English (167). Once the family is established in New Jersey, they replace the Latina/o tradition of celebrating
Three Kings' Day with a Christmas tree and presents bought at Sears and Pen-
ney's, to be opened American-style on the twenty-fifth of December (186–87).

This insistence on abandoning Puerto Rican cultural traditions and sub-
stituting the American customs promoted through media images reveals the
immigrants' belief that they can reinvent themselves as full-fledged Americans.
One Christmas, when Marisol is thirteen, she receives an invitation to Christmas Eve dinner at the home of a well-to-do friend from school. She sees the
invitation as an opportunity to show how well she fits in, for she "wanted
more than anything to believe that people like the Rosellis could accept [her]
as one of their own" (189). While acceptance by an established family like the
Rosellis (ironically, of immigrant background themselves) is desirable, the
primary economic goal of Marisol's family is to gain entry into the American
middle-class. After buying a home in the suburbs, Marisol and her father
assemble a perfectly color-coordinated interior with the help of the Sears cata-

logue, complete with "curtains, sheets, throw rugs, and cushions matched in the best middle-class American taste" (283–84). In Ortiz Cofer's novel, even home decoration functions as a means of indicating identification with the values of this highly visible sector of United States society. By joining countless other middle-class American families who have replicated the perfectly matched Sears decor in their own homes, Marisol's family proclaims the success of their "de-ethnicization." Here the dynamic between visibility and invisibility is evident, for the family tries to erase their ethnic hypervisibility in their drive to gain access to American middle-class economic power.

Although the characters in *García Girls* and *The Line of the Sun* initially believe that assimilation is a worthy and attainable goal, the immigrant children in particular become aware that the process exacts a high price. Ramona's and Chucha's mistrust of white Americans suggests that on the respective islands there is an implicit awareness of the power of American culture to erase all differences, to whitewash over the visible traces of one's culture of origin. For some immigrants, this threat to their identity assumes a tangible form in the United States. Carla, the oldest García daughter, experiences the family's move to America as an event of devastating loss. While for her family "[t]he day the Garcías were one American year old" is cause for celebration, Carla thinks of the anniversary as commemorative of "the day [she] lost everything" and wishes only to be allowed to go home (150). Earlier her sister Sandi had had a premonition of the magnitude of this loss as her family was hastily preparing to flee the Island. When instructed to choose one toy to take with her to the United States, Sandi realized that "nothing quite filled the hole that was opening wide inside [her]. . . . Nothing would quite fill that need, even years after" (215).

The characters' rejection of their cultural origins may cause them to feel that they have lost their anchor or center. In both novels, middle-class suburbs are seen as the ultimate space of assimilation, a sort of "black hole" where the disappearance of the Latina/o self is a real (and for some immigrants, desirable) possibility. In *García Girls*, the Dominican relatives attending a party for Carlos García held in daughter Sofía's suburban home arrive "with tales of how they'd gotten lost on the way; the suburbs were dark and intricate like mazes with their courts and cul-de-sacs" (35). This portrayal opposes the popular (Anglo-American) view of suburbs as neat, orderly, *white* spaces. The images reveal the vague menace that American dominant culture represents for many immigrants, in spite of the allure of assimilation.

For Ramona in *The Line of the Sun*, the home her husband buys in the New Jersey suburbs embodies spiritual loss, the absence of the cultural anchors she had relied on for survival on the mainland. This house contrasts sharply with "El Building," the tenement previously inhabited by the narrator's family along with numerous other Puerto Rican immigrants. In Ramona's perception the suburban houses — "the square homes of strangers" — are like television sets: "you could see the people moving and talking, apparently alive and real, but when you looked inside it was nothing but wires and tubes" (172–73). While Ramona is away on a visit to Puerto Rico, the narrator and her father decorate their new home in "soothing hues," although Marisol suspects that her mother may be unhappy without her saints and "the brilliant reds and greens and yellows that reminded her of her lost Island paradise" (284). Unknowingly Marisol and her father participate in the elimination of excess (agitating, flamboyant colors in this case), an erasure that the dominant culture requires in order to sustain the illusion of harmony and homogeneity. When Ramona returns to settle into the new neighborhood, her reaction is negative as her daughter had feared. As Marisol observes, her mother "had come back from her real home to a place that threatened to imprison her. In this pretty little house, surrounded by silence, she would be the proverbial bird in a gilded cage" (285).

The metaphor of a bird in a gilded cage is significant in the context of immigrant narrative for its correspondence to the situation of the immigrant who has managed to "make it" to the suburbs. Beautiful surroundings (again, by middle-class Anglo-American standards) cannot mask the fact that both bird and immigrant are trapped, isolated from others of their kind; equally demoralizing is their inability to communicate. Ramona, with her limited English skills, has little contact with the outside world and is destined to remain confined and lonely. By contrast, the García daughters learn quickly that English offers them a means of gaining acceptance in their alien environment. At first Carla apologizes repeatedly to people for her poor English even though she "hated having to admit this since such an admission proved, no doubt, the . . . point that she didn't belong here" (156). Yolanda, who acknowledges having been a terrible student in the Dominican Republic, discovers that English offers her a place where she can establish herself, and she becomes an enthusiastic writer: "[I]n New York, she needed to settle somewhere, and since the natives were unfriendly, and the country inhospitable, she took root in the language" (141). Both the García girls and Marisol in *The Line of the Sun* realize that by gaining proficiency in English they acquire competence and power in a cultural space that their less bilingual parents can only endure "either with the bravura of the Roman gladiator or with . . . downcast-eyed humility" (171).

These immigrant children only gradually realize that acquisition of a new language is an arduous and seemingly endless task with powerful emotional implications. In *García Girls,* after one of Yolanda's high school teachers describes her as "vivacious," Yolanda concludes that she must initially treat even apparent compliments with suspicion if they involve unknown vocabulary. Revealing the uncertainty produced by the immigrant's linguistic weaknesses, Yolanda reflects that "English was then still a party favor for me — crack open the dictionary, find out if I'd just been insulted, praised, admonished, criticized" (87). Later, one of Yolanda's college classmates arrives late to class; based on the sound of his name, Rudolf Brodermann Elmenhurst III, Yolanda assumes that he has just rushed in from his barony somewhere in Austria.[13] When "Rudy" turns out to be an all-American heartbreaker with "a scarred, masculine, bad-boy face," Yolanda laments her tendency toward what she calls the "immigrant's failing, literalism" (89).

Yolanda's fascination with language leads her to major in English, another possible port of entry into Anglo-American society. Yet she is continually frustrated by being an outsider to the language with its multiple layers of meaning, and by extension feels alien to the dominant culture represented by her classmates:

> For the hundredth time, I cursed my immigrant origins. If only I too had been born in Connecticut or Virginia, I too would understand the jokes everyone was making on the last two digits of the year, 1969; I too would be having sex and smoking dope . . . and I would say things like "no shit," without feeling like I was imitating someone else. (94–95)

Yolanda's perception of herself as a mere imitator of American college student behavior — as a cultural impostor — suggests that language has a significant performative capacity in the assimilation process.

Clearly learning English offers important material benefits to immigrants, including access to education, employment, and the political process. Yet for many of Ortiz Cofer's and Alvarez's characters a sense of loss accompanies the supplanting of Spanish by English. As sociologist Juan Flores comments, for ethnic communities "using English is a sign of being here, not necessarily of liking it here or of belonging" (43). For some characters, the association between language and culture is so close that their sense of self is intimately linked to the language they use. In *García Girls,* a Dominican character who lives on the island argues that a person's innermost emotional responses can only be expressed in his/her first language. He tells Yolanda that in spite of her many years in the United States, "in the midst of some profound emotion, one would revert to one's mother tongue"; and to determine which language defines Yolanda's "true" cultural identity, he asks her what language she loves in (13).

Yolanda's inability to answer this question reflects the confusion her bicultural identity continues to evoke, a turmoil that simmers for years before erupting during her marriage to an Anglo-American man. For Yolanda, the threat of erasure is perceived most intensely at the site of language. Consequently, she relates her husband's incomprehension of her native tongue to the suppression of her identity, of her self, for he fails to understand even the significance of her nickname "Yo":

> "*I*" — she pointed to herself — "rhymes with the *sky!*"
> "But not with *Joe!*" John wagged his finger at her . . .
> "*Yo* rhymes with *cielo* in Spanish." Yo's words fell into the dark, mute cavern of John's mouth. *Cielo, cielo,* the word echoed. And Yo was running, like the mad, into the safety of her first tongue, where the proudly monolingual John could not catch her, even if he tried (72).

Yolanda is so traumatized by the schism that the competing languages produce in her psyche that she does indeed go mad, requiring hospitalization for a nervous breakdown. Although she recovers, she is destined to be defined by the split sense of self that is her legacy as a bilingual/bicultural individual.

THE PERSISTENCE OF NOSTALGIA

The immigrant children in *The Line of the Sun* and *García Girls* view the constant interaction of cultures and languages — the performative facet of identity — as a challenge to be met. Their parents' generation, by comparison, tends to respond to the persistent sense of being alien to their adoptive culture with intense nostalgia and longing for the past. In a sense, the parents still perceive their cultural identity to be "located" in the *patria*. Critics of mainland Puerto Rican literature have observed that the homeland can assume mythical status; Eliana Rivero compares Nuyorican idealization of Borinquen, "a beautiful, Eden-like island," "the fatherland of pristine origins," with the exaltation of Aztlán found in some Chicano literature (1985, 179). Many mainland Puerto Rican writers of the early 1970s, who were influenced by the political and cultural awakening of the late 1960s, portrayed the island as the source of a true racial or ethnic identity.[14] In both *The Line of the Sun* and *How the Garcia Girls Lost Their Accents*, the original immigrants perpetuate the notion that island culture is completely distinct from (and in many ways superior to) American culture. They view the homeland as the place where the native culture survives intact, unsullied by contact with foreigners, unthreatened by change. The homeland thus operates as one of the Latina/o community's important "collective fictions."

In Ortiz Cofer's novel and in Alvarez's to a lesser extent, the original immigrant generation shows symptoms of the "virus" of nostalgia and homesickness that Paul Tabori calls *bacillus emigraticus*.[15] In *The Line of the Sun*, the narrator Marisol observes that for the Puerto Rican women in her family's apartment building, the main topic of conversation (besides their husbands and children) was the island: "They would become misty and lyrical in describing their illusory Eden. The poverty was romanticized and relatives attained mythical proportions in their heroic efforts to survive in an unrelenting world" (174).[16]

The immigrants' idealization of the island in comparison to harsh American reality reflects their assumption that at home their ancestral culture existed in a pure, uncontaminated state. Yet *The Line of the Sun* and *García Girls* show that both Puerto Rican and Dominican cultures are infused with Anglo-American cultural signs. In the novels, evidence of the pervasive American influence on Caribbean culture appears in the island-dwellers' references to the United States. Although New York City, "the only place most of them had heard of anyone from Puerto Rico going to" (*Line of the Sun* 149), is distant, the powerful American presence permeates everyday life in Puerto Rico and the Dominican Republic and has become part of island culture at all socio-economic levels.[17]

The Puerto Rican characters in *The Line of the Sun*, most of whom are poor *campesinos*, are subject to United States colonization both in life-style (they depend on an American-owned sugar refinery for their meager living) and in their perception of the mainland. For these characters America is an idealized utopia where everyone has television sets and drives big cars (148); as Marisol's grandmother marvels, " 'The way people come up with miracles in Nueva York, the Lord Jesus will probably be spotted there next' " (40). In contrast to the lush, tropical paradise of the island, America is "la tierra de nieve" where snow is purported to fall from the sky like grated coconut and to taste like vanilla ice cream (152). For the villagers, snow is legendary, a motif that embodies the magical aura surrounding America and the seemingly limitless possibilities offered by life there. The narrator's uncle describes the mystique of snow:

When Guzmán thought of America . . . he saw a great city . . . with ornate, tall structures and wide streets all in white with *nieve, nieve*. In Spanish the word sounded exotic because so little spoken. It called forth pure breezes and crystalline lakes, and cleanliness not possible where people sweat all the time. (106)[18]

Guzmán's and his fellow villagers' association of the United States with whiteness, cold, and cleanliness reflects the pervasiveness of mass media images of America as a racially "pure" and homogenized society.

Likewise, the Dominican characters living on the island in *García Girls* dwell in the imposing shadow of American culture and politics. Here, too, snow and New York are recurring motifs; most discussions of the United States include a reference to snow or to one of the various New York landmarks that are known to all. Chucha, the Garcías' Haitian servant, describes America as "that place they were always telling me about with the talcum powder flowers falling out of the clouds and the buildings that touch Damballah's sky" (223). Even island Catholicism is influenced by the mystique of America. Another servant shows the daughter Carla her prized photo of "a powerful American Virgin" — a postcard of a robed woman "with a sharp star for a halo and a torch in her upraised hand" standing in front of "a fairytale city twinkling with Christmas lights" (260).

The wealthy Dominican characters in *García Girls* are also fascinated by American cultural icons, whose influence apparently transcends socioeconomic class. True to their privileged upbringing, the García daughters are more impressed with American consumer culture than with the Statue of Liberty. Yolanda hopes one day to visit the United States to see snow but also to experience the wondrous F. A. O. Schwarz department store. For the Dominican oligarchy depicted in the novel, American consumer goods are considered highly desirable, and education acquired in the United States is also prized by the wealthy families who send their children to Ivy League schools. A less visible and more sinister manifestation of United States penetration into Dominican space takes the form of U.S. government intervention in Dominican political affairs. An aborted plot to overthrow the dictator Trujillo, instigated and organized by the State Department and involving several García family members, is the catalyst for the series of events leading to the family's flight from the island.

This evidence that Puerto Rican and Dominican cultures are in fact "contaminated" by outside influences is elided in the immigrant characters' vision of their islands. Their insistence on the cultural purity of the homeland is an example of what Werner Sollors calls "mythological ancestry construction"

(1986, 235). In *The Line of the Sun,* the physical and emotional distance from the island that causes the Puerto Rican migrants' longing for home also makes their memories more idealized than accurate. These characters, and previous generations of immigrants, have responded to the virus of homesickness by attempting to replicate their cultural homeland within American space. They maintain this imitation of Puerto Rico in "El Building," the New Jersey tenement where Marisol lives with her family after their arrival from the island. Marisol describes El Building as an "ethnic beehive" where life is lived at a high pitch, a "microcosm of island life with its intrigues, its gossip groups, and even its own spiritist" (170–71). El Building serves as a sort of fortress of Puerto Rican tradition and solidarity for its inhabitants; Marisol observes that "it was as closely knit a community as any Little Italy or Chinatown" (171).

The *bodega* across the street supplies the residents of El Building with scarce Puerto Rican delicacies like green bananas, breadfruit, and *yuca,* and the building itself is filled with smells and sounds familiar to the islanders. For Marisol, the smells in particular evoke vague memories of a place she hardly remembers; one evening around dinnertime she inhales the aroma of fried plantains, beans and "the ever-present rice" and wonders "if [her] mother's Island smelled the same as El Building at dinner time" (182). Religious paraphernalia is likewise employed by the inhabitants of El Building to maintain a powerful tie to their homeland:

> Fortified in their illusion that all could be kept the same within the family as it had been on the Island, women decorated their apartments with every artifact that enhanced the fantasy. Religious objects imported from the Island were favorite wall hangings. Over the kitchen table in many apartments hung the Sacred Heart. . . . And Mary could always be found smiling serenely from walls. (172)

In El Building, each traditional meal that is prepared, each spiritist meeting, each burst of island music can be read as a performative act that perpetuates this illusion that authentic Puerto Rican culture is being maintained. The image of cultural essence fostered by this community can nonetheless be deconstructed through a close reading of the performances originating in El Building. Marisol herself becomes aware that the transplanted *patria* established in El Building is no more a space of "true" Puerto Rican culture than is the idealized island of the migrants' nostalgia:

> The smells of beans boiling in a dozen kitchens assailed my nostrils. Rice and beans, the unimaginative staple food of all these people who re-

created every day the same routines they had followed in their mamá's houses so long ago. Except that here in Paterson, in the cold rooms stories above the frozen ground, the smells and sounds of a lost way of life could only be a parody. (223)

Marisol reads the migrants' replication of Puerto Rican routines as a parody of island life, performed on the "stage" of El Building. Later, after the spiritist meeting that ends in fiery disaster, she describes the residents as "vanquished, doleful as children caught in a forbidden game — pathetic in their absurd costumes" (268). When the tenement community is viewed as parody, as "a bizarre facsimile of an Island *barrio*" (220), the complexity of El Building's relationship to the Puerto Rican culture that it imitates is made visible.

Mikhail Bakhtin describes parody as "the creation of a *decrowning double; it is that same 'world turned inside out'* " (1984, 127). He argues that parody is thus ambivalent, having the capacity to communicate a spectrum of tones ranging from reverent acceptance to parodic ridicule (1981, 77). While Bakhtin's principal objects of study were prenovelistic parodies of sacred texts, his demonstration of how parody operates to deauthorize official languages has relevance for El Building's simulation of the homeland. The migrant parents' faithful replication of Puerto Rican culture is indicative of the "reverent acceptance" that Bakhtin asserts is as much a part of parody as is mockery. Marisol's "ethnic" reading of El Building has a different slant. Her ridicule of El Building reveals her bicultural generation's skepticism and highlights the coexistence of vastly different parodic practices: as critique by Marisol, and as veneration of island culture by the original migrants.[19] Marisol's attitude toward El Building is similar to Rosa's negative reaction to the Cuban Club in *The Greatest Performance* (see chapter 3). In both instances the immigrant children view the attempted replication of the homeland by their parents' generation as at best a bad imitation, and at worst a farce. In these contexts, the characters' skepticism of blind loyalty to the social codes of their ancestral culture makes their ethnic perspective apparent.

Marisol's observation that "the smells and sounds of a lost way of life could only be a parody" hints that the migrants' near-reverence for their ancestral culture may in fact mask a challenge to the authority of the official discourse of cultural identity. "Puerto Rican identity" is, like all nationalisms, a discourse whose dominance depends upon it being endorsed without question.[20] Marisol's interpretation of El Building as parody demythologizes the venerated Puerto Rican cultural essence endorsed by her compatriots. Her reading thus casts in a skeptical light the notion of "Puerto Ricanness" as a naturalized or definable attribute.

The repeated performances of Puerto Rican cultural heritage by the inhabitants of El Building are a sort of cultural "drag" not unlike the gender imitation that Judith Butler interrogates. As I discussed in the preceding chapters, drag purports to be the imitation of an original feminine essence that cannot, in fact, be considered the rightful property of the female sex. Drag, Butler claims, ultimately reveals that gender "is a kind of imitation for which there is no original" (1991, 21). Applying Butler's theory to cultural identity, El Building's Puerto Rican "drag" reproduces the system of impersonation by which *any* cultural identity is assumed: through repetition of performative acts. The Puerto Rican migrants in *The Line of the Sun*, in attempting to re-create their island, are in fact imitating an illusory cultural essence. What the residents of El Building produce is a parody of an effect — "Puerto Ricanness" — that is itself a social construction.[21] Marisol's critique of El Building reveals the tension between the Puerto Ricans' nationalism and the performativity of ethnic culture and identity.

Part of Marisol's skepticism is directed at the apparent need for endless repetition of traditional Puerto Rican codes, as her previous comments about the omnipresent religious artifacts in El Building indicate. The necessity of these repeated performances further hints that this cultural construct is highly unstable. In my discussions of *City of Night* and *The Mambo Kings Play Songs of Love* (see chapters 2 and 3), I argued that such compulsive repetition never fully constitutes identity. As Butler asserts, the very need for repetition reveals the impermanence of identity (1991, 24). This view of identity coincides with Bhabha's notion of culture as constructed through the ongoing performances of daily life. In El Building, this process involves the reproduction of the practices, smells, and sounds of the Puerto Rican way of life. Marisol challenges the notion of a definable ancestral culture that can be transposed intact to the American milieu and preserved within the migrant enclave. Her critique reveals that El Building is a simulation of the island, a space haunted by "the absent presence of the originating ancestral source" (Boelhower 95), a substitute *patria* modeled after a homeland that exists primarily in the migrants' nostalgia-tinted imagination.[22]

The fragility of this simulated homeland becomes starkly apparent when it is threatened by American dominant culture in *The Line of the Sun*. The first-generation migrants' preservation of traditional customs — to retain aspects of their heritage that they perceive as nonnegotiable — often involves transgression of American cultural norms. Religion, for example, is closely linked with cultural identity and is generally included as a characteristic through which an ethnic group may distinguish itself from the dominant culture. The close historical connection between ethnicity and religion becomes apparent when the word "ethnic" is traced to a Greek root (*ethnikos*) meaning "nation" and "heathen."[23]

In *The Line of the Sun*, the catastrophic fire that destroys El Building results in part from the ill-fated transposition of island spiritism to American cultural space. This tragic incident serves as a dramatic allegory for the conflict between ethnic cultural practices and American norms. Traditional Caribbean spiritism—with its loud chanting, complex rituals, and use of brilliantly-colored costumes and ceremonial fire—contrasts sharply with the staidness of American mainstream religion, causing the former to be judged an extreme example of ethnic excess. In a more hospitable context, the spiritist meeting organized by the women of El Building could very well have been carried out without mishap. Instead, the volatile combination of a deteriorating old building, emotionally charged participants (the neighborhood was being subjected to increasing police harassment), and far too many people crowded into a tiny apartment, plus an ample dose of ceremonial fire, is a formula for disaster. A neighbor explains to Marisol why the women believe so fervently in the necessity of the meeting; he points out the foreignness of their practices by Anglo-American standards:

> "[Y]ou should know this about Island women, not little *Americanitas* like you. . . . They believe that we have invisible friends, these spirits of theirs. . . . They mean well, but here in America their hocus-pocus only complicates things. Can you imagine trying to explain to our crewcut *policía*, the one giving us the third degree at Cheo's, that the meeting Saturday is to ask for assistance from the dead?" (246)

The dangerous "hocus-pocus" practiced by the residents of El Building is evidence of the migrants' refusal to discard island beliefs. The resulting tragedy draws attention to the tenuousness of both the Puerto Ricans' position in American society and their access to their cultural origin. Frustrated by economic problems, discrimination, and alienation—the persistent concerns of immigrants and members of other minority groups—the women of El Building decide to seek the help of spirits. Yet, as the neighbor's reference to the "crewcut *policía*" indicates, the Puerto Ricans' belief in the spirit world marks them as culturally unintelligible according to the norms of the Anglo-American majority. When the spiritist meeting ends in fiery disaster, the community's private ceremony turns into a public spectacle, a hypervisible performance of ethnic excess.

The meeting thus functions as a performative act that enables the dominant "audience" to produce ethnic subjects in order to regulate (and subjugate) them. The erasure of this ethnic community from the American cultural map can be read as an allegory for dominant culture's neutralization of excess that endangers social stability. At the same time, the devastation of El Building signals the demise of the migrants' illusion of a cultural "home" that is impervious to change or destruction.

In contrast to their parents' generation, the immigrant children in *The Line of the Sun* and *García Girls* have relatively vague memories of the island. Their goal is to feel at home in the United States by learning to navigate the bicultural and bilingual space they inhabit as ethnic U.S. Latinas. Even so, at times the sensation of displacement resulting from constant negotiation between cultures motivates this generation to seek a ground — a sort of ontological stability — in the *patria*. At the beginning of *García Girls,* Yolanda has suffered a full-fledged identity crisis and has concluded that she needs to spend some time in the Dominican Republic to find herself. Her failed marriage to an Anglo has left her feeling fragmented, her head, heart, and soul disconnected, like "three persons in one Yo" (78). Once on the island, she claims to have found a peace of mind that life in America never offered her: "Standing here in the quiet, she believes she has never felt at home in the States, never" (12). In college Yolanda's difficulty in conforming to American dating practices had already convinced her that she would never fit in. After an evening of resisting her boyfriend's sexual advances that ends with his stinging accusation that she is "worse than a fucking Puritan," Yolanda experiences the full impact of her emotional diaspora: "I saw what a cold, lonely life awaited me in this country. I would never find someone who would understand my peculiar mix of Catholicism and agnosticism, Hispanic and American styles" (99). Yolanda's confusion about her sexuality arises from conflict between the conservative codes of female sexual behavior of her upper-class Dominican upbringing, and the far more liberal American sexual mores. Her body becomes the battlefield where this cultural clash is played out, where the intersection of gender and ethnicity is clearly marked. For Yolanda and other Latinas, as for Mario in *The Greatest Performance,* cultural identity is inscribed on the body.

A similar sense of turmoil and alienation had earlier motivated the youngest García daughter, Sofía, to remain on the island after her sisters returned to the States at the end of their yearly summer pilgrimage. Attributing all her adolescent traumas to the experience of exile, Sofía declares that "the States aren't making me happy" (116). She goes so far as to transform herself into a proper Dominican *señorita,* complete with ultrafeminine attire, dramatic makeup, "a jangle of bangles and a cascade of beauty parlor curls" (117), and the requisite possessive, macho boyfriend. To Sofía's dismay, her "Americanized" sisters read her performances of femininity as Latina excess and are ruthless in their efforts to deprogram her. Sofía, like her sister Yolanda, imagined that by returning to her cultural roots she would be able to escape the sense of fragmented identity that she had experienced intensely as an outsider in the United States.

Marisol in *The Line of the Sun* shares this sense of "homelessness" that is intrinsic to the immigrant experience. Because her father is in the Navy, Marisol's family is more financially secure than their neighbors in El Building, yet less so than her Catholic school classmates. As a result, she feels like an outsider to both groups: "I was already very much aware of the fact that I fit into neither the white middle-class world of my classmates at Saint Jerome's nor the exclusive club of El Building's 'expatriates' " (177). Marisol, like the García girls, begins to imagine that life would have been far better for her on the island, for there she would know who she was instead of living in cultural limbo. Although she has no recollection of Puerto Rico, she nevertheless resents having been denied the opportunity to live there:

[L]istening to stories about [my uncle's] life on the Island, and hearing Ramona's constant rhapsodizing about that tropical paradise — all conspired to make me feel deprived. I should have grown up there. I should have been able to play in emerald-green pastures, to eat sweet bananas right off the trees, to learn about life from the women who were strong and wise. (222)

Forced to depend on the accuracy of her uncle's and her mother's rose-colored memories, Marisol does not see that the island as they portray it is a fiction. In the midst of her struggles to define her identity, Puerto Rico symbolizes the home that she can never find on the mainland.

WRITING FAMILY HISTORY:
THE INVENTION OF THE ETHNIC SELF

In spite of Marisol's critical attitude toward El Building, the community nevertheless provides her with a sense of roots. El Building's ethnic cohesiveness serves to assuage the residents' fear of fragmentation and loss of history. It may be tempting to consider ethnic communities as no more than a temporary stop along immigrants' inevitable trajectory toward assimilation, a haven where nostalgia keeps the homeland alive. Yet Marisol's commentary on El Building indicates that as a migrant child, she is involved with the ethnic community in a more complex manner. Her critique of the migrants' re-creation of "home," even as she derives pleasure and security from living there, is a performance through which she asserts her subjectivity as an ethnic U.S. Latina.

Both *The Line of the Sun* and *How the García Girls Lost Their Accents* ultimately challenge the notion that the immigrants can recover their cultural origins through a return, real or symbolic (by means of nostalgia), to the homeland. For the García daughters, their Dominican identity at times assumes the form of a diffuse, nonexclusive *hispanidad*. Carla, the eldest, develops a hankering for Mexican peasant blouses when she discovers her Hispanic roots (41), while the second daughter, Sandi, identifies with Spanish culture as embodied by a group of flamenco dancers she sees performing. Her reaction to the dancers is visceral: "Sandi's heart soared. This wild and beautiful dance came from people like her, Spanish people" (185). Her parents similarly prefer to elide the specificity of their island heritage and ground themselves in their conquistador ancestors "from the green, motherland hills of Spain" (197). The Garcías' Eurocentric view of their identity may be a response to generalized discrimination against Latinos in the United States, reflecting a desire to dissociate themselves from lower-class Latin American immigrants and Chicanos. Indeed, on more than one occasion the García women are shocked to discover that the family name, which on the island had guaranteed instant recognition and respectful treatment, has no importance whatsoever in the United States.

For the Garcías, tracing their cultural roots is a sort of *mise en abîme,* a search for an origin that is perpetually out of reach. In general, the characters in *The Line of the Sun* and *García Girls* are frustrated in their attempts to anchor themselves in Puerto Rican or Dominican culture, or even to establish a ground in a generalized Hispanic past. Whether they like it or not, they are in the United States to stay; yet complete assimilation—the assumption of an imagined American identity—eludes them as well. As ethnic Americans, their cultural identity is being constantly performed and invented in their movement between Puerto Rican and American, Dominican and American. Through the girls' "peculiar mix of . . . Hispanic and American styles" their dynamic *ethnic* identity emerges and evolves. The patterns of resistance and accommodation that are woven into the narrative fabric of *The Line of the Sun* and *García Girls* offer glimpses of the ongoing process of negotiation that constitutes ethnicity.

In both novels, situations in which the immigrant children are involved in conflicts between traditional island values and dominant American norms show such an ethnic subjectivity emerging. The García girls struggle to cope with what they perceive to be excessive conservatism on the part of their parents. In spite of their proassimilation stance, Carlos and Laura García, like the residents of El Building, hope that "all could be kept the same within the family as it had been on the island" (*Line of the Sun* 172).[24] When the García girls try to persuade their mother to allow them to do normal American-type things like going to a shopping mall or to a movie, she dismisses them with " 'The problem with you girls . . .' " From Yolanda's perspective, the problem "boiled down to the fact that [the girls] wanted to become Americans and their father—and their mother, too, at first—would have none of it" (135). Even after the family has lived in American suburbs for several years, the parents continue to enforce policies that their daughters find highly inappropriate: "The rules were as strict as for Island girls, but there was no island to make up the difference" (107).

The García girls discover that their immigrant parents' moral conservatism seems anachronistic when transplanted into the more liberal American social space. Their emotional attachment to the homeland is considerably weaker than that of their parents; this distance causes them to view the Old World rules with skepticism. The García parents decide that their daughters need additional exposure to traditional Dominican ways, and they arrange for the girls to spend summers on the island to reinforce their ties with *la familia*. The girls nevertheless suspect that a larger scheme is involved:

The hidden agenda was marriage to homeland boys, since everyone knew that once a girl married an American, those grandbabies came out jabbering in English and thinking of the Island as a place to go get a suntan. (109)

This fear that the grandchildren will grow up without an emotional connection to the island is an interesting counterpoint to Dr. García's supposedly positive attitude toward the benefits of assimilation (e.g., access to political office). The contradiction implies that even the gung-ho parents are ambivalent about the consequences of assimilating. For the parents, assimilation signifies the replacement of one culture by another, the absolute erasure of Dominican identity as a new, American identity is assumed.

Because immigrant children narrate both novels, the portrayals of parental opinions and attitudes are constructs that reflect the narrators' biases. The parents, as depicted by the García girls and Marisol, are indifferent to the questions of identity that cause their children so much turmoil. The García girls' reaction to their mother's inventions calls attention to this generation gap:

They resented her spending time on those dumb inventions. Here they were trying to fit in America among Americans, they needed help figuring out who they were, why the Irish kids whose grandparents had been micks were calling them spics. Why had they come to this country in the first place? Important, crucial, final things, and here was their own mother, who didn't have a second to help them puzzle any of this out, inventing gadgets to make life easier for the American Moms (138).

While what drives their mother is the necessity of invention, the daughters struggle to cope with problems that they consider to be of greater consequence, such as understanding the racist hierarchy among immigrant groups. Ironically, this hierarchy, like their mother's gadgets, is also the product of American invention.

Marisol in *The Line of the Sun* feels similar confusion in dealing with her inescapably bicultural reality. She concludes that while she will act as "interpreter of the world" for her nonassimilated mother, her identity will remain in constant flux: "[T]hough I would always carry my Island heritage on my back like a snail, I belonged in the world of phones, offices, concrete buildings, and the English language" (273). In spite of Marisol's desire to integrate fully into the American milieu, she acknowledges that she cannot completely sever her ties to her ancestral culture.

This process of navigating the space between cultures appears to continue indefinitely. The legacy of the García girls' strict upbringing haunts them for years, at times manifesting itself in uncertainty and contradictory behavior. A lover complains to Yolanda that he feels "caught between the woman's libber and the Catholic señorita" (48); once again, Yolanda's "ethnic body" is the site of negotiation between American sexual liberation and traditional island moral codes.[25] Both novels suggest that the assimilated "American" identity to which many immigrants aspire is as much an illusion as is their idealized vision of the homeland. As Edna Acosta-Belén asserts, the affirmation of a Puerto Rican identity in the United States "has demonstrated that the core of this purported experience is not the mythical 'melting pot' or fusion of other cultures with a mainstream Anglo-American cultural current" (986). The cultural angst shared by the García daughters in *How the García Girls Lost Their Accents* and Marisol in *The Line of the Sun* is thus the result of the shifting subject positions that they assume in relation to their ancestral culture and American culture as they perceive it.

The immigrant parents in *García Girls* at times regard American dominant culture as a vaguely malevolent presence that threatens the survival of their traditional island values and beliefs. In *The Line of the Sun* the threat of cultural erasure is given far more literal form when the fire in El Building forces the ethnic community to disperse. The fire in *The Line of the Sun* acts as metaphor for the message of dominant society to immigrants: melt down (i.e., assimilate) or be excluded. The homogenizing capability of dominant American culture is such that the immigrant who hopes to survive and succeed must conform to certain standards that often conflict with those of his/her native culture. Yet this same fear that one's cultural identity is at risk is the generating force at the heart of ethnic literature.[26] In immigrant writing like the novels of Ortiz Cofer and Alvarez, resistance to the potential loss associated with American "success" produces the works' recuperative character.

These two novels do not merely create a static cultural encyclopedia of Puerto Rican or Dominican identity; they portray the emergence of a distinctly ethnic subjectivity. In so doing, their narrators also deconstruct the immigrant "success story" that their parents have strived to emulate. Russian immigrant Mary Antin's autobiography *The Promised Land* (1912) is a classic illustration of this notion of leaving one's ancestral culture behind. In her introduction she declares, "I was born, I have lived, and I have been made over . . . I am absolutely other than the person whose story I have to tell" (xix). The invention of ethnic identity in Ortiz Cofer's and Alvarez's novels likewise involves the remaking of the narrators. Through the writing process, they gain increased understanding of their biculturalism, which in turn transforms them into persons who are distinct from those whose story they tell. Even so, Antin's project of eliminating her foreign "excesses" in order to become Americanized implies a finality that Marisol and the García girls would not claim to have achieved.

The Line of the Sun and *How the García Girls Lost Their Accents* might best be described as "ethnic success stories." The narrators' resistance to total assimilation distinguishes the novels from immigrant success stories, even as their writing—their "authorized" performances of ethnic difference—gains them entrance into the American cultural milieu. By questioning both immigrant nostalgia and assimilation ideology, Ortiz Cofer's and Alvarez's novels construct an ethnic space that resists being subsumed into the American mainstream. Because cultural productions are performative—"spectacles" that also possess the generative capacity of speech—the novels themselves could be considered ethnic performances.

Miguel Algarín describes this performative function of cultural productions, in reference to Nuyorican literature: "The future will be procured by what we do that is cultural in the present, so that we are not so much chasing the tradition of a culture as we are putting it down" (1981, 90). *The Line of the Sun* and *García Girls* highlight the role of writing in the invention of cultural tradition and of ethnic identity when the narrators examine their personal motivation to become writers. Both Marisol and Yolanda express a desire to impart order to the fragmented memories of their immigrant past and to reconcile these with their ethnic present. Witnessing their mothers' responses to cultural displacement provides some inspiration for both girls. In *The Line of the Sun*, Ramona asks her daughter, " '[D]o you think there will ever be a bridge across the water to my Island?' " (285). She does not suspect that Marisol herself will build such a bridge symbolically, through her writing, a space where the island and the mainland, Puerto Rican and American cultures, will be intertwined.

Yolanda's mother is concerned less with returning to the island than with modifying reality in the United States. As mentioned above, through Laura García the motif of invention is developed. Laura's inability in America to gain the recognition that automatically came from being a member of the de la Torre clan at home motivates her to seek acknowledgment through her designs. Laura attempts to distinguish herself — and to gain access to economic power — by inventing gadgets that will change the lives of Americans. Yolanda considers her mother's creations to be little more than a waste of time and energy:

> "But what's the point?" Yoyo persisted.
> "Point, point, does everything need a point? Why do you write poems?"
> Yoyo had to admit it was her mother who had the point there. Still, in the hierarchy of things, a poem seemed much more important than a potty that played music when a toilet-training toddler went in its bowl (138).

In fact, the similarity between Laura's gadgets and Yolanda's poems is far greater than the daughter imagines, for both are attempts to transform quotidian reality.

As the narrators of *García Girls* and *The Line of the Sun* piece together memories and retellings of past events, they begin to realize that writing their stories will require a significant amount of invention. With this discovery they recognize that the distinction between history and fiction is blurred. At best, the author or storyteller can only piece together fragments of the past. The task of the writer who seeks to produce a coherent vision of the past has a parallel in the first-born child's reconstruction of the family history as described in *García Girls*. That is, the writer of history begins from a blank page not unlike "the clean slate of the oldest making the past out of nothing but faint whispers, presences, and tones" (*García Girls* 216).

The recurrent references to invention in these immigrant novels suggest that the notions of invariable history and definable cultural origins should be problematized. Foucault, along with other poststructuralist thinkers, challenges both notions through his examination of discourse and the construction of history. In *The Archaeology of Knowledge,* he argues that history is a web of interwoven discursive practices, organized through systems that establish statements as events and determine their survival in "the great mythical book of history" (128). He calls these systems the "archive" and contends that we can never claim dominion over the discourses the archive regulates. On the contrary, the archive reveals that "our history [is] the difference of times, our selves the difference of masks" (131). Foucault's view of history coincides with the perspective eventually reached by the narrators of *García Girls* and *The Line of the Sun:* They realize that their immigrant history is rife with discontinuities and that their cultural origin can never be recovered but only invented. Moreover, Foucault's description of self as the difference of masks resonates with the notion of ethnic identity as a succession of performances.

García Girls alludes to the specificity of the "history as fiction" concept for the immigrant writer. The day the García family flees the island, their servant Chucha speculates about the girls' future in the United States: "They will be haunted by what they do and don't remember. But they have spirit in them. They will invent what they need to survive" (223). This necessity of invention is the legacy of immigrants, for access to their homeland and ancestral culture, which they view as the source and foundation of their history, is limited or nonexistent. Marisol, at least, has a trunk filled with bits of her writing that will aid her in chronicling the story she wants to tell. Even so, she acknowledges the role that creativity will play: "One day I would have the courage to put it all together. . . . Perhaps I would start the story in the present and go back, giving myself more and more freedom to invent ways of telling it" (287). The immigrant children — Yolanda García, Marisol — are in fact "haunted by what they do and don't remember," and through writing they strive to fill in the gaps.

Ultimately the narrators of both novels recognize that their writing participates in the creation of history, although Yolanda and Marisol begin composing their stories in the hopes of gaining self-awareness. Yolanda grows up to be "a curious woman, a woman of story ghosts and story devils, a woman prone to bad dreams and bad insomnia" (290) and writes to exorcise her demons. Similarly, Marisol views her trunk full of writings, many of which focus on her uncle Guzmán, as a puzzle that could reveal many things about her own life (287). She concludes that "the only way to understand a life is to write it as a story, to fill in the blanks left by circumstance, lapses of memory, and failed communication" (290); the life to which she refers could as easily be her own as that of her uncle. Both narrators finally dispel the notion that their history can exist without creative involvement on their part.

By acknowledging that as they assemble the fragments of their past they are also making up stories, these narrators undermine their own narrative authority. *The Line of the Sun* closes with an anecdote about Guzmán in which his new wife makes him swear that he will never sin again. Obediently he kneels and makes the promise, and Marisol concludes the narrative by declaring, "Right at that point, when he and I tell our best lie, I say, this is the end" (291). Yolanda García, too, associates writing with lies, for one of her persistent demons is a black cat that she periodically hears "wailing over some violation that lies at the center of my art" (290).

The narrators' confessions of unreliability diminish their status as purveyors of truth, underscoring the fallacy in reading their narratives as simple representations of verifiable history. Instead, these works indicate that the poststructuralist challenge to interpretation and narrative authority may have particular implications for ethnic literature. Michael Fischer has found this type of self-consciousness to be characteristic of recent ethnic autobiographical fiction. He asserts that these works call attention to their own fictive nature through narrators that comment on the writing process (232). This self-reflexivity in turn encourages the reader to participate in the production of the text. The performative nature of immigrant novels such as *The Line of the Sun* and *García Girls* is affirmed through their narrators' seduction of the reader into the interpretive process. In addition, their narrators' admissions of questionable veracity support the notion that no narrator ever possesses the "truth" of his/her story or experience. In the introduction to *Memory, Narrative, and Identity*, the editors observe that memory disrupts linear, conventional narratives and introduces multiple voices and perspectives. As *The Line of the Sun* and *García Girls* show, this use of multiple voices "allows for a narrative exploration of the past that rejects or circumvents positivistic assumptions about truth and history" (Singh et al. 18).

While self-conscious narrative and the deconstruction of narrative authority are hardly unique to ethnic fiction, the function of both techniques is noteworthy in ethnic writing because of their destabilizing effect on identity categories. Lacking access to historical truth, the ethnic subject can only express a position with respect to events as he/she observes them. The narrators of *The Line of the Sun* and *García Girls* assume a variety of such subject positions, at times identifying with their island cultural heritage through the nostalgia of others, at times critiquing that nostalgia and proclaiming their solidarity with the ideology of assimilation. Both Ortiz Cofer's and Alvarez's novels challenge the essentialism that results when isolated performative acts or stances are taken to be representative of the comprehensive content of any identity category — "Puerto Rican," "Dominican," "American," "ethnic

Latina/o." The novels suggest that even immigrant children like Marisol and the García girls are not remade as fully assimilated Americans. Their ancestors' reminiscences and attempts to simulate island life likewise fail to provide the narrators with access to a cultural essence around which to build their identity. Evidence of this ethnic voice can be detected at the level of narrative structure as well in *The Line of the Sun*. The text is divided into two sections, one taking place in Puerto Rico and the other in the U.S. These two cultural spaces are held in tension by the narrative voice, which links the sections and negotiates between them in much the same way as the ethnic subject creates and inhabits a space between cultures.[27]

"Child of the Americas," the poem by Puerto Rican-born Aurora Levins Morales cited in the epigraph of this chapter, offers an eloquent portrayal of subjectivity at the intersection of diverse cultures. The poetic persona declares that "Africa is in me, but I cannot return . . . Taíno is in me, but there is no way back . . . Europe lives in me, but I have no home there . . . " Self is presented as the result of *mestizaje*, the weaving together of disperse ancestral threads — African, indigenous, European. The poem acknowledges the impossibility of "going home," that is, of claiming an identity anchored solely in one of these cultural heritages. Levins Morales's poem proposes that identity is not a definable essence nor a relic of the past to be preserved. This movement between cultures, vividly depicted in *The Line of the Sun* and *How the García Girls Lost Their Accents*, is fundamental to the construction of ethnic identity. Ethnicity — as elusive as the family histories that the narrators seek to write — is an ongoing process of invention that links past, present, and future.

FIVE

THE "BOOM" IN U.S. LATINA/O FICTION

Performing Magical Realism in The Love Queen of the Amazon *and* So Far from God

Era como si Dios hubiera resuelto poner a prueba toda
capacidad de asombro, y mantuviera a los habitantes de
Macondo en un permanente vaivén entre el alborozo y el
desencanto, la duda y la revelación.[1]
— GABRIEL GARCÍA MÁRQUEZ, *Cien años de soledad*

Does the concept of performance have implications not only for identity — gender, ethnicity, sexuality — but also for the literary text itself? Cultural performances are generated at the level of social interaction and personal/group identity, but also through the writing process itself.
These performances can perpetuate the illusion of cultural essence according
to how the social or literary text is read. Drag produces the illusion of feminine
essence; in much the same way, certain literary works project an aura of
essential "Latino-ness." The preceding chapters focused on the constitution of
gender and cultural identity through performative acts associated with essential femininity, masculinity, and Latina/o culture. Now I wish to explore the
way that a set of *literary* codes — in particular, the aesthetic of the Latin American "Boom" — has similarly begun to be interpreted as a sign of Latina/o
essence.

Mainstream reviews of U.S. Latina/o prose from the past decade offer ample evidence that such essentializing of Latina/o literature and culture is becoming widespread. In 1985, the *Los Angeles Times* review of Chicana writer
Cecile Pineda's novel *Face* claimed that "Pineda will be compared to Cortázar,
Borges and Márquez."[2] Reviewer Andrei Codrescu's comments on *Raining
Backwards* (1988), by U.S. Cuban Roberto Fernández, are more critical; Codrescu declares that the novel would have been greatly improved if "the echoes
of Gabriel García Márquez that run like a ritual motif through it had been
made conscious and dealt with intelligently" (27). Cristina García is even

more blunt in her review of Pineda's *The Love Queen of the Amazon* (1992), describing the novel as "a pale imitation of the glorious style of the best Latin American literature" (2).

In a 1992 article on U.S. Latina/o fiction writers, *Hispanic* magazine's assistant editor Martha Frase-Blunt alleges that both critics and publishers fall into the trap of stereotyping in their efforts to understand the writers' popularity among mainstream readers. Thanks to the Boom writers, Frase-Blunt asserts, Hispanic culture and history have found an enthusiastic audience in the United States. As a result, however,

> [t]he term "magic realism" seems to have become a catch-all in the literary world to describe a "Latin American" style of fiction in which real action is tinged with dreamlike surrealism . . . [C]ritics are inclined to use a broad brush to apply the term to any contemporary U.S. Hispanic writer who delves into the emotional side of life. (32)

In the same article, Guatemalan-American writer Francisco Goldman (*The Long Night of White Chickens,* 1992) expresses dismay at publishers' insistence on defining U.S. Latina/o writing as magical realist: "They will paste the words 'García Márquez' onto every single book jacket—they even did it to me. I kept telling them 'I don't do magic realism' " (32). Victor Perera's review of Goldman's novel indicates that critics are influenced by such labeling. Perera suggests that Goldman's novel is burdened by superfluous "magic realist" passages and speculates that such passages may have been retained "to bolster the book's claim to Marquezian stature" (8). The assumption underlying these characterizations and critiques of Latina/o fiction is that García Márquez and his Latin American contemporaries are the standard to which U.S. Latina/o writing should be held.

The term "magical realism" as used indiscriminately by mainstream reviewers to describe Latina/o fiction is only superficially related to the literary aesthetic associated with Jorge Luis Borges, Alejo Carpentier, and many of the Boom writers of the 1960s. Critics have responded to these works with extensive scholarship on "magic realism," as the term was coined in 1925 by German art critic Franz Roh to describe the postexpressionist painting of the 1920s. Although both the origin of magical realism and its definition remain unresolved issues of scholarly debate,[3] a general understanding of some characteristics of this type of writing can be derived from existing criticism. In a 1948 essay, Arturo Uslar Pietri asserted that magical realism simultaneously engages quotidian existence and its mysterious aspects; it is marked by "la consideración del hombre como misterio en medio de los datos realistas" (161–62).[4] Twenty years later, Luis Leal similarly observed that the impulse behind such writing is the exploration of the mysterious within empirical reality (1967, 232).

A similar current in U.S. Latina/o fiction became apparent as early as 1971 with the publication of Rudolfo Anaya's novel *Bless Me, Ultima*.[5] Anaya's novelistic portrayal of rural Chicana/o life and folklore, set in northern New Mexico, offered readers access to mythical, magical, and spiritual aspects of Chicana/o culture. In the course of the young narrator's coming-of-age process, he learns of his people's belief in the Golden Carp and later sees the mythical creature; he witnesses the power of both the local *curandera* (healer) Ultima, and the evil work of *brujería* (witchcraft); and he discovers that "the more I knew about people the more I knew about the strange magic hidden in their hearts" (101). A line from the first page of *Bless Me, Ultima* conveys the notion of mutable temporality for which Boom fiction is famous, as the narrator intones, "Time stood still, and it shared with me all that had been, and all that was to come" (1).

Bless Me, Ultima set the precedent for subsequent Latina/o fiction that would likewise incorporate so-called magical realist elements. Ron Arias's 1975 novel *The Road to Tamazunchale*, for example, is the story of the fantastic adventures of Fausto Tejada, an elderly Chicano living in East Los Angeles. During don Fausto's final days the protagonist cruises the streets of Los Angeles with a young *cholo*, travels to colonial Peru to meet with the viceroy, is visited periodically by his deceased wife, and successfully escorts a group of undocumented workers across the Tijuana-California border. Contrasting Arias's novel with previous Chicano realist fiction, critic Eliud Martínez calls *The Road to Tamazunchale* a work of the "new reality" in which "vision and fantasy, hallucination and dream are celebrated" and "[e]verything imaginable and even the impossible are possible" (14). Other critics have examined the close resemblance between Tomás Rivera's narrative techniques in ... *y no se lo tragó la tierra* (1971) and Juan Rulfo's in *Pedro Páramo* and *El llano en llamas*, as well as the echoes of Borges and García Márquez in *The Road to Tamazunchale*.[6]

In addition to the "magical realist" aspects of some Latina/o fiction, the Latin American ancestry of U.S. Latina/o writers seems to make comparisons of their writing with Latin American literature inevitable. Because the Boom novels are the most widely known literary works from Latin America, they are generally the sole point of reference when such comparisons are drawn. The publication and distribution of the works of Julio Cortázar, Carlos Fuentes,

García Márquez, Mario Vargas Llosa, and other Boom writers brought Latin American magical realism to the attention of a worldwide readership. Doris Sommer and George Yúdice summarize the impact these writers produced:

> Latin Americans dazzled the reader with crystalline lucidities (Borges), moving renderings of madness (Sábato, Cortázar) and violence (Vargas Llosa), larger than life portrayals of power and corruption (Fuentes, García Márquez), ebullient baroque recreations of tropical culture (Carpentier, Souza, Amado, Cabrera Infante, Sarduy). (190)

As early as 1970, the Boom novels were already viewed as a literary corpus that projected certain characteristics. John S. Brushwood mentions narrative strategies that deviate from logical sequence, subvert the normal correlation of cause and effect, and produce an impression of simultaneity (19). Sommer and Yúdice also note Boom novels' self-consciousness about the writing process as well as their self-reflexivity with regard to cultural and national identity (197).

In spite of the diversity of contemporary Latin American literature, Boom fiction continues to be viewed as the quintessential Latin American writing. Brushwood claims that García Márquez's narrative style, along with Borges's stories, have become the prevailing stereotypes of Latin American fiction: "They represent what readers expect — in the United States and in other countries" (13).[7] In addition, a number of critics have argued that magical realism is the true literary expression of Latin American "reality." These critics underscore the importance of the Latin American sociohistorical context in the emergence of this type of writing. Alejo Carpentier, in his "Prólogo" to *El reino de este mundo* (1949), offers observations on what he calls "*lo real maravilloso*" of Latin American reality. Carpentier asserts that

> por la virginidad del paisaje, por la formación, por la ontología, por la presencia fáustica del indio y del negro, por la Revelación que constituyó su reciente descubrimiento, por los fecundos mestizajes que propició, América está muy lejos de haber agotado su caudal de mitologías. (10)[8]

He adds that in this setting, the powerful religious faith of the populace creates favorable conditions for belief in miracles, which he describes as unexpected alterations of reality (7). The hybrid religious practices produced by the fusion of European Catholicism with African and indigenous religions in Latin America would seem to support this notion of a uniquely Latin American spirituality. Part of the "magic" of magical realism can be attributed to the exoticness of *santería*, spiritism, visions, and apparitions; in comparison to mainstream

Anglo-European religions, these practices and phenomena may seem foreign or even bizarre.

In a 1984 essay entitled "Fantasy and Artistic Creation in Latin America and the Caribbean," García Márquez likewise highlights the close connection between Latin American "reality" and the nature of the writing that the region has produced. Citing examples of the amazing eccentricities of various Latin American dictators, the astounding violence of the area's storms, and the powerful superstitions and legends, he claims that the most difficult task of Latin American artists has been "making their reality credible" (1985, 13). His view coincides with Carpentier's assessment of the Latin American *real maravilloso*; García Márquez declares that "nothing has ever occurred to me, nor have I been able to do anything, that is more awesome than reality itself" (1985, 15).

These observations highlight the importance of acknowledging the specific sociohistorical circumstances from which Latin American Boom fiction emerged. In addition to being rooted in a reality that García Márquez characterizes as "boundless," "incredible," and "unbelievable," many of the works bear the traces of contemporary Latin American political and economic issues. Yet it is problematic to extrapolate from these comments and conclude that magical realism somehow captures the "essence" of Latin American culture. The international literary community's obsession with magical realism is evidence of this tendency to condense a complex, diverse culture into simplistic formulas and stereotypes.[9] Ironically, the "presumed creator of the magical realist genre," as Elías Miguel Muñoz refers to García Márquez, has expressed skepticism about the seemingly interminable analysis and imitation of magical realism. Muñoz notes that in a 1989 writing workshop, García Márquez commented that he finds the term *realismo mágico* redundant and the concept ludicrous; he believes that there is no "magical" reality, but simply *la realidad* (1995, 180).

Nevertheless, comparisons of U.S. Latina/o fiction with García Márquez's characteristic style are merited in some cases. Recently, a veritable flurry of U.S. Latina/o novels have been published that unquestionably imitate magical realism and incorporate other formal and thematic elements associated with the Boom. Many of the passages of Judith Ortiz Cofer's *The Line of the Sun* that are set in Puerto Rico parody magical realism (see chapter 4). The villagers' reverence for the mythical snow of the North, their powerful spiritism, and the descriptions of the island — "Everything was too lush, too green, too hot. Every rock's underside was creeping with life" (161) — are all clearly reminiscent of *Cien años de soledad*.

In both *The Line of the Sun* and Esmeralda Santiago's *When I Was Puerto*

Rican (1993), the powerful U.S. presence in the imagination of the island evokes fanfare and a mystique much like that surrounding the periodic arrival of the gypsies in Macondo. In Santiago's novel, the objective of U.S. officials is to modernize the island, including the indoctrination of the *campesinos* in proper nutrition and health practices. Instead, the Americans' educational sessions, complete with a giant set of teeth, charts of the major food groups, and graphic, oversized visuals of lice and tapeworms, produce consternation among the inhabitants of the town of Macún. The Puerto Rican characters are faced with modernity in the form of scientific knowledge and developments (the narrator comments that the officials "used ornate Spanish words that we assumed were scientific talk for teeth, gums, and tongue" [65]). These invasions of "progress" are surrounded by the same aura of irreality with which *Cien años de soledad* is infused; the inhabitants of both Macún and Macondo remain in a perpetual "vaivén entre el alborozo y el desencanto" in which "nadie podía saber a ciencia cierta dónde estaban los límites de la realidad" (*Cien años* 268).[10]

These Marquezian anecdotes appear in literary texts rather than in everyday life, yet they evoke an association with Latina/o culture in much the same way as do "real" ethnic performances (traditional practices, language usage, and so on). That is, such portrayals of an exotic, primitive cultural "origin" operate as performances that make Latina/o identity readable. The representation of Latin American–style religious faith in Latina/o fiction is likewise an ethnically coded spectacle that is staged in the text.[11] Many of the "magical realist" mythologies of Latin American culture are preserved in the folklore of Latina/o communities in the United States through stories of miraculous occurrences and the spiritual world. This folklore expresses cultural difference from the dominant Anglo-American culture, which allows magical realism in U.S. Latina/o writing to be read as an ethnic sign.

In Cristina García's 1992 novel *Dreaming in Cuban, santería* also functions as ethnic performance by enabling the U.S. Cuban protagonist to reestablish a connection to her ancestral culture. One day when Pilar's college-student existence seems particularly meaningless, she enters a Park Avenue *botánica* run by an ageless man who looks "as if his ancestors were royal palms" (200). The proprietor immediately identifies her as a daughter of Changó and gives her holy water, an assortment of herbs with which to bathe, and a white candle. Pilar follows his instructions after returning to her room at the university:

> I light my candle. The bath turns a clear green from the herbs. It has the sharp scent of an open field in spring. When I pour it on my hair, I feel

a sticky cold like dry ice, then a soporific heat. I'm walking naked as a beam of light along brick paths and squares of grass, phosphorescent and clean. . . . On the ninth day of my baths, I call my mother and tell her we're going to Cuba. (203)

In effect, Pilar's performance of the ritual highlights her ethnic difference — *santería* is practiced outside the margins of Anglo-American culture — as it rekindles her desire to seek out her Cuban roots.[12]

Magical realism is not the only feature for which contemporary Latin American fiction is renowned. As mentioned above, readers and critics have come to view experimentation with narrative structure, and with the representation of time in particular, as emblematic of Boom fiction.[13] The peculiar temporality that develops in *Cien años de soledad* has become a hallmark of the Boom:

Muchos años después, frente al pelotón de fusilamiento, el coronel Aureliano Buendía había de recordar aquella tarde remota en que su padre lo llevó a conocer el hielo. (59)[14]

Los acontecimientos que habían de darle el golpe mortal a Macondo empezaban a vislumbrarse cuando llevaron a la casa al hijo de Meme Buendía. (331)[15]

This easily recognizable narrative style has begun to appear in U.S. Latina/o fiction as well. Oscar Hijuelos's third novel, *The Fourteen Sisters of Emilio Montez O'Brien* (1993), is rife with narrative sequences that mimic the style of *Cien años de soledad*:

[S]he had invented or allowed herself to drift into a most pleasant and unladylike dream — the pleasurable memory of which would come to her even years later, when she, a much older woman, would turn to look at the glowing aqua-blue dial of an electric clock and then into a mirror, remembering. (23)

Margarita would never suspect or even begin to imagine that some years later she would be walking up those very same steps to a reception, blushing and laughing. (55)

This manipulation of narrative is also found in *The Line of the Sun* ("Ramona and Rafael were to be man and wife not a full year after they faced each other on Mamá Cielo's porch" [83]). Whether the intent of Hijuelos's and Ortiz Cofer's writing is parodic ridicule or reverent imitation of García Márquez's narrative style, either form of mimicry establishes a dialogic relation between U.S. Latina/o and Latin American fiction.[16]

Thus some Latina/o texts simply imitate Boom fiction's best-known techniques; the *Rayuela*-like narrative structure of Ana Castillo's *The Mixquiahuala Letters* (1986), as well as the mind-boggling array of Boom references in Cecile Pineda's *The Love Queen of the Amazon* (1992), are additional examples of this type of intertextuality. In Castillo's *So Far from God* (1993), on the other hand, the juxtaposition of magical realism, Spanish Golden Age-style chapter titles, New Mexican regional dialect, and Chicano folklore produces a text that performs a pan-Latino cultural identification.

In an attempt to identify the "essence" of U.S. Latina/o fiction, critics may fail to note the differences in the ways Boom aesthetics are deployed, or even the fact that by no means all Latina/o writing has a magical realist bent. Some Latina/o writing does clearly copy Boom styles, and some critics do haphazardly label works as magical realist. Regardless of the source, these repeated "performances" of magical realism at the level of writing have begun to give the impression that U.S. Latina/o literature has an invariable style and that Latina/o culture has a mystical essence. But such an essence is an illusion, just as there is no *Latin American* essence behind Boom fiction, the "original" that U.S. Latina/o magical realism imitates. This stylistic and thematic imitation appears to reaffirm the novels' essential "Latino-ness," yet it can be read as a form of drag that parodies the very notion of Latina/o cultural essence.

Two recent novels by Chicana writers, Cecile Pineda's *The Love Queen of the Amazon,* and Ana Castillo's *So Far from God,* are excellent examples of this type of drag spectacle. Both novels have been labeled by critics and their publishers as magical realism, and both works unquestionably appropriate aesthetic codes associated with the Latin American Boom. In effect, the texts act as stages upon which their writers display a collection of "costumes": Latino signs such as magical realism, Boom stylistic techniques, markers of *chicanismo,* and so on. Significantly, the excessiveness of these signs points to the illusory quality of the cultural essence that they ostensibly reflect. In this chapter, I argue that such "impersonation" of Boom fiction calls attention to the fact that Latina/o culture is *not* monolithic. This phenomenon differs considerably from the performances of gender and cultural identity that I have discussed throughout this book. Nevertheless, these novels offer insights into Latino/a culture that add a new dimension to my exploration of the performative aspects of culture and identity.

PARODY, PASTICHE, AND THE (UN)MAKING
OF HISTORY: *THE LOVE QUEEN OF THE AMAZON*

No existe el concepto del plagio: se ha establecido que todas las obras son obra de un solo
autor, que es intemporal y es anónimo.[17]
— JORGE LUIS BORGES, "Tlon, Uqbar, Orbis Tertius"

Based on external appearances, Cecile Pineda's elaborately conceived *The
Love Queen of the Amazon* could easily be read as a translation of a previously unknown Latin American Boom novel.[18] Both the novel's title and its
cover design, a quasi-surrealist illustration of a voluptuous, jewel-bedecked
nude, floating on her back over lush aquatic flora and flanked by two oversized
orchids, suggest such a reading. The plot — a fanciful tale of a beautiful young
Peruvian woman who marries a renowned but obsessive writer and transforms their mansion into a bordello of mythical stature — is built around concerns and motifs that are common to other contemporary Latin American
novels.

The novel's epigraph, "Working Women," by Chicana poet Gina Valdés,
establishes an immediate link with Chicana/o literature as well. Yet aside from
the common motif of prostitution in both the poem and the novel, the connection between Latin American and U.S. Latina/o contexts is not explicitly developed in the text. *Love Queen* is most visibly a sort of condensed encyclopedia
of Boom fiction; it borrows liberally from Boom stylistic codes (magical realism, nonlinear temporal structure, and so forth), themes, and character types.
Shortly after the protagonist, Ana Magdalena, meets her suitor, Federico
Orgaz, strange coincidences begin to suggest that the novel is anything but a
straightforward chronicle of their life together. Their courtship consists of
outings in which Federico reads to Ana Magdalena from the manuscript he is
working on, with her mother, Andreina, acting as chaperon. During one of
these excursions, Andreina makes the startling discovery that events from her
life of the previous day are beginning to appear in the pages of Federico's novel.
Little by little it becomes evident that the narrator of Pineda's text is none other
than Federico himself. He describes to Ana Magdalena his vision for the novel:
" 'I'm going to give the world a major work, a stunning romance. . . . I'm going
to call it *The Love Queen of the Amazon*. And you, my darling, will provide
just the right touch of inspiration!' " (115). The title thus refers not only to Ana
Magdalena and her bordello, but also to Federico's "masterpiece," for woven
into *Love Queen* is the story of the novel's production.

Once this quirky homodiegetic narrator[19] is taken into account, the function of the novel's blatant and overstated references to Boom fiction becomes clearer. Federico's approach to producing a masterpiece is to imitate the writing of the Latin American masters. Like the narrator of Hijuelos's *The Fourteen Sisters of Emilio Montez O'Brien*, he mimics the narrative style made famous by García Márquez and other Boom novelists. *Love Queen* begins, almost predictably, with the lines "Many years later, when there was little doubt left, people still marveled . . . " (3), and it is sprinkled with similar allusions to *Cien años de soledad:*

It was there Ana Magdalena first laid eyes on the young dockhand who was later to lend a hand shaping her destiny (6).

In future years, Andreina would perversely remember the arrival of Doña Eduviges, not as the answer to all their woes, but as a towering inconvenience (38).

Just as in *Cien años de soledad*, this peculiar temporal construction hints at a narrator who is fully involved in the novelistic present but also possesses full knowledge of the future.

Federico quickly introduces magical realism into the narrative through his description of Ana Magdalena's birth. One day during the ninth month of her pregnancy, Andreina falls asleep while taking a bath to relieve her discomfort; she awakens to discover that "[s]wimming vigorously in water tinged a delirious aquamarine by her ruptured amniotic fluids was a sturdy female infant whose back was entirely covered with downy black hair" (4). Ana Magdalena's unusual birth and amazing swimming ability are just the beginning of a series of extraordinary events that parody García Márquez's style. Federico includes the requisite levitating character, following the precedent set by Remedios La Bella and the priest in *Cien años de soledad*. In *Love Queen*, the floater is Federico's elderly mother Clemencia. One evening after dinner, Ana Magdalena is startled to see her mother-in-law floating serenely up the stairs to her room, "her feet . . . gliding a full inch above the floor" (144).

Apparently miracles are commonplace in the town of Malyerba ("Bad Weed"), for the amazing occurrences elicit only mild reactions and even annoyance from the people. The narrator expresses something resembling fatigue with all the fantastic goings-on, foreshadowing the revival of a comatose character with "they were about to witness another in a long and tiresome string of miracles" (123). Here the narrator himself hints that the novel has an element of parody, which unfortunately is not exploited further. The sheer excess of magical realist episodes that he includes suggests that he views the Latin American *real maravilloso* with a certain reverence but also, in Mikhail Bakhtin's words, "with irony, with a smirk" (1981, 69). This simultaneous deployment of opposing parodic practices makes *Love Queen* neither a convincing critique of magical realism nor an homage to it. Instead, through the proliferation of miracles the text parodies the notion of a magical Latin American essence.

In addition to its profusion of magical realism, *Love Queen* engages in a dialogic relationship with Latin American fiction by means of its appropriation and manipulation of Boom motifs. Ana Magdalena's bordello, for example, has a clear antecedent in Vargas Llosa's *La casa verde* and an even earlier precursor in José Eustasio Rivera's *La vorágine*. "La Nymphaea" is a postmodern variation of the classic brothel, decorated in an array of styles that includes the look of a nineteenth-century convent, Art Nouveau, Toulouse-Lautrec, and Ali Baba and the Forty Thieves.[20] In fact, La Nymphaea occupies what was previously a Capuchin convent; it owes its present existence to the confiscation of church property by the dictatorship of 1910. The fictional Latin American country continues to be ruled by a dictator, the "President Plenipotentiary, Caudillo-for-Life, El Señor Magnífico, Ochoa-Vicente y Ruiz" (159). A minute four-foot six-inch man with bristling, "statesmanly" mustaches, El Magnífico is a pastiche of the dictator characters portrayed in such Latin American classics as *El señor presidente*, *El otoño del patriarca*, *Yo, el supremo*, and *El recurso del método*.[21]

Long before the dictator makes his appearance in the novel, a reference to the oppressive political climate of the country evokes yet another comparison with contemporary Latin American fiction. In *Cien años de soledad* the disappeared train filled with banana workers is a sharp criticism of worker repression and exploitation by the United Fruit Company. In *Love Queen*, similarly, the narrator remarks that the music master of the convent where as a girl Ana Magdalena is interned "would finally reach the peak of his ambition as an army executioner in suppression of the miners' strike" (11). Intertextuality with the Colombian novel is further developed through the similarities between the towns of Malyerba and Macondo, as *Love Queen* continues *Cien años'* parody of the sluggish pace of Latin American modernization. Federico begins the second chapter by pontificating, "In those days, progress had yet to visit Malyerba. Potholes had not yet been invented" and proceeds with a treatise on the relative scarcity of vehicles: "[A]s a general rule, the wheel has always exhibited a certain bashfulness making its appearance in the New World, its relative merits being still in dispute" (21). In Malyerba, however, modernization is a minor concern, for in this town flukes of nature quickly assume epic proportions. A year of incessant rain brings Malyerba an unusual affliction reminiscent of Macondo's plagues of insomnia and forgetfulness: a "pestilential tide of prophets" that gathered "like starlings, clustering everywhere . . . clogging the flooded thoroughfares, shouting and expostulating, hawking rosaries, holy pictures, and miracle water from Lourdes" (181).

After incorporating the obligatory plague into his novel, Federico seems uncertain as to what to do with it. In fact, much of the narrative of *Love Queen* is constructed of contrived and flimsily connected anecdotes that allow Federico to fulfill what he considers to be the requirements of a great novel. Thus in Malyerba, as in Macondo, time has a strange plasticity: "Like putty, it could expand or contract. It could ball itself into a knot or, equally, stretch out in long, elastic strings, metaphorically speaking" (57). Federico takes some of his most extreme creative liberties with regard to the narration of history, freely juxtaposing chronologically disparate moments in an ambitious but ultimately superficial critique of positivism, capitalism, and imperialism. Ben Franklin makes a brief appearance at La Nymphaea one stormy evening; later Charles Darwin and Horatio Alger also pay visits to the bordello. By conflating distinct moments in history, Federico produces a pastiche that underscores the illusory nature of historical "truth."

Federico's portrayal of Alger, whose motto is "Hard work, service with a smile—long as business is good, it means you're in the Lord's grace" (183), allows him to insert a jab at the Protestant work ethic. Hints of sociopolitical critique of United States and multinational capitalist practices appear at numerous other points in the text. After Ana Magdalena transforms the mansion into her own brothel, she resorts to taking out a loan with well-nigh impossible terms from the shadowy "International Fiduciary Fund." The *yanquis* have already made their presence felt in Malyerba in other ways, although they avoid contact with the natives by isolating themselves in their own city surrounded by a cyclone fence. Sergio Ballado, Ana Magdalena's lover, comments that because of the *norteamericanos'* single-minded notion of order, " '[w]hen a hill is in the way, they just flatten it and build a swimming pool' " (199).

For reasons unknown, Federico discards a passage of his manuscript in which the dying Simón Bolívar experiences first-hand the *yanquis'* condescending attitude toward Latin Americans.[22] He may have decided to omit this anecdote because its political critique is too direct. Like a true postmodern writer, Federico toys with political commitment but ultimately keeps his narrative ambiguous by leaving out overly forceful passages. Nevertheless, the novel is infused with the traces of resistance to exploitation caused by U.S. foreign and domestic policy.[23]

Regardless of Federico's political stance, his editorial decisions are clearly influenced by his desire for fame. His original vision for *The Love Queen of the Amazon* was impressive:

Suddenly, spread out before him, Federico beheld the magnificent sweep of the novel which was sure to bring him fame, and considerable fortune, which might even place him in line for international acclaim. . . . He would chronicle the history of a house of pleasure. . . . A parade of the great men of history: La Perouse, Diderot, Voltaire, the firebrands of revolution. . . . The march of progress led by the great stockmen of Argentina. . . . It would all be there, a splendid tapestry of hemispheric history. (150)

His objective as a writer is to produce a totalizing panorama of the historical formation of Latin American cultural identity. Federico's insistence on maintaining complete authorial control becomes evident during a literary soirée to which Ana Magdalena and her mother are invited. Federico engages in a heated argument with Euclides da Cunha about the writer's responsibility to avoid "unorthodox digressions" in his narrative. He claims that Twain and Sterne were inferior writers in this respect, and he blames their failures on deficient literary preparation:

"What can anglos know of our great literary tradition handed down from generation to generation by our great and illustrious Hispanic forebears? I say to hell with white spaces! . . . Fabulation is what is needed, the endless and obsessive elaboration of the narrative line to form labyrinthine arabesques, polyhedrons, dodecahedrons of astonishing and dizzying complexity" (58).

Federico clearly follows his own advice; da Cunha remarks that Federico's writing is so full of prevarications that " 'It's a wonder there's anyone left patient enough to turn the pages' " (58). In effect, the narrator appropriates the "language" of the Boom as part of his effort to capture the essence of Latin American culture in one literary masterpiece. In his ambitious attempt, Federico creates a simulacrum of Boom fiction that is pure artifice: a facade without substance, a grandiloquent pastiche, a novelistic drag show. Lamentably, *Love Queen* fails for the same reason: The clever intentions behind the novel produce a generally tedious and unsatisfying narrative.

There is a significant problem with this notion that Federico's material comes from the Latin American writers. Although it is impossible to determine precisely when the events of Pineda's novel take place, it appears that Federico writes *Love Queen* before the Boom classics would have been published. Technically, then, only *Pineda's* text can be considered an imitation of Boom fiction. Pineda invents a precursor to the Boom writers — Federico — whose style, as evaluated in the late 1990s, is best described as an obvious imitation of these same writers. This narrative trick recalls Borges's deconstruction of the notion of influence in his short essay, "Kafka and His Precursors," particularly his observation that "every writer *creates* his own precursors" (201).[24] In a paradox of influence, Federico creates Boom "precursors" who actually *follow* him. His stylized language is situated in an impossible context, a time when such language was not readable as a marker of Boom fiction. Clearly, a late-twentieth-century postmodern consciousness lurks behind the novel. Within Federico's universe, *Love Queen* must be read as pastiche, defined by Fredric Jameson as "the identical copy for which no original has ever existed" (66).

Federico gradually begins to recognize that the scope of his project is beyond his (or any other writer's) capability. He realizes that the task he has set for himself is endless, in part because he finds that he is unable to control his own manuscript:

> [T]he more he typed, the more the manuscript seemed to acquire a mysterious life all of its own. He discovered that the same episodes had a nasty habit of reappearing in later chapters. . . . Whenever he stumbled on another such duplication, he had to begin typing all over again. (214)

This view of the writing process, with its echoes of Borges's circular, labyrinthine prose, allows Federico to avoid final responsibility for his narrative which, to his dismay, he can never complete.

The consequences of self-referentiality are discussed by Roberto González Echevarría in an essay on contemporary Latin American fiction. González Echevarría observes that in many Boom novels, the author's figure laments his lack of narrative authority; as a result, "his importance diminishes and he is even cancelled out as the source of creation and ultimate knowledge" (71). Thus by including the story of how the work itself is written, the narrator erases the boundaries between reality and fiction. Federico, initially deluded by the failed premise of nineteenth-century realist writers like Galdós and Flaubert, gradually becomes aware that he can never gain more than fleeting access to Latin American reality. He nevertheless refuses to acknowledge that this absence of authorial control is intrinsic to the writing process. Instead, Federico blames his frustration with *Love Queen* on Ana Magdalena, whom he accuses of withholding information about her bordello that would have been a rich source of material for his novel:

> "You could at least have told me about the courtroom! And the torture chamber! And the hot-air balloon! And even the confessional! But no, you simpering little viper, you keep the best material to yourself! Now I have to rework the whole thing!" (248)

Rather than accept that any literary attempt to comprehensively represent reality is destined to fail, Federico concludes that he must rewrite *Love Queen*. In spite of his erudition and philosophical approach to literature, he is blind to a fundamental truth about novelistic discourse: that it can never capture the totality of culture, or of history, or of human existence. Bakhtin's observations about novelistic discourse offer a plausible explanation for this "shortcoming" of the text. He argues that the novel is the literary form that most closely approximates the complex interaction of languages that fills social space. Yet this same ongoing dialogue gives novelistic images "their openendedness, their inability to say anything once and for all or to think anything through to its end" and leaves the text indeterminate and uncontrollable (1981, 365).

This approach to narrative emphasizes the performative nature of both writing and culture: Writing cannot capture reality or definitive truths but can only act as a performance that may produce the *illusion* of essence. Federico has no control over his narrative of Latin American culture because the culture itself is constantly evolving; it cannot be encapsulated, frozen, in a literary text. He does have occasional revelations about the transcendence of the writing process in comparison to the finished product. With his publisher pressuring him to complete his manuscript, he discovers that he has resisted closing down Ana Magdalena's bordello because then "there would be very little left to write, and writing, well, dear God, it was the very air he breathed" (208). La Nymphaea has been Federico's source of anecdotes in his ongoing effort to write Latin American history. Consequently, to close the brothel would be to dismantle a site where the performativity of culture is visible, a site whose everyday practices are the substance of Federico's grand literary *oeuvre*.

Federico does not recognize the implications of his frustrating experience with *The Love Queen of the Amazon*, even though it challenges the very premise on which he based his literary endeavor. His dream of single-handedly narrating the continent, of creating "a splendid tapestry of hemispheric history" with a huge cast of characters — conquerors, missionaries, "firebrands of revolution," the great stockmen of Argentina, the "*señoritos* of the single crop" (150) — is unattainable. Federico's insistence on beginning his project anew reveals his conviction that producing the definitive manuscript is only a matter of acquiring the right information. Yet the essence of Latin American culture that he believes his novel can capture is illusory; he is destined to fail even if he endlessly rewrites the text. As I have argued in previous chapters, repetition of performative acts can never fully establish the essence of culture or gender.[25] Moreover, Federico contests his own narrative authority when he blames Ana Magdalena for the shortcomings of his manuscript. In this way the novel supports the notion that Latin American culture cannot be articulated in one voice but rather is always "an interplay of heterogeneous discourses" (Sommer and Yúdice 198).

By generating a pastiche of Boom fiction, *The Love Queen of the Amazon* challenges the status of Boom writing as an official discourse of Latin American identity and culture. This pastiche both underscores and reveals the problematic nature of the dialogic relationship between U.S. Latina/o and Latin American fiction, a connection that is first highlighted by the novel's epigraph. Federico flounders miserably in his attempt to write a definitive, all-encompassing history of Latin American culture; his failure can be read as a veiled warning against essentialist characterizations of either literature. To assume, for example, that to be "authentic" a U.S. Latina/o novel must reflect an ethnic essence (which *Love Queen* does not), or must somehow incorporate magical realism, is to impose artificial limitations on a diverse body of writing. At worst, magical realism risks becoming a superficial Latino performance with no more substance than the backless "Infanta" costume in the Velázquez room of Ana Magdalena's bordello.

PERFORMING *CHICANISMO* IN *SO FAR FROM GOD*

Times *had* changed. . . . Wasn't it possible that miracles, too, had changed?
— JOHN RECHY, *The Miraculous Day of Amalia Gómez*

In contrast to *The Love Queen of the Amazon*, Ana Castillo's 1993 novel *So Far from God* takes place in a typically U.S. Latina/o setting: the northern New Mexico town of Tomé.[26] The novel is nonetheless connected to a larger Latin American context by its title, which is taken from a quote about Mexico attributed to Porfirio Díaz. Castillo's work shares other similarities with Pineda's, specifically a proliferation of what the publisher's blurb calls "homegrown magical realism," and the occasional passage written in García Márquezlike narrative style. In fact, one reviewer suggests that these elements make *So Far from God* a more readable alternative to *Cien años de soledad,* claiming that Castillo's novel

> [distinguishes] itself from its South American predecessors by its chatty, accessible *Norteño* language and relentless good humor. Give it to people who always wanted to read *One Hundred Years of Solitude* but couldn't quite get through it. (Kingsolver)

This family saga of a working-class Chicana named Sofia and her four daughters does contain a healthy dose of extraordinary events. Around Tomé, humans exhibit animal behaviors and vice versa; third daughter Fe discovers that her fiancé, like his sheepherder ancestors, has acquired "the odd affliction of bleating" (175). Even the local crows' unusual habit of smoking discarded cigarette butts from their perch on telephone wires elicits neither surprise nor curiosity from the townspeople (199). In the first chapter, furthermore, Sofia's youngest daughter dies, but during her funeral she revives and flies up to the church roof. From this position she informs the stunned crowd that she has been to hell, to "pulgatorio," and to heaven. After this announcement, "[w]ith the delicate and effortless motion of a monarch butterfly the child brought herself back to the ground" (24). The amazing feat earns her the name of "La Loca Santa," which the people shorten to "La Loca" when they find that she refuses to grant blessings or perform miracles on demand.

Such incidents involving magical elements of Latino Catholicism and folk-lore operate as visible performances of Chicano/Latino identity in the novel. For in spite of (or perhaps because of) the seemingly insurmountable obstacles that the characters encounter, their belief in miracles and in the spiritual world forms one of the community's most powerful collective fictions. Insofar as mystical Catholicism is viewed as a foundation of Chicana/o culture, "magical realist" religious performances affirm and establish solidarity with Chicana/o cultural identity. Superstition, magic, and spirits — the inexplicable — are in-compatible with rational Western thought; consequently, such performances are a form of opposition to Anglo-European positivist paradigms.

In *So Far from God,* the quantity of miraculous and inexplicable events and the narrator's matter-of-fact manner of recounting them mark the community as unmistakably different from Anglo-American society.[27] The mainstream medical establishment lends no credence to the story of La Loca's resurrection; doctors at the Albuquerque hospital to which Sofi takes the revived child conclude that she is most likely an epileptic (25). Whether or not such phe-nomena can be attributed to the community's lack of access to up-to-date medical care, faith healing and miracles — *lo maravilloso* — are an accepted part of everyday life in Tomé. One character recalls that as a child he was convinced that La Loca's resurrection was a trick, "the way all children view the magical, which to them falls within the realm of possibility" (192). As an adult, he comes to share the other characters' belief that miraculous events are a reasonable outcome of their religious devotion.

The second daughter, Caridad, seems to be powerfully connected to the spirit world, for she is at the center of several magical occurrences. A brutal attack by an unknown assailant leaves the young woman alive but mutilated, "a nightmare incarnated" (33) who will have to be cared for as long as she lives. Nevertheless, a few months after the assault the entire family witnesses the miraculous sight of Caridad,

> walking soundlessly, without seeming to be aware of them, across that room. . . . Furthermore, it wasn't the Caridad that had been brought back from the hospital, but a whole and once again beautiful Caridad. (37)

In general, the narrator makes no attempt to offer logical explanations for the magical events that take place in Tomé, presenting them simply as everyday, collective occurrences.[28]

The narrative style of *So Far from God* complements the novel's magical realist bent, particularly through its appropriation of the now ubiquitous Marquezian temporality:

> Eventually it would be revealed that none of the women in that family was without some unusual trait . . . (58)

> . . . in a few months she would be satisfied to find that her hunch about Fe was right . . . (136)

> [T]hat month would always be remembered by everyone who had known her as the one in which la Fe died right after her first anniversary (171).

While the narrator's intention may be to parody Boom fiction, the novel lacks the ironic distance that Federico's dual role as character and narrator generates in *The Love Queen of the Amazon*. As I showed above, Federico unwittingly renders Boom discourse devoid of meaning — by making excessive use of it — even as he venerates it, and he becomes an anguished victim of his own lack of originality. In *So Far from God*, the narrator liberally borrows but the text lacks the self-referentiality that Federico adds to Pineda's narrative. In addition, Tomé's miraculous occurrences are removed from the Latin American context that critics have argued is inseparable from magical realism. Consequently, the novel's "magical realism" seems only superficially connected to the distinctly North American circumstances in which the narrative is grounded.

While the two novels share the common denominator of Boom aesthetics, *So Far from God*'s focus on specific problems faced by a rural Chicana/o community lends the novel a more overtly political tone than that of *Love Queen*. Castillo's commentary on issues of racism and economic exploitation in U.S. society serves as a reminder that ethnicity is not simply free-wheeling performance, an act over which the ethnic subject has full control. The fictionalized incidents of victimization to which the novel alludes call attention to the sociohistorical forces that operate to disenfranchise ethnic and racial minority groups. For instance, the racist essentialism that makes it difficult for Latinos to be recognized as individuals in American society is illustrated by the character Francisco's experience in Vietnam. He is subjected to ethnic stereotyping that erases difference between members of minority groups. His platoon nicknames a Navajo soldier "Chief," while Francisco is called "Chico" and a Puerto Rican soldier is given the doubly derogatory nickname of "Little Chico." The narrator points out that "to the white and black soldiers all 'Spanish boys' were 'Chico'" (94).

The day-to-day difficulties with which the characters of *So Far from God* struggle, as well as the larger social problems that affect them, combine to produce a serious threat to the very existence of their community. For the characters, as for members of many minority communities in the United States, this threat takes the form of a lack of economic resources and consequent loss of family land, exploitation by large corporations, environmental hazards, and assimilation. The novel suggests that the narrator is trying to rescue New Mexico Chicana/o identity from oblivion, to halt or at least call attention to the inexorable erasure of her people's cultural tradition. Her strategy is to construct a sort of encyclopedia of local Chicana/o folklore and oral tradition that also engages religious, historical, political, and feminist issues.

In spite of the novel's generally upbeat tone, much of the action involves occurrences that reveal the fragility of the characters' existence. Sofi's decision to run for mayor of Tomé (a position that has never existed before) is motivated by her frustration with the downward spiral that the town is taking. A primary problem is the gradual disappearance of the family farms that have supported the people for generations; the narrator explains that the recent influx of "outsiders," that is, gringos, is largely responsible for this.[29] The people of Tomé find themselves threatened not only by harsh economic conditions that make their small farms impractical but also by exploitation by the large corporations that have made their way into the area. Fe's horrible (and ultimately fatal) experience working at a company called Acme International highlights the vulnerability of the Chicanos to this type of manipulation and abuse. She is required to work with toxic chemicals and dies of cancer, the victim of a system that mercilessly exploits its purposely uninformed workers. Other townspeople are likewise exposed to mysterious health hazards that cause them to sicken and animals to die; here the narrator's critique is aimed at governmental and corporate negligence with regard to toxic waste disposal.[30] Toward the end of the novel, the community uses a highly culture-specific venue, the local Good Friday procession, to stage a dramatic protest. This year, the townspeople alter their traditional reenactment of Christ's final hours to produce a twentieth-century Chicana/o revision of the Way of the Cross. Instead of Mary meeting Jesus, the women wear photographs of their loved ones who have died from exposure to toxic chemicals.[31] At each station along the procession's route, the crowd stops to hear people speak about the abuses that are "turning the people of those lands into an endangered species" (242). In lieu of Jesus bearing the cross, a man speaks about the countless Hispano families living below poverty level; later three Navajo women talk about the effects of uranium contamination on the reservation. The line between past and present begins to blur to create an eerie effect of simultaneity:

Veronica wiped the blood and sweat from Jesus' face. Livestock drank and swam in contaminated canals. . . .
The women of Jerusalem consoled Jesus. Children also played in those open disease-ridden canals where the livestock swam and drank and died from it. . . .
Nuclear power plants sat like gargantuan landmines among the people, near their ranchos and ancestral homes. Jesus was nailed to the cross. . . .
No, no one had ever seen a procession like that one before. (242–44)

Thus *So Far from God* weaves together contemporary social problems and an age-old ritual of northern New Mexico Catholics. This procession, with its fusion of biblical past and the community's present, is evidence of the performativity of culture. The people themselves transform religious tradition by reinventing a time-honored ritual to respond to their immediate needs.

In addition to its focus on the economic and environmental problems that afflict many minority communities in the United States, Castillo's novel presents another hotly debated "ethnic" issue: assimilation. Two of Sofi's daughters, Fe and Esperanza, make concerted efforts to leave Tomé behind. Yet these characters both die tragically; the text thus appears to suggest that attempting to "perform" as an Anglo can be lethal. Fe's demise clearly alludes to the hazards of assimilation. Her decision to work for Acme was prompted by her desire for a middle-class life-style that the majority of Tomé's inhabitants could never hope to attain. Of Sofi's four daughters, Fe is the one most driven to assimilate and join the ranks of the Anglo-American middle-class she sees portrayed in the media. She is light-skinned, although the narrator interjects that Fe "was not nearly as white as she thought she was" (157–58). As an adult she begins systematically acquiring the symbols of the "good life": a husband — she marries her accountant cousin Casimiro ("Casey") — a new car, and a tract home filled with new furniture. Yet Fe's dreams of assimilation are shattered by her untimely death at the hands of the very company that she had seen as her ticket out of Tomé, away from what she perceives to be the backwardness of her cultural heritage.

Fe's devastating story serves as a metaphor for the manner in which the allure of assimilation contributes to the deterioration of close-knit Chicana/o communities like the one portrayed in *So Far from God*. The narrator points out that the younger generations of Tomé, unable or unwilling to earn a living as their ancestors did, go to Albuquerque or other cities to work, go to college out of state, or are sent out of the country with the army (139). Eldest daughter Esperanza has increasing difficulty embracing Catholicism and the concomitant miracles that her family accepts without question. The simultaneous sudden recoveries of Caridad and Fe (who screamed nonstop for months after being jilted by her first fiancé) finally convince Esperanza that the things that go on in her family defy her comprehension:

> Caridad's and Fe's spontaneous recoveries were beyond all rhyme and reason for anyone, even for an ace reporter like Esperanza. It was time to get away, Esperanza decided, far away. (39)

Unlike the majority of the characters, for whom inexplicable phenomena and leaps of faith are an essential part of their culturally specific belief system, Esperanza's tolerance for mystical occurrences has been exceeded. In effect rejecting the notion that because she is Chicana she must perform in accordance with these beliefs, Esperanza leaves Tomé in order to reinvent herself. Her pursuit of a successful career, which takes her ever farther from her community, involves a certain amount of "Anglo cross-dressing," of drag, to produce the illusion of assimilation. Assimilation is also presented as a grave threat: Esperanza's dreams of a career as a news anchorwoman take her to the Middle East, where she is kidnapped and killed. Her departure from the community is a sign of the inevitable transformation of Chicana/o cultural identity. Esperanza does not cease to be Chicana by going away; rather, she begins performing a variant of *chicanismo* that is vastly different from that practiced by Tomé's inhabitants.

So Far from God is thus firmly grounded in tangible social, economic, and political problems faced by Chicanos and other minority groups. The novel appears to suggest that such communities can only survive through solidarity and unified effort. When the people of Tomé begin organizing a cooperative to bolster the town's deteriorating economic base, the narrator observes that "it became a debate of either everyone doing it all together or nobody doing anything at all" (146). The narrator's didactic chronicle is her response to the forces that threaten the people of Tomé. Her narrative seeks to ensure the survival, in literary form, of this beleaguered community's culture. In this sense the text follows the paradigm that Juan Bruce-Novoa has observed in Chicana/o literature in general, a literature which he claims is a reaction "to a threat of Chaos, of the culture disappearing into something other than itself" (1982, 212). As an "almanac of Chicanismo"[32] infused with local Chicano folklore and language, *So Far from God* rescues the people's cultural tradition from complete disappearance.

At the same time, the novel can be read as a challenge to the notion of static, monolithic Latina/o identity that is the conventional foundation for resistance. The text's anti-essentialism becomes apparent through the sheer excess of the novel's diverse Chicano/Latino performances, as well as through the narrator's own critique of Chicana/o culture. Like Federico in *The Love Queen of the Amazon,* this narrator has a propensity for wanting to cover all bases. She mixes lofty sounding chapter titles à la Cervantes with local dialect, recipes, and folk remedies, weaving in constant feminist and political commentary. The result is an exhaustive, overly ambitious compendium of Chicano/Latino performances, a complex and ultimately tiresome chronicle that links centuries of *hispanidad.*

The novel's imitation of narrative techniques associated with *Cien años de soledad* and other Boom fiction is an easily recognizable reference to Latin American literature. Unlike *Love Queen,* however, *So Far from God* copies a variety of literary styles in addition to Boom stylistics. The narrator also draws upon Spanish Golden Age literature as inspiration for her rambling, detailed chapter titles. These elaborate titles — "An Account of the First Astonishing Occurrence in the Lives of a Woman Named Sofia and Her Four Fated Daughters; and the Equally Astonishing Return of Her Wayward Husband" — immediately establish dialogue with *Don Quixote.* The titles are nevertheless firmly grounded in the twentieth-century in spite of their archaic veneer, making references to Clark Gable, channeling, and "Ectoplasmic Return." They also include recognizable markers of *chicanismo:* the Penitentes of New Mexico, La Llorona, *santeros,* and *curanderas* appear in different chapter titles. Within the narrative itself, the narrator's connection to the Chicana/o community is fortified by the performative effect of her use of colloquial speech patterns. The narrative is sprinkled with double negatives ("nobody could say nothing about it" [21], "she did not see nothing too unusual" [44]) and regional expressions in Spanish (*mitotera, nomás, metiche*). The narrator engages in other performances that show off her knowledge of folk culture, such as describing the local *curandera*'s home remedies and La Loca's favorite recipes. That is, she emphasizes the practices of everyday life through which cultural tradition is transmitted. By faithfully transcribing the remedies as told to her by doña Felicia, the narrator reinforces the association between Chicana/o culture and oral tradition. Many of the remedies include elements of faith-healing — spiritual cleansings, the placing of an egg on the patient's stomach to reveal the location of a digestive obstruction, and so forth. Thoroughly "nonscientific," the remedies make Latina/o folklore visible and accessible to monolingual mainstream readers through the narrator's act of naming them. When contrasted to the scientifically substantiated treatments of the American health care industry, these remedies work as performances of ethnic difference.

La Loca's recipes for *carne adovada, posole,* and *bizcochitos* likewise provide a vehicle for the narrator to demonstrate her cultural solidarity with the community.[33] She periodically adds her own recommendations to the recipes ("for our purposes here, I am adding specific measurements myself" [167]), and provides running commentary on the history of the dishes and other related trivia. These folksy comments serve to establish a certain intimacy with readers unfamiliar with the local culture. At the same time, they allow the narrator to reaffirm her insider status in the Tomé Chicana/o community. This "Chicana cooking show hostess" narrative style is reminiscent of the narrator of Laura Esquivel's *Como agua para chocolate.* It is one of the voices that the narrator employs to present her encyclopedia of Chicano/Latino culture. She switches from this chatty style to an almost scholarly discourse to explain the historical background of community traditions like the Holy Week procession. She attributes the persistence of this ritual, which is foreign to Anglo-American culture, to the Spanish Catholic church's powerful influence over northern New Mexico during the colonial period. As a result, she declares, "neither Mexican nor U.S. appropriation diluted the religious practices of the descendants of the Spaniards who settled there . . . such is their fervent devotion" (74).

Yet even as the narrator is celebrating and valorizing Chicano/Latino tradition through these varied performances, she turns a critical eye toward the culture. In some respects this narrator resembles the character Esperanza, for both dare to question traditional cultural mythologies: the belief in divine intervention, the sexist power structures of the Chicana/o community, and the Catholic church. Following La Loca's "death," the narrator calls attention to the blind faith that is an integral part of the culture of Tomé. The parish priest admonishes the townspeople that "we must not show our lack of faith in Him at these times and in His, our Father's fair judgment," and Sofi's neighbors attempt to console her with "[T]he Lord alone knows what He does!" (22). These empty words provide little comfort for the distraught mother; the narrator vividly portrays Sofi's sense of the futility of her faith:

> Why? Why? That's exactly what Sofi wanted to know at that moment — when all she had ever done was accept God's will. As if it hadn't been punishment enough to be abandoned by her husband, then — for no apparent reason and without warning . . . her baby was taken away! Oh, why? Why? That's all she wanted to know. (22)

For the irreverent narrator, Catholic dogma is anything but sacred. While describing Sofi's founding of M.O.M.A.S. (Mothers of Martyrs and Saints), the narrator does a feminist reading of Catholic history that calls attention to the exclusion of women from the church hierarchy. By the end of the novel a rumor has begun to circulate that M.O.M.A.S. officials are requiring anatomical proof that board members are indeed female. The narrator finds this particularly ironic in light of the knowledge that at one time papal candidates were required to prove that they were *not* women:

> After all, just because there had been a time way back when, when some fregados all full of themselves went out of their way to prove that none among them had the potential of being a mother, did it mean that there *had* to come a time when someone would be made to *prove* that she did? (251)

Her feminist critique extends to Chicana/o cultural icons as well, in particular the legendary figure of La Llorona. She blames sexist misinterpretation for the bad rap that La Llorona has acquired among "her people," proposing that "La Llorona in the beginning (before men got in the way of it all) may have been nothing short of a loving mother goddess" (163). Sofi's recollection of the numerous Chicanas she has known who were forced to raise their children alone — "none of them had ever tried to kill their babies" (161) — challenges La Llorona's image as a horrific *madre terrible*.

The narrator's vindication of La Llorona is part of her exposé of the sexism of Chicana/o cultural tradition. She is particularly merciless with respect to cultural norms that associate femininity with passivity and submission. Within the text's fictional world, Sofi becomes a subversive feminist voice. She refuses to embrace the culturally inscribed role of passive female and resists stoically accepting fate. On the contrary, the tragedies and crises that afflict Sofi's family during the course of the novel awaken her rebellious spirit. She takes the bold step of running for mayor of Tomé after concluding that this is the only way to achieve positive changes for the community. Empowered by the idea of influencing the town's destiny, Sofi begins a campaign to enlighten the townspeople. She points out the futility of their victim stance by evoking the memory of Esperanza, who in her Chicana radical days often said that the community would continue to be "poor and forgotten" unless it took action (139). Castillo places the message of Chicana/o empowerment — "we [need] to go out and fight for our rights" (142) — firmly in the hands of a female character. In so doing, she carries on the legacy of a long line of Chicana feminists who by rejecting traditional constructs of femininity strive to de-essentialize Chicana/o identity.[34]

So Far from God's numerous anecdotes of magical realism and Catholic mysticism suggest an essential Chicano/Latino connection to the spiritual world as well. Yet the narrator's irreverent feminist reading of the collective fictions of Chicana/o culture deals a blow to the idea of an unchanging core of cultural mythologies. The need for repeated performances of Chicano/Latino identity in the novel further underscores the inaccessibility of the essence that these performances supposedly reflect. Once again Judith Butler's theory of gender illuminates the issue of cultural identity, particularly her insistence that such repetition establishes "the *instability* of the very category that it constitutes" (1991, 18). As I have argued in previous discussions, Latina/o cultural identity, like gender, must be constantly reinforced and reenacted. Here the repetition takes the form of the array of anachronistic cultural codes, all eminently readable as "Latina/o" signs, with which the narrator fills her story.

This profusion of disparate discursive styles and narrative techniques, of tidbits of Chicana/o folklore and history, resembles a collection of costumes in which Castillo "dresses" the story of Tomé. In this sense, *So Far from God* is effectively a novelistic Latina/o drag show. The writer costumes the community's narrative as a Golden Age *novela*, as a Boom novel, as a Chicana/o social protest treatise, and as a *telenovela* spanning several decades and involving a typically large cast of characters. These stylistic drag costumes are associated with widely diverging historical contexts, making the text more pastiche than parody.[35] *So Far from God* does not copy a single literary style but simultaneously mimics a number of styles; like *Love Queen,* it cannot be considered an imitation of a definable original.

The stylistic and narrative complexity of *So Far from God* allows the novel to engage, in varying degrees, many of the central issues of this study. Through its critique of Tomé's collective fictions, the text challenges traditional Latina/o constructs of gender and cultural identity. Grounded in the everyday practices of an endangered Chicana/o community, the novel vividly portrays the tension between cultural tradition and the forces that continuously transform culture. Thus *So Far from God* attests to the performative nature of ethnic identity. Close reading of the text's melange of stylistic devices — the "costumes" that mask the absence of Latina/o essence — lends additional support to the concept of drag as a metaphor for identity.

READING BEYOND THE MAGIC

On the surface, both *The Love Queen of the Amazon* and *So Far from God* appear to be thoroughly "Latino" texts, based on their easily recognizable references to pan-Latina/o culture. Yet neither novel promotes a homogenized view of Latina/o cultural identity, for close reading uncovers an intrinsic anti-essentialist quality in both texts. The narrator of *Love Queen* dreams of writing an all-encompassing novelistic history of Latin America that will embody the essence of the culture. Ironically, Federico's nonrealist representation of narrative events — the proliferation of magical incidents, the nonlinear conception of time — alludes to the elusiveness of the reality he aspires to capture. In spite of his valiant efforts to retain complete narrative authority he finds that he cannot control the text. Like his nineteenth-century realist precursors, he can only present a fragmentary, partial rendering of his grand project.

As a literary device, magical realism provides the verbose, eccentric Federico with an alternative to traditional realist narrative. In addition, appropriation of magical realism and other Boom stylistic devices in *Love Queen* establishes a dialogic relationship between U.S. Latina/o and Latin American fiction. In effect, Pineda's novel affirms the connection that is often made between the two literatures. At the same time, the text challenges some critics' assumption that U.S. Latina/o literature is American ethnic writing with a Latin American essence. This tendency is evident in Kingsolver's review of *So Far from God,* which depicts the novel as a sort of Latin American "lite," and the numerous other reviews highlighting the Marquezian tendencies of the works they describe.

So Far from God nevertheless differs from *Love Queen*'s no-holds-barred pastiche of Latin American magical realism and Boom writing. In Castillo's novel, in contrast to Pineda's, "magical realism" is firmly rooted in a United States *ethnic* problematic. In this work, miraculous occurrences have strong spiritual connotations, and references to Latino Catholicism and folklore make the miracles highly visible performances of Latina/o excess. *So Far from God*'s narrator produces a compendium of the ongoing performances — miracles, folk tales, faith healing, regional dialect — that constitute the collective identity of Tomé. The narrative thus serves to symbolically rescue the community from disappearance by bringing its culture to life through the text. Yet it cannot be considered a nostalgic paean to Chicano tradition, for it offers feminist resistance to the intrinsic sexism of many of the cultural mythologies. In this sense, *So Far from God* implies that resistance can be generated without relying on monolithic identity projects that exclude members of the community. The fundamental ideology behind the protests in which the character Esperanza participated during her "Chicana radical" days — "working to change the 'system' " (142) — is still valid. However, the view of identity that those protests expressed has been revised, allowing new forms of resistance to be articulated.

In spite of their obvious differences, the novels I have discussed in this chapter are nevertheless part of U.S. Latina/o fiction's magical realist "boom." I have shown how critics in mainstream publications tend to view magical realism as the essence of Latin American literature and to emphasize the miraculous and/or mystical elements in Latina/o novels. The result is the unjustified and ultimately damaging homogenization of works containing a miracle or two. Because they stand out as recurring examples of Latina/o excess, these miracles or magical occurrences operate as performances that produce the illusion that the U.S. Latina/o canon has a magical realist essence as well. To overlook the diverse contexts that generate these performances is to disregard both the complexity of this writing and the social, historical, and political factors that distinguish it from Latin American literature. While some U.S. Latina/o fiction may indeed contain elements that are reminiscent of Latin American magical realism, these narrative "performances" are only one aspect of U.S. Latina/o literature.

My readings of *The Love Queen of the Amazon* and *So Far from God* have shown how both works deconstruct the notion of cultural essence. These two novels indirectly suggest a more comprehensive view of Latina/o culture and identity for the 1990s, a view that accounts for the power of tradition but also acknowledges the inexorable force of day-to-day performative acts. Latina/o identity cannot be captured in a literary work, like Federico's grandiose project, much less in a phrase like "magical realism." It is dynamic, multifaceted, a "permanente vaivén" between history and the continuous, everyday rewriting of Latina/o culture.

CONCLUSION

The Show Must Go On

It seems somehow contradictory to append a "conclusion" to a project that purports to show the fundamentally *inconclusive* character of identity. Nevertheless, I wish to end this book — this "performance" — with a few closing comments on reading U.S. Latina/o fiction and culture. My work with Latina/o fiction has been motivated by a desire to show that this rich and diverse literary corpus is *not* the product of a lone "supreme creator" who lurks behind its pages, as Ilán Stavans has suggested. While I have identified connections among these works of Latina/o fiction, the texts cannot be described as homogeneous. On the contrary, the commonalities they share — identity as theme and subtext, performance and drag as metaphors for identity — highlight the dynamic, ever-changing nature of culture.

It is crucial, in my opinion, for critics to acknowledge the performative aspects of identity and culture but also to recognize the significance of history and tradition. In order to do justice to Latina/o literature, we must be wary of binary paradigms of resistance and identity. At the same time, we must take care to avoid extreme anti-essentialist characterizations that treat subjectivity as purely act or show and fail to address sociohistorical factors. My objective has been to seek a middle ground, a space between these poles, not out of indecision nor in an attempt to accommodate all possible critical positions. The texts themselves, through their interweaving of cultural tradition with ongoing day-to-day performances and negotiation, suggest a reading strategy that accounts for both the pedagogical and the performative aspects of culture.

How, then, can my emphasis on drag—the anti-essentialist metaphor par excellence—be justified? I am convinced that deploying cross-dressing as metaphor for cultural identity need not imply that identity is detached from political or material issues. The key facet of drag that I have emphasized is its capacity to parody rigidly defined identity categories. To critique the notion of Latino essence is not to deny the effects of sociohistorical forces (racism, oppression) nor to dismiss or denigrate collective fictions. Indeed, to some extent the illusion of ethnic essence is a result of these same forces. The spiritism of the Puerto Rican characters in *The Line of the Sun,* Rosa's melodramatic music in *The Greatest Performance,* the miracles in *So Far from God,* and characters' non-Anglo physical features contribute to this illusion because they are all deemed "excess" in American society.

My critique of cultural essence by means of the performance and drag metaphors does, however, call attention to the identities that traditional Latina/o paradigms exclude. Within Chicana/o, Puerto Rican, and Cuban enclaves like the ones portrayed in the novels, excess erupts in the form of challenges to the collective fictions that are the foundation of community identity. One such cultural fiction becomes apparent through the exile nostalgia of some of the immigrant characters in *The Line of the Sun, How the García Girls Lost Their Accents,* and *The Greatest Performance.* Identity, for these characters, is grounded in an idealized homeland that is paradiselike and culturally pure; survival of the ancestral culture depends on the perpetuation of these nationalist mythologies.

Such cultural nationalism can produce exclusionary standards of ethnic authenticity that are highly problematic, particularly with respect to gender and sexuality. In *The Greatest Performance,* the tradition-bound members of the Club Cubano José Martí judge the unconventional life-style of the lesbian protagonist Rosa to be not only unfeminine, but also "un-Cuban." The gay and lesbian subjectivities developed in Ortiz Taylor's and Rechy's fiction are likewise "culturally unintelligible" according to traditional Chicana/o gender constructs. In other works, futile efforts to definitively establish identity through endlessly repeated performances make the texts themselves resemble symbolic drag shows. Cesar's hyperbolic masculinity in *The Mambo Kings Play Songs of Love,* Federico's interminable manuscript in *The Love Queen of the Amazon,* and the narrator's Chicano/Latino pastiche in *So Far from God* are clear examples of such repetition. The drag motif in *The Greatest Performance* offers a provocative alternative to the notion of stable identity categories. If we envision *all* identity as a sort of ongoing drag show, as parodic imitation of a nonexistent original, then no configurations of ethnicity, gender, or sexuality can be judged culturally inauthentic.

My readings of the novels highlight moments of resistance that oppose the concept of static cultural identity. The immigrant daughters in *The Line of the Sun* and *How the García Girls Lost Their Accents* discover that their cultural "home" is neither the island nor mainstream America, that their sense of self is forged through negotiation and invention. *City of Night, Faultline,* and *Southbound* likewise focus on the liberating potential of movement between communities. These views of Latina/o identity contest the artificial standards and limitations generated by attempts to define authentic Chicana/o or U.S. Cuban or mainland Puerto Rican identity. By calling attention to the role of performance in culture, the critical perspective that I propose acknowledges the perpetual change that is intrinsic to all cultures.

The face of U.S. Latina/o literature will continue to evolve as well, with the publication of new texts and the recovery/discovery of previous writings. Latina/o culture is constantly being reinvented through these works; as the narrators of several of the novels discover, writing offers a space in which ethnicity can be explored. In the closing passage of *The Line of the Sun,* Marisol concludes that "the only way to understand a life is to write it as a story" (290). By looking to the past and writing her life story, she begins to chronicle the continuous series of performances that constitute her identity as a mainland Puerto Rican.

Yet ethnic writing is not limited to the retrospective compiling of past performances. Rosa's promise to Mario at the end of *The Greatest Performance* hints at the potential of ethnic texts to liberate identity from the constraints of cultural tradition and authenticity: "I will create this place where you can be who you've always wanted to be, Marito. . . . This moment of greatness, I will create it" (151). There are many such "moments of greatness" in the novels that I have studied, when the narrative moves into uncharted cultural territory. All Latina/o literature occupies an ever-expanding space in which identity is perpetually under construction through performances that challenge the artificial boundaries separating cultures, genders, and races. There is no "supreme creator" of these texts. What thrives behind these pages, what breathes life into them, is a cultural space without limits. The show *will* go on as the many U.S. Latina/o stories continue to be told.

NOTES

Chapter 1

1. Debate continues about the most appropriate term to designate persons of Latin American descent residing in the United States. The denomination "Hispanic" was sanctioned for official U.S. government use in 1968 and was gradually adopted in the cultural and business spheres. The term has been widely criticized, however, for its negative political connotations. Juan Flores and George Yúdice describe "Hispanic" as "an identity label imposed by the politicized statistics of the Census Bureau and the market who seek to target particular constituencies for political and economic manipulation" (80n).

   In addition, Latinos have noted the Eurocentric bias of "Hispanic," which denies the hybrid cultural and racial heritage of most Latin Americans. In recognition of the validity of these criticisms, I have chosen to employ the gender-inclusive "U.S. Latina/o," or simply "Latina/o," in this study. For varying perspectives on this complex issue, see Asunción Horno-Delgado, Eliana Ortega, Nina M. Scott, and Nancy Saporta Sternbach, eds. *Breaking Boundaries: Latina Writings and Critical Readings* (Amherst: University of Massachusetts Press, 1989), 2–23; Margarita B. Melville, "Los hispanos: ¿clase, raza o etnicidad?" *Hispanos en los Estados Unidos*, Rodolfo J. Cortina and Alberto Moncada, eds. (Madrid: Ediciones de Cultura Hispánica, 1988), 131–45; Carlos Muñoz, Jr., *Youth, Identity, Power: The Chicano Movement* (London: Verso, 1989), 10–11; and Ramón Gutiérrez and Genaro Padilla's vindication of the term "Hispanic" in *Recovering the U.S. Hispanic Literary Heritage* (Houston: Arte Público, 1993), 17–18.

2. Seminal critical works include Edward Simmen, ed., *New Voices in Literature: The Mexican American* (Edinburg, Tex.: Pan American University, 1971); Octavio Ignacio Romano-V., ed., *Voices: Readings from El Grito, 1967–1973* (Berkeley:

Quinto Sol Publications, 1973); Carlos Monsiváis, "Literatura comparada: Literatura chicana," *Fomento Literario* 1 (1973): 42–48; Juan Bruce-Novoa, "Freedom of Expression and the Chicano Movement," *La Luz* (Sept. 1973): 28–29; idem, "The Space of Chicano Literature," *De Colores* 1, no.4 (1975): 22–42; idem, "Literatura chicana: La respuesta al caos," *Revista de la Universidad de México* 29, no.12 (1975): 20–24; Philip Ortego, ed., *The Chicano Literary World 1974* (Las Vegas: New Mexico Highlands University, 1975); Miguel Algarín, "Nuyorican Language," *Nuyorican Poetry: An Anthology of Words and Feelings* (New York: Morrow, 1975), 9–27; and Félix Cortés, Angel Falcón, and Juan Flores, "The Cultural Expression of Puerto Ricans in New York City: A Theoretical Perspective and Critical Review," *Latin American Perspectives* 3, no.3 (1976): 117–50.

3. See Juan Flores, "Puerto Rican Literature in the United States: Stages and Perspectives," *ADE Bulletin* 91 (Winter 1988): 39–44; Edna Acosta-Belén, "Beyond Island Boundaries: Ethnicity, Gender, and Cultural Revitalization in Nuyorican Literature," *Callaloo* 15, no.4 (1992): 979–98; Ramón Saldívar, *Chicano Narrative: The Dialectics of Difference* (Madison, Wis.: University of Wisconsin Press, 1990); Tey Diana Rebolledo, *Women Singing in the Snow: A Cultural Analysis of Chicana Literature* (Tucson, Ariz.: University of Arizona Press, 1995); Rafael Pérez-Torres, *Movements in Chicano Poetry: Against Myths, Against Margins* (Cambridge, England: Cambridge University Press, 1995); Eliana Rivero, "Cubanos y cubanoamericanos: perfil y presencia en los Estados Unidos," *Discurso literario* 7, no.1 (II semestre 1989): 81–101, and "(Re)writing Sugarcane Memories: Cuban Americans and Literature," *The Americas Review* 18, no.3–4 (1990): 164–82.

4. A substantial number of anthologies following this model have been published in the last fifteen years. See Gary D. Keller and Francisco Jiménez, eds., *Hispanics in the United States: An Anthology of Creative Literature*, 2 vols. (Ypsilanti, Mich.: Bilingual Review/Press, 1980–82); Nicolás Kanellos, ed., *A Decade of Hispanic Literature: An Anniversary Anthology* (Houston: Revista Chicano-Riqueña, 1982); Alma Gómez, Cherríe Moraga, and Mariana Romo-Carmona, eds., *Cuentos: Stories by Latinas* (New York: Kitchen Table Press, 1983); María del Carmen Boza, Beverly Silva, and Carmen Valle, eds., *Nosotras: Latina Literature Today* (Binghamton, N.Y.: Bilingual Review/Press, 1986); Evangelina Vigil-Piñón, ed., *Woman of Her Word: Hispanic Women Write*, 2d ed. (Houston: Arte Público, 1987); and Harold Augenbraum and Margarite Fernández Olmos, eds., *The Latino Reader: From 1542 to the Present* (New York: Houghton Mifflin, 1997).

5. Exceptions include Rivero 1985; Eliana Ortega and Nancy Saporta Sternbach, "At the Threshold of the Unnamed: Latina Literary Discourse in the Eighties," in *Breaking Boundaries: Latina Writings and Critical Readings*, Horno-Delgado et al., eds., 2–23 (Amherst: University of Massachusetts Press, 1989); and some of the essays in Miguel Falquez-Certain, ed., *New Voices In Latin American Literature/ Nuevas voces en la literatura latinoamericana* (Jackson Heights, N.Y.: Ollantay Press, 1993). In *Recovering the U.S. Hispanic Literary Heritage*, editors Gutiérrez and Padilla have assembled essays on various Latina/o literatures; however, all but two of the seventeen articles focus on the works of a single group.

6. See Luis Leal, "Mexican-American Literature: A Historical Perspective," *Modern Chicano Writers*, Joseph Sommers and Tomás Ybarra-Frausto, eds. (Englewood Cliffs, N.J.: Prentice-Hall, 1979), 18–30; Francisco Lomelí, "Po(l)etics of Recon-

structing and/or Appropriating a Literary Past: The Regional Case Model," in *Recovering the U.S. Hispanic Literary Heritage*, Ramón Gutiérrez and Genaro Padilla, eds., 221–39 (Houston: Arte Público, 1993); and Juan Bruce-Novoa, "Naufragios en los mares de la significación: De *La Relación* de Cabeza de Vaca a la literatura chicana," *Notas y comentarios sobre Alvar Núñez Cabeza de Vaca*, Margo Glantz, coordinadora (México, D.F.: Grijalbo, 1993), 291–308.

7. The *Actos* of Valdez's Teatro Campesino, created and performed by California farmworkers from 1965 to 1967, played an important role in the consciousness-raising of other workers and later of a larger public. As Teatro Campesino evolved during the late 1960s and 1970s, its repertoire was expanded to include other issues of significance to the Chicano community. For more detailed information on Chicano theater of this period see articles by Huerta; Cárdenas de Dwyer; and Yarbro-Bejarano (1979). Quinto Sol Publications, whose stated objective was to promote Mexican-American writing, was founded in 1967 by a group of University of California-Berkeley intellectuals. "El Plan Espiritual de Aztlán," a pivotal document formulated at the National Chicano Youth Liberation Conference in 1969, declares, "We must insure that our writers, poets, musicians, and artists produce literature and art that is appealing to our people and relates to our revolutionary culture" (cited in Richard García 110).

My objective in this introductory chapter is not to provide an in-depth analysis of Chicana/o literary history, but to situate recent texts within a basic historical framework. Informative overviews of Chicana/o literature and the recognition of Chicana/o writing as a literary corpus in the 1960s and 1970s include Tomás Ybarra-Frausto, "The Chicano Movement and the Emergence of a Chicano Poetic Consciousness," *New Scholar* 6 (1977): 81–109; Carl R. Shirley and Paula W. Shirley, *Understanding Chicano Literature* (Columbia, S.C.: University of South Carolina Press, 1988); Juan Bruce-Novoa, "Chicano Literary Production, 1960–1980," *RetroSpace*, 75–90; Teresa McKenna, "Chicano Literature," A. LaVonne Brown Ruoff and Jerry Ward, eds., *Redefining American Literary History* (New York: Modern Language Association of America, 1990), 363–72; Raymund A. Paredes, "Mexican-American Literature: An Overview," in Gutiérrez and Padilla's *Recovering the U.S. Hispanic Literary Heritage*, 31–51; and Francisco A. Lomelí, "Contemporary Chicano Literature, 1959–1990: From Oblivion to Affirmation to the Forefront," *Handbook of Hispanic Cultures in the United States: Literature and Art*, Francisco Lomelí, ed. (Houston: Arte Público Press, 1993), 86–108.

8. As Miguel Algarín declares in the introduction to the 1975 anthology *Nuyorican Poetry*, "The experience of Puerto Ricans on the streets of New York has caused a new language to grow: Nuyorican" (15). For further information on the emergence of mainland Puerto Rican literature, see Juan Flores; Alfredo Matilla, "Breve panorámica de las letras puertorriqueñas en los Estados Unidos," *Explicación de textos literarios* 15, no.2 (1986–87): 19–31; Edna Acosta-Belén, "Puerto Rican Literature in the United States," A. LaVonne Brown Ruoff and Jerry W. Ward, eds., *Redefining American Literary History* (New York: Modern Language Association of America, 1990), 373–78; and Frances R. Aparicio, "From Ethnicity to Multiculturalism: An Historical Overview of Puerto Rican Literature in the United States," *Handbook of Hispanic Cultures in the United States: Literature and Art*, Francisco Lomelí, ed., 19–39.

9. Effects of this two-way migration on mainland Puerto Rican culture and identity are discussed in Eduardo Seda Bonilla, "¿Qué somos: puertorriqueños, neorriqueños o nuyorriqueños?" *The Rican: Journal of Contemporary Puerto Rican Thought* 2 (1974): 81–107; Efraín Barradas, "Puerto Rico acá, Puerto Rico allá," *Revista Chicano-Riqueña* 8 (Summer 1979): 46–56; Manuel Maldonado-Denis, *The Emigration Dialectic: Puerto Rico and the U.S.A.* (New York: International Publishers, 1980); and Juan Flores, John Attinasi, and Pedro Pedraza, Jr., "'La Carreta Made a U-Turn': Puerto Rican Language and Culture in the U.S., *Divided Borders: Essays on Puerto Rican Identity* (Houston: Arte Público, 1993), 157–83.

10. Criticism by Eliana Rivero, one of the more prolific critics of U.S. Cuban writing, reflects this perspective, as does the introduction to *Veinte años de literatura cubanoamericana: Antología 1962–1982* by Silvia Burunat and Ofelía García. See also Carolina Hospital, "Los atrevidos," *Linden Lane Magazine* 5, no.4 (1987): 22–23; Gustavo Pérez-Firmat, "Transcending Exile: Cuban-American Literature Today," *Occasional Papers Series Dialogues* 92 (December 1987): 1–13; and Nicolás Kanellos, "Cuban-American Literature," *The Hispanic Almanac: From Columbus to Corporate America* (Detroit: Visible Ink Press, 1994), 409–13. More comprehensive information on the historical development of U.S. Cuban literature may be found in two recent studies by Rodolfo J. Cortina, "Cuban Literature of the United States: 1824–1959," in Gutiérrez and Padilla, *Recovering the U.S. Hispanic Literary Heritage*, 69–88, and "History and Development of Cuban American Literature: A Survey," in Lomelí, *Handbook of Hispanic Cultures in the United States: Literature and Art*, 40–61.

11. These comments are intended to offer a limited and highly simplified overview of the formation of the three largest U.S. Latina/o communities. Providing a more in-depth historical analysis of the Latina/o presence in the United States is beyond the scope of this study. For background on Chicana/o history, Rodolfo Acuña's *Occupied America: A History of Chicanos* (New York: Harper and Row, 1988) is considered seminal; see also Richard García, ed., *Chicanos in America, 1540–1974* (Dobbs Ferry, N.Y.: Oceana Publications, 1977), which includes a detailed chronology and important historical documents; Juan Gómez-Quiñones's interpretation of borderland political history, *Roots of Chicano Politics, 1600–1940* (Albuquerque: University of New Mexico Press, 1994) and his study of political reform efforts, *Chicano Politics: Reality and Promise, 1940–1990* (Albuquerque: University of New Mexico Press, 1990); Carlos Muñoz, Jr., *Youth, Identity, Power: The Chicano Movement* (London: Verso, 1989), an in-depth analysis of the different facets of the Movement; and the important essays on Chicana issues and history in Adela de la Torre and Beatriz Pesquera, eds., *Building with Our Hands: New Directions in Chicana Studies* (Berkeley: University of California Press, 1993). Historical studies of Puerto Rican communities on the mainland include Virginia Sánchez Korrol's ground-breaking *From Colonia to Community: The History of Puerto Ricans in New York City, 1917–1948* (Westport, Conn.: Greenwood Press, 1983); Juan Flores, *Divided Borders: Essays on Puerto Rican Identity* (Houston: Arte Público, 1993), which contains insightful commentary on Puerto Rican culture; Clara Rodríguez, *Puerto Ricans Born in the U.S.A.* (Boston: Unwyn Hyman, 1989); and the valuable essays in Clara E. Rodríguez, Virginia Sánchez Korrol, and José O. Alers, eds., *The Puerto Rican Struggle: Essays on Survival in the United States* (Maple-

wood, N.J.: Waterfront Press, 1980). The history of the U.S. Cuban community is discussed in Mirien Uriarte-Gastón and Jorge Cañas Martínez, eds., *Cubans in the United States* (Boston: Center for the Study of the Cuban Community, 1984); several informative essays in Damián Fernández, ed., *Cuban Studies Since the Revolution* (Gainesville: University Presses of Florida, 1992); and Carlos Ripoll, *Cubanos en los Estados Unidos* (New York: Las Américas, 1987). See also Alfredo Padilla, ed., *Handbook of Hispanic Cultures of the United States: History* (Houston: Arte Público, 1994); Edna Acosta-Belén and Barbara R. Sjostrom, eds., *The Hispanic Experience in the United States: Contemporary Issues and Perspectives* (New York: Praeger, 1988); and Frank Bean and Marta Tienda, eds., *The Hispanic Population of the United States* (New York: Russell Sage Foundation, 1987).

12. The paradigm described by Sollors persisted in criticism of Chicana/o texts at least through the mid-1980s. Eliana Rivero's description of Chicana/o literature in her article "Hispanic Literature in the United States: Self-Image and Conflict" exemplifies this tendency:

> Chicano literature . . . is by essence and definition a literature of self-search and a literature of social protest. Chicanos see themselves as searching for their authentic past, their roots in Indian and Spanish-Mexican culture, and they resent and resist cultural domination by what they perceive as the Anglo intruder in their ancestral homelands. (1985, 178–79)

13. An example of the politics of ethnic authenticity generated by the "group-by-group" approach can be observed in critic Frank Chin's distinction between "real" and "fake" Asian American literature. In his 1991 essay "Come All Ye Asian American Writers of the Real and the Fake," Chin accuses Amy Tan, Maxine Hong Kingston, and David Henry Hwang of faking "all of Asian American history and literature" (3). Shirley Geok-lin Lim has written several excellent articles contesting such standards of Asian-American authenticity; see "Assaying the Gold: Or, Contesting the Ground of Asian American Literature," *New Literary History* 24 (1993): 147–69.

14. Recent Latina/o fictional works that have received considerable attention from mainstream readers and reviewers include Oscar Hijuelos's Pulitzer Prize–winning novel *The Mambo Kings Play Songs of Love* (1989), Julia Alvarez's *How the García Girls Lost Their Accents* (1991), Víctor Villaseñor's *Rain of Gold* (1991), and Cristina García's *Dreaming in Cuban* (1992). See also my comments on the U.S. Latina/o "Boom" in chapter 5.

15. Ironically, in an earlier review of four U.S. Latina/o novels–*Alburquerque* (Rudolfo Anaya, 1991), *Dreaming In Cuban* (Cristina García, 1992), *Cantora* (Sylvia López-Medina, 1992), and *The Greatest Performance* (Elías Miguel Muñoz, 1991)–Stavans had commented on the heterogeneity of the U.S. Latina/o population. Referring to the four novels, he asked,

> Does it make sense to speak of their creators simply as Hispanic? . . . Wouldn't it be better to approach Chicanos, Puerto Ricans, Cubans, Dominicans, and others by referring to their own national backgrounds? Does anybody refer to Italian, German, French, and Spanish authors with the single category of European writers? (1992, 5)

Such an approach acknowledges that U.S. Latina/o identity is not monolithic. However, Stavans assumes a connection between the writer and his/her national culture that may be tenuous at best, particularly for Latinos whose families have resided in the United States for two or more generations. His proposal also fails to account for diversity based on gender and class and ignores the complex nature of national identity.

16. See Dorinda Moreno, "Mujer de la Raza," *La Mujer es la tierra/La tierra la vida* (Berkeley: Casa Editorial, 1975), 27; Berta Ornelas, *Come Down from the Mound* (Phoenix, Ariz.: Miter, 1975); Bernice Zamora, "Notes from a Chicana Coed," *Caracol* 3 (1977): 19; Mirta Vidal, "Women: New Voice of La Raza"; and Lorna Dee Cervantes, "Para un Revolucionario," in *Emplumada* (Pittsburgh: University of Pittsburgh Press, 1981).

My use here of the term *Chicano,* rather than the more inclusive Chicana/o, is intended to reflect the male-centered view of cultural identity implicit in the nationalist ideology. The ideology referred to as Chicano cultural nationalism emerged from the Chicano student movement, in particular the March 1969 National Chicano Youth Liberation Conference. At this conference, activist Rodolfo "Corky" Gonzales set forth his nationalist vision of Chicano identity, declaring that "nationalism is the key to our people liberating themselves" (cited in Steiner 385). The resolutions developed by Gonzales and his adherents, which took the form of "El Plan Espiritual de Aztlán," espoused a "new" Chicano identity based on symbols of traditional Mexican culture and the rejection of Anglo-American cultural domination. See Carlos Muñoz, Jr., *Youth, Identity, Power: The Chicano Movement* (London: Verso, 1989), 75–78.

17. In "Calculated Musings: Richard Rodríguez's Metaphysics of Difference," Rosaura Sánchez describes Rodríguez as "an ethnic writer estranged more from his own collectivities than from dominant society" whose works "serve to perpetuate dominant fantasies about marginalized populations and to legitimate the status quo" (172). Sánchez uses Rodríguez as evidence that a writer's ethnic status alone "does not imply an alternative perspective" (171). See also Arturo Madrid, "The Miseducation of Rich-heard Road-ree-guess," *Maize* 5, no.3/4 (Spring-Summer 1982): 88–92; Tomás Rivera, "Richard Rodríguez's *Hunger of Memory* as Humanistic Antithesis," *MELUS* 11, no.4 (Winter 1984): 5–13; Ramón Saldívar, "Ideologies of the Self: Chicano Autobiography," *Diacritics* 15, no.3 (Fall 1985): 25–34; Alfredo Villanueva-Collado, "Growing Up Hispanic: Discourse and Ideology in *Hunger of Memory* and *Family Installments,*" *The Americas Review* 16, no.3–4 (Fall-Winter 1988): 75–90; Lauro Flores, "Chicano Autobiography: Culture, Ideology, and the Self," *The Americas Review* 18, no.2 (Summer 1990): 80–91; and Rolando J. Romero, "Spanish and English: The Question of Literacy in *Hunger of Memory,*" *Confluencia* 6, no.2 (Spring 1991): 89–100.

18. "appear tranquil and nostalgic" (my translation).

19. For in-depth discussion of gay and lesbian Latino/a identities, see chapters 2 and 3.

20. Bruce-Novoa began to develop his anti-essentialist arguments in "Freedom of Expression and the Chicano Movement" (1973) and "Canonical and Non-Canonical Texts" (1986); both may be found in *RetroSpace.* See also his "Dialogical Strategies, Monological Goals: Chicano Literature" in *An Other Tongue: Nation and Ethnicity in the Linguistic Borderlands,* Alfred Arteaga, ed., 225–45.

21. See Angie Chabrám's analysis of culturalist variants of Chicana/o literary criticism in "Conceptualizing Chicano Critical Discourse" in *Criticism in the Borderlands: Studies in Chicano Literature, Culture, and Ideology*, Héctor Calderón and José David Saldívar, eds., 127–48.

22. According to Hall, psychoanalysis — particularly Freud's insistence that "social, cultural and political life cannot be understood except in relationship to the formations of the unconscious life" — made a profound contribution to the displacement of a stable sense of identity (1989, 11).

23. Ricardo Ortiz similarly emphasizes the role of memory and desire in identity formation in his essay "Sexuality Degree Zero: Pleasure and Power in the Novels of John Rechy, Arturo Islas, and Michael Nava." Ortiz describes identity as "fundamentally an effect of the self's troubled relation to memory and desire," constructed at the "intersection of power and pleasure, of history and desire" (123).

24. Recently, more scholarship has been devoted to the recuperation and/or "discovery" of U.S. Latina/o texts that had been previously ignored for a variety of reasons. One example is the Recovering the U.S. Hispanic Literary Heritage Project, organized by Arte Público Press and the University of Houston and sponsored by the Rockefeller Foundation. The project is dedicated to recovering works by Latina/o writers that have remained unpublished. This literature, which includes a variety of oral forms, began to flourish during the sixteenth century. As Roberta Fernández points out in the introduction to her annotated bibliography *Twenty-Five Years of Hispanic Literature in the United States 1965–1990*, publication of these works "will challenge the canon of the literatures of the Americas" (7).

25. Pérez-Torres's theoretical apparatus in *Movements in Chicano Poetry* likewise highlights parallels between Chicana/o and postcolonial discourses. Pérez-Torres comments that "[a]lthough Chicano literary criticism has not as yet been widely discussed as a postcolonial discourse, similar tensions and discontinuities are at work in both forms of discourse" (28).

26. I have greatly simplified Bhabha's complex analysis of this tension and the "contested conceptual territory" it generates. The core of his argument is that

> the people are the historical "objects" of a nationalist pedagogy, giving the discourse an authority that is based on the pre-given or constituted historical origin *in the past;* the people are also the "subjects" of a process of signification that must erase any prior or originary presence of the nation-people to demonstrate the prodigious, living principles of the people as contemporaneity. (145)

27. Even the widely accepted term "dominant culture" is problematic, insofar as it essentializes both American and minority cultures and reinforces a questionable paradigm of binary opposition. For the purposes of this study, I will employ the expression with the understanding that the concept of "dominant culture" is an inescapable essentialism like those Diana Fuss identifies in *Essentially Speaking*.

28. From *The Practice of Everyday Life* (1984).

29. The novels that I include in this study are Sheila Ortiz Taylor's *Faultline* (1982) and *Southbound* (1990), and John Rechy's *City of Night* (1963); Oscar Hijuelos's *The Mambo Kings Play Songs of Love* (1989) and Elías Miguel Muñoz's *The Greatest Performance* (1991); Judith Ortiz Cofer's *The Line of the Sun* (1989) and Julia Alvarez's *How the García Girls Lost Their Accents* (1991); and Cecile Pineda's *The*

Love Queen of the Amazon (1992) and Ana Castillo's *So Far from God* (1993). These novels are described in more detail at the end of this chapter.

30. Butler's view of gender coincides with Michel Foucault's theory that institutional discourses and regulative strategies produce the subjects that they identify as transgressive. See volume 1 of Foucault's *The History of Sexuality,* especially "Right of Death and Power over Life."

31. William Boelhower points out that "ethnic" and "American" are not separately definable; they are involved in a dialogic relation such that "the energy of ethnic/American contact seems to generate the language of identity in the form of an endless production of questions" (27).

32. The bibliography on racism and heterosexism/homophobia in American society is far too extensive to cite here. Important discussions of these issues include Michael Omi and Howard Winant, *Racial Formation in the United States: From the 1960s to the 1990s* (New York: Routledge, 1994); Adrienne Rich, "Compulsory Heterosexuality and Lesbian Existence," in Ann Snitow, Christine Stansell, and Sharon Thompson, eds., *Powers of Desire: The Politics of Sexuality* (New York: New Feminist Library, 1983), 177–205; John D'Emilio and Estelle B. Freedman, *Intimate Matters: A History of Sexuality in America* (New York: Harper, 1988); and Gay Left Collective, eds., *Homosexuality: Power and Politics* (London: Allison and Busby, 1980).

33. Phelan's observations on representation and image corroborate this linkage of visibility and invisibility. She argues that the assumed political power of visibility and the concomitant impotency of invisibility are in fact a false binary, that "[t]here is real power in remaining unmarked; and there are serious limitations to visual representation as a political goal" (6).

34. See introductory comments in chapter 2.

35. A number of lesbians of color have critiqued the Anglocentric tendencies of U.S. lesbian communities. Chicana writer Cherríe Moraga's *Loving in the War Years* includes a discussion of Third World lesbians' disillusionment with racism in the women's and gay movements of the late 1970s and early 1980s. According to Moraga, "the 'white' modifier [was] implied and unstated" in the majority of these groups (127). Several writers in Moraga's and Anzaldúa's anthology *This Bridge Called My Back* express similar sentiments. Native American writer Chrystos notes that in the 1980s racism and intolerance of cultural difference persisted among lesbian feminists, many of whom "seemed to throw off the outer trappings of their culture and were very vocal in criticizing it" (69). Audre Lorde's seminal essay, "The Master's Tools Will Never Dismantle The Master's House," is a powerful early exposé of racism in radical lesbian/feminist groups (Moraga and Anzaldúa 98–101).

In "Chicano Men: A Cartography of Homosexual Identity and Behavior," Tomás Almaguer identifies several factors that contributed to the formation of gay and lesbian communities whose character was overwhelmingly white and middle-class. Almaguer asserts that economic and racial advantages made Anglo-American gays and lesbians "*relatively* better situated than other homosexuals to endure the hazards unleashed by their transgression of gender conventions and traditional heterosexual norms" (87).

Chapter 2

1. Angie Chabrám's essay "Conceptualizing Chicano Critical Discourse" in *Criticism in the Borderlands: Studies in Chicano Literature, Culture, and Ideology*, Héctor Calderón and José David Saldívar, eds., provides insightful commentary on the evolution of Chicano criticism during the past twenty-five years.

2. The daunting obstacles that early Chicana writers had to overcome in order to have their works published and recognized reflects the gender-based hegemony of the artistic community. Further discussion of the marginalization of Chicanas can be found in Moraga; Chabrám-Dernersesian; Horno-Delgado et al.; María Herrera-Sobek and Helena María Viramontes, eds., *Chicana Creativity and Criticism: Charting New Frontiers in American Literature*, first published in *The Americas Review* 15, no.3/4 (1987):1–190; Norma Alarcón, "Traddutora, Traditora: A Paradigmatic Figure of Chicana Feminism," *Cultural Critique* 13 (Fall 1989): 57–87; and Sonia Saldívar-Hull, "Feminism on the Border: From Gender Politics to Geopolitics," in Calderón and Saldívar's *Criticism in the Borderlands: Studies in Chicano Literature, Culture, and Ideology*, 203–20.

3. I have appropriated Judith Butler's notion of cultural intelligibility as developed in *Gender Trouble*. According to Butler, culturally intelligible practices of gender identity are those limited by "the rigid codes of hierarchical binarisms," by rules "that are partially structured along matrices of gender hierarchy and compulsory heterosexuality" (1990, 145). I propose that within ethnic communities, culturally intelligible identities are likewise defined by codes of hierarchical binarisms. As a result, minority subject positions — those that challenge prevailing androcentrism or heterosexism, for example — would be culturally *unintelligible*.

4. I interpret Almaguer's expression "modern gay man" to imply a man involved in a same-sex relationship in which both participants are seen as gay. His research indicates that such an identity category, strictly speaking, is not generally acknowledged by Latinos.

5. Anzaldúa suggests that lesbians of color in general are subjected to this sexual repression: "For the lesbian of color, the ultimate rebellion she can make against her native culture is through her sexual behavior. She goes against two moral prohibitions: sexuality and homosexuality" (1987, 19). Jewelle Gomez, an African-American writer and critic, concurs in her assessment of the exclusion of the work of black lesbians from studies of black writers:

> Our work implies, at the very least, the acceptance of an intrinsically sexual aspect of black women's lives. And because that sexuality is directed toward other women it implies a complete independence from male spheres of influence. (50)

6. Namascar Shaktini calls the lesbian a "revolutionary signifier," asserting that "as sexual subjects and nonwives, lesbians cannot exist for the sex-gender system; we are, by our very existence, a double contradiction of this system" (291). See also Lourdes Argüelles and Anne M. Rivero, "Gender/Sexual Orientation Violence and Transnational Migration: Conversations With Some Latinas We Think We Know," *Urban Anthropology* 22, no.3/4 (1993): 259–75.

7. I do not wish to imply that male homosexuality is structured exclusively around anal penetration, only that in the Latina/o popular imagination anal sex between men attracts an inordinate amount of attention.

8. See, for example, Floyd Salas's *Tattoo the Wicked Cross* (1967); Oscar Zeta Acosta's *The Autobiography of a Brown Buffalo* (1972) and *The Revolt of the Cockroach People* (1973); and Elías Miguel Muñoz's *Crazy Love* (1988), as well as *The Greatest Performance* (1991, discussed in chapter 3).

9. In Chicana/o narrative, John Rechy's ten novels are noteworthy, from *City of Night* (1963) to *Our Lady of Babylon* (1996), as well as Arturo Islas's *The Rain God* (1984) and *Migrant Souls* (1990), Michael Nava's *How Town* (1993), Sheila Ortiz Taylor's three novels, and Terri de la Peña's 1992 novel *Margins*. Although not works of fiction, Richard Rodríguez's *Hunger of Memory* (1982) and *Days of Obligation* (1992) and Gloria Anzaldúa's *Borderlands/La Frontera* (1987) also offer insights into the Chicano/a gay/lesbian problematic.

10. Even establishing historical parameters for Chicana/o identity has generated substantial debate among critics of Chicana/o literature. One critical perspective identifies the inception of a Chicana/o ethnic consciousness in the chronicles of sixteenth-century Spanish explorers like Alvar Núñez Cabeza de Vaca; another designates the 1848 annexation of northern Mexico as the founding moment of a Chicana/o ethnic minority. Still other critics consider Chicana/o identity to have been defined through 1960s Movement politics. For summaries of these perspectives, see Luis Leal's "Mexican American Literature: A Historical Perspective," in *Modern Chicano Writers,* Joseph Sommers and Tomás Ybarra-Frausto, eds. (Englewood Cliffs, N.J.: Prentice-Hall, 1979); and Raymund Paredes's "Mexican-American Literature: An Overview" and Francisco Lomelí's "Po(l)etics of Reconstructing and/or Appropriating a Literary Past: The Regional Case Model," in *Recovering the U.S. Hispanic Literary Heritage,* Ramón Gutiérrez and Genaro Padilla, eds.

11. George Lipsitz, "'That's My Blood Down There': Strategic Anti-Essentialism in Popular Music," paper presented at the University of California Humanities Research Institute, Irvine, October 29, 1992.

12. See Foucault's "Right of Death and Power over Life," in *The History of Sexuality,* volume 1.

13. In addition to *Faultline* and *Southbound,* Ortiz Taylor has written the novel *Spring Forward/Fall Back* (1985), the poetry collection *Slow Dancing at Miss Polly's* (1989), and *Imaginary Parents* (1996).

14. In the acknowledgments to *Southbound,* Ortiz Taylor thanks Juan Bruce-Novoa "for helping me find my way back to the Chicano community."

15. Sedgwick elaborates on this notion of an ethnic/cultural/religious parallel to the gay/lesbian closet. She considers the oppressions directed against these groups to be analogous "in that the stigmatized individual has at least notionally some discretion ... over other people's knowledge of her or his membership in the group." The principal difference between the two cultural contexts, according to Sedgwick, arises from the "clear ancestral linearity and answerability" of ethnicity or religion as opposed to the lack of a similar traceable heritage for gays and lesbians (75).

16. Recent discussion of the construction of identity in the works of multiracial artists has further problematized the notion of discrete racial and/or ethnic communities. See Elena Tajima Creef, "Performing Theory: Women Warriors, Punk Geishas, and

Mixed-blood Asian-American Theater," paper presented at the University of California Humanities Research Institute, May 18, 1993; Ai, "On Being 1/2 Japanese, 1/8 Choctaw, 1/4 Black, and 1/16 Irish," *Ms*, May 1978; Velina Hasu Houston, "On Being Mixed Japanese in Modern Times," *Pacific Citizen*, Dec. 20–27, 1985, section B, as well as her unpublished collection of poetry, "Green Tea Girl in Orange Pekoe Country."

17. This shifting is possible for Arden in part because she is able to pass as straight, as nonethnic, and so on; minorities with nonwhite physical features cannot pass. The hegemony of whiteness in U.S. society generates the racist oppression to which such minority groups are subjected, oppression that Arden is able to avoid.

18. Novels by Rechy have been judged "non-Chicano" by both Raymund Paredes and Philip Ortego; on the other hand, both Juan Bruce-Novoa and Charles Tatum have consistently included Rechy's works in their discussions of the Chicano novel. Regardless of the content of his novels, Rechy clearly identifies himself as Chicano, as his comment to James Giles reveals: "You can't know, Jim, the crap of being a Chicano in all the ugly little Texas towns where all they know, or have ever known, is hate!" See Giles, "Religious Alienation and 'Homosexual Consciousness' in *City of Night* and *Go Tell It on the Mountain*," *College English* 36, no.3 (November 1974): 369–80; Paredes, "The Evolution of Chicano Literature," in *Three American Literatures*, Houston Baker, Jr., ed. (New York: Modern Language Association, 1982), 33–79; and Ortego, "The Chicano Literary Renaissance," *Social Casework* 52, no.5 (May 1971): 294–307.

19. For the purposes of this study, American "dominant" culture will indicate the white heterosexual majority, whose authority is reinforced by legal, religious, and scientific discourses.

20. Beaver elaborates on this assertion:

> Homosexuality poses a uniquely peculiar challenge to cultural stability because it seems to threaten the genetic cycle itself and the whole elaborate coding of binary sexuality. So it must be ruthlessly disarmed of its disruptive power. (109)

21. This passage exemplifies the frequent disregard for rules of standard English grammar that characterizes Rechy's writing in *City of Night*. This experimental stylistic device produces a desultory effect that seems to reflect the narrator's defiance of structures of authority and his celebratory stance toward anarchy.

22. An incisive novelistic interrogation of the participation of institutional discourses (psychoanalytic, sociological, medical) in the construction of homosexuality is Manuel Puig's *El beso de la mujer araña* (1976). In this novel, Puig juxtaposes a series of footnotes containing data on homosexuality, drawn from a variety of sources, and a fictional dialogue between two men in an Argentine prison. The outcome of the extended conversation between the two prisoners—a *loca* accused of solicitation and a political activist accused of revolutionary activity—is the deconstruction of the authority of the official discourses and the "truth" about homosexuality that they promote.

23. This character's reference to "growing wings" probably alludes to the image of the gay male as "fairy." However, there is evidence that the character speaking is Latino, for he is described as "not tall, very well built, *dark*" (36, emphasis mine), in

which case the reference could also be to the Spanish epithet *pájaro* (bird). The possibility that this character is Latino lends additional significance to the distinction he makes between being queer and straight, for the "rules" he promotes reflect the Latino *activo/pasivo* paradigm described by Almaguer.

24. An interesting parallel to this assertion of masculinity within a context of male homoeroticism is found in Nuyorican writer Piri Thomas's 1967 autobiography *Down These Mean Streets*. In one scene, the narrator and a group of his buddies go to the apartment of three Latino drag queens; the "maricones" (faggots) then ply the men with liquor, marijuana, and money in exchange for sex. Marta Sánchez points out that in this instance,

> the conventional relationships of the gendered active/female polarities are, in actuality, inverted because the *machos* become the male prostitutes who perform a paid service for the men in drag they mock. . . . Piri's adventure to engage in homosexuality without losing his male identity fails because he and his friends get situated in the passive sexual role (HRI presentation, March 2, 1993).

Rechy's characters, likewise, assume the traditionally female passive role—they are the sexual objects of other men—in their sexual trade, challenging their own claims to masculinity.

25. This classification of a male as homosexual is made strictly on the basis of object choice rather than sexual aim; as anthropologist Roger Lancaster points out, in the United States "homosexual desire itself, without any qualifications, stigmatizes one as a homosexual." In "Subject Honor and Object Shame: The Construction of Male Homosexuality and Stigma in Nicaragua," *Ethnology* 27, no.2 (1987): 116. Cited in Almaguer 77. Eve Sedgwick acknowledges that this overwhelming emphasis on same-sex desire in Anglo-European perceptions of homosexuality is a puzzling historical development:

> It is a rather amazing fact that, of the very many dimensions along which the genital activity of one person can be differentiated from that of another . . . precisely one, the gender of object choice, emerged from the turn of the century, and has remained, as *the* dimension denoted by the now ubiquitous category of "sexual orientation." (8)

26. This song, "Que llueva, que llueva, la Virgen de la Cueva" is in fact sung by children throughout Latin America.

27. A significant part of the novel deals with the narrator's struggle to come to terms with the aspects of his cultural heritage that his Mexican mother represents. That is, Jim's Chicano identity is made visible largely through interactions with his family. He refers to the "stifling Mexican Catholicism" that enabled his mother to endure the abuses of his father, "a Catholicism from whose hollowness Jim had all but extricated himself already" (67). (This character's attitude toward his religious upbringing resonates with Richard Rodríguez's extensive critique of Catholicism in *Hunger of Memory*.) The sight of yellow flowers through a window reminds him of his family's yearly Día de los Muertos pilgrimages to the cemetery, where his mother would place huge chrysanthemum wreaths on the graves of her dead son and daughter, Salvador and Esperanza (97). Later he mentions his mother's recol-

lections of her happy youth in Chihuahua, where she was once called "the loveliest girl in Mexico" by a Mexican general (150).

While Jim's fluency in Spanish reflects his Chicano background, the principal site of contestation of cultural identity is his difficult relationship with his mother. Throughout the novel he is involved in intense conflict between a need for independence, and a sense of obligation to care for his mother and respond to her obsessive love for him. Consequently, Jim's cultural identity is constantly being played out through a dynamic of rejecting his ethnicity (in the form of his mother) and being drawn irresistibly back to it.

28. As I have pointed out, in the early 1960s "Chicano identity" had not been recognized as a cultural-political construct. This should be taken into account when considering the visibility of gay identity in *City of Night* and the relative invisibility of Chicano ethnic subjectivity; in 1963, an audience for "Chicano performances" did not exist.

29. Cited in Butler 1990, 137.

30. I elaborate this connection between repetition and the construction of masculinity in my discussion of *The Mambo Kings Play Songs of Love* in chapter 3.

31. Important work in this area has been done by black gay and lesbian critics such as Audre Lorde, Barbara Smith, and Essex Hemphill in their examination of the homophobia implicit in black identity politics.

32. *City of Night* focuses on oppression in 1960s American society. Nonetheless, recent anti-immigrant and anti-gay campaigns (California's Proposition 187, anti-homosexual legislation in Colorado and Oregon) and moves to dismantle affirmative action indicate that little progress has been made against racial and ethnic discrimination and homophobia.

33. Roland Barthes's observations in *S/Z* on the ephemeral quality of truth affirm this relationship between repetition and the inaccessibility of essence. Truth, in Barthes' words, "is what is at the *end* of expectation . . . for expectation is a disorder: disorder is supplementary, it is what is forever added on without solving anything, without finishing anything. . . . Truth is what completes, what closes" (76).

Chapter 3

1. "Cuban-American" is widely used to refer to Cuban émigrés who have taken up residence in the United States since the 1959 Cuban Revolution, and to their children in particular. When the term "U.S. Cuban" appears in this book I have used it intentionally to underscore the problematic nature of hyphenated identity labels as assigned to U.S. Latinos. Such labels (Cuban-American, Mexican-American, and so on) take "America" to be synonymous with the United States, an assumption that ignores the geographical and historical reality of the continents that comprise the Americas. Furthermore, these labels fail to reflect the multicultural dimension of the identity category "American" by implying that members of U.S. ethnic groups are distinct from "Americans." See Manzor-Coats for a more in-depth discussion of this issue.

2. Achy Obejas's short story, "We Came All the Way From Cuba So You Could Dress Like This?" alludes to the nationalistic fervor and influence of the exile community. Enumerating the "things that can't be told" about her family's refugee existence during the 1960s and 1970s, the U.S. Cuban narrator mentions that refusing to

donate money to exile groups "only invited questions about our own patriotism" (124).
3. Rodolfo J. Cortina's essay "Cuban Literature of the United States: 1824–1959" is an informative overview that calls attention to the works of numerous lesser-known writers. The majority of the Cuban immigrants who arrived during the first two decades after the revolution were members of the middle and professional classes and were disillusioned with the Castro regime (if not openly opposed to the revolution). Their economic and political status thus differentiated them from typical working-class immigrants as well as from many other U.S. Latinos.
4. The 1980 U.S. Census reported approximately 600,000 Cuban-born persons residing in the United States; by the 1990 census, the number had increased to more than 1,000,000.

As Mary S. Vásquez comments with respect to what she calls the "highly interesting critical polemic" surrounding U.S. Cuban literature,

[t]he diversity of views regarding U.S. Cuban writers, ethnicity, and the mainstream is an indicator of the vitality and multiplicity of the Cuban experience in the United States, literary expressions of it, and critical approaches to this ever-growing body of literature (34).

See also Rivero 1989 and 1990.
5. There is nevertheless a powerful and vocal faction of the U.S. Cuban community whose members staunchly refuse to consider themselves ethnic Americans. As David Rieff points out in *The Exile: Cuba in the Heart of Miami*, to do so

would have meant finally submitting to the proposition that . . . the decades of wishing for return, of tasting it in one's dreams . . . had all been for naught. It would have meant saying not just that the exile was over . . . but that there had never really been an exile except in the mind of Miami. (30)

6. Born in New York to Cuban parents, Hijuelos has received considerable recognition for his fiction, including the Pulitzer Prize for *Mambo Kings*. In 1985, Eliana Rivero observed that the U.S. Latina/o literary community had yet to achieve the kind of mainstream recognition that the awarding of a major American literary prize would indicate. In light of *Mambo Kings'* success, Rivero's words seem almost prophetic:

Perhaps it will be the lot of future generations of Hispanics to witness the granting of an important *American* literary award to one of their authors. . . . Whether this can be possible . . . only time and history will tell. (1985, 190)

7. Muñoz was born in Cuba in 1954 and immigrated to the United States in 1969. He has also published two collections of poetry (*En estas tierras/In This Land*, 1989; *No fue posible el sol*, 1989) and numerous scholarly essays on Latin American and U.S. Latina/o literature. His fourth novel, *Brand New Memory*, is forthcoming.
8. So perfectly, in fact, that Ricky and Lucy finally realize their dream to make it in Hollywood through Ricky's portrayal of a typical Don Juan character.
9. The intertextuality with Cuban exile writer Edmundo Desnoes's novel *Memorias del subdesarrollo* (*Inconsolable Memories*), which focuses on the early years of the revolution, should be noted. In both Desnoes's text and *The Greatest Performance*,

the first-person narrators use the concept of "underdevelopment" (cultural, intellectual, social) ironically in showing that they are indeed capable of transformation and revolutionary thought. In spite of this irony, both narrators nevertheless view the past (Desnoes's memories of before the revolution, Rosa's memories of her life before Joan) as underdevelopment.

10. Likewise, Flavio Risech observes that many Latinos have discovered that "admission into American-style queerness requires that they leave at the door the garments of their *latinidad,* acquiring in the process a deracialized status" (538).

11. See Butler 1991, 21 and 24, as well as chapter 1 of this study.

12. Pérez-Firmat's observations about Cuban culture in *The Cuban Condition* cast doubt on the accuracy of Cesar's essentialized depiction of the Cuban character. Basing his comments on close readings of *criollista* narratives, Pérez-Firmat notes that

> [w]hat characterizes Cuban culture is mutability, uprootedness. Indeed, given this state of affairs, it might not even be appropriate to speak of a Cuban "culture," since the term implies a fixity of configuration that is belied by the fluidity of the Cuban situation. (1989, 23)

He reiterates this view in *Life On the Hyphen,* declaring that "Cuban culture has always lacked a stable core or essence" (15).

13. See Norman Mailer's essay, "Superficial Reflections on the Hipster," in *The White Negro* (1957).

14. David Rieff describes several political organizations in Miami whose objectives reflect the same nostalgia and idealism that are parodied in the Cuban Club José Martí. Among these are the Cuban-American National Foundation, referred to in its fund-raising brochures as "the crucible of all the ideals and love of all Cubans" who are members of "one big family" sharing a "historic responsibility" (117); the Sugar Growers' Association, a group of prerevolution Cuban sugar business owners who are working on plans to get their holdings returned to them (81–82); and the Municipios de Cuba en el Exilio, whose members "held regular elections to the councils and mayoralties of towns most of those doing the voting had not set eyes on for at least twenty years" (137).

15. These pamphlets are written with the same tone that will infuse much of what is written and said about Cuba within the émigré communities for the next three decades. The essentialism intrinsic to this official discourse of nostalgia is an outgrowth of the nationalism that bonds exiles to one another, in Edward Said's words:

> Triumphant, achieved nationalism then justifies, retrospectively as well as prospectively, a history selectively strung together in a narrative form: thus all nationalisms have their founding fathers, their basic, quasi-religious texts, their rhetoric of belonging, their historical and geographical landmarks, their official enemies and heroes. (359)

The nationalistic discourse of static Cuban cultural identity is contested by the everyday performances of the people who continuously transform the culture.

16. This scene closely resembles Risech's depiction of family dinners in typical anti-Castro Cuban homes in Miami. Risech comments that the "constant refrain" at

such gatherings is "[t]he fossilized rhetoric of *Añorada Cuba,* the lament for a pre-Castro Cuba that never really existed, a mythical Cuba where everyone had wealth, health and high culture" (531).

17. This view of female identity has, of course, been challenged since the early days of feminism. See chapters 1 and 2 for my discussions of Latinas and male-centered definitions of self.

18. "I should've married that girl back in Cuba! Now there was a quiet girl who never bothered me, she knew where her bread was buttered. . . . She always left me alone" (141).

19. The repeated performances throughout the text of Nestor's anguished *bolero,* "Beautiful María," underscore the failure of this ideal of womanhood. The women with whom Cesar and Nestor are involved in Cuba refuse to passively submit to them. Cesar's wife Luisa leaves him because of his incorrigible womanizing, and Nestor's lover María abandons him when he begins asserting his male authority by mistreating her. Even so, the text's androcentric discourse ultimately prevails; in spite of their apparent independence, both women marry other men shortly after breaking up with Cesar and Nestor. Meanwhile, the Castillo brothers seem to perceive themselves not as oppressive machos but as innocent victims of women's unjustified intolerance.

20. As Lillian Manzor-Coats asserts in an essay on gender constructs in U.S. Cuban theater, in Cuban culture "maleness is culturally coded as hypermaleness; the difference between macho — the hypersimulation of maleness — and male disappears" (165). Mario discovers that to be a Cuban male is to act macho. The absence of this "hypermaleness" is not readable as male behavior and thus is associated with effeminacy/homosexuality.

21. See my discussion of Tomás Almaguer's article on homosexuality in Latina/o cultures in chapter 2.

22. In her fantasies, Rosa impersonates powerful, oppressive male authority figures. The pastichelike quality of these paragons of masculinity underscores the constructedness of male gender identity.

23. Ileana Fuentes explores the pervasiveness of these gender constructs in Cuban culture in her study *Cuba sin caudillos.* She argues that "nuestra nación está contaminada de un virus antiquísimo y omnipotente, al que se le ha dado el nombre de machismo, el cual se nutre, se regenera, y se fortalece a diario de la siquis individual y colectiva del pueblo cubano" (our nation is contaminated by an ancient and omnipotent virus, which has been given the name of *machismo,* and which is nourished, regenerated, and strengthened daily by the individual and collective psyche of the Cuban people) [my translation], 28.

24. These camps were established in 1965 and were called Unidades Militares de Ayuda a la Producción (UMAP). Lourdes Argüelles and B. Ruby Rich observe that the camps were "aimed at safeguarding the revolution and guaranteeing the public good" and consider them to be evidence of the "growing crescendo of antihomosexual rhetoric" (691). The UMAP camps were in operation only until the end of 1967. However, the more recent expulsion of supposed homosexuals during the 1980 Mariel boatlift indicates that vestiges of institutionalized homophobia have persisted in Cuba.

25. Excess is inevitably linked to lack, as I pointed out in chapter 1. In *Mambo Kings*

this relationship is played out through Cesar's sexual excesses and the sense of absence, of impending loss, that drives him.

26. In this way, the novel highlights the tenuous nature of historical truth. As Foucault argues in *The Archaeology of Knowledge*, the complexity of the description of historical "events" is made evident through interrogation of the field of discourses surrounding statements that are made. The primary focus of Foucault's theory of history is not the historical events per se but rather the description of discursive events in order to respond to the question, "[H]ow is it that one particular statement appeared rather than another?" (27). By revealing the interplay of discourses that is involved in the documentation of history — the reordering and fabrication of memories that takes place — *Mambo Kings* articulates a challenge to its own narrative authority.

27. In his essay "Reflections on Exile," Said declares that "[p]erhaps this is the most extraordinary of exile's fates: to have been exiled by exiles: to relive the actual process of up rooting at the hands of exiles" (361).

28. The space that Rosa and Mario create embodies the same sort of liberation as that celebrated by Lourdes Argüelles in her testimonial essay, "Crazy Wisdom: Memories of a Cuban Queer." In this retrospective piece about an Afro-Cuban lesbian spiritist, Argüelles writes of lessons learned from "crazy wisdom masters," teachers whose lives "constantly challenge conventional wisdoms and ordinary morality" and whose teachings "seem to empty the body and mind of crippling biographical and cultural baggage" (199–200).

Chapter 4

1. I use "immigrant literature" to indicate works by foreign-born writers who have settled permanently in the United States. Obviously this broad definition includes works that other critics would classify as ethnic literature. Indeed, a number of critics assert that immigrant and ethnic literatures can be distinguished from one another by comparing their characteristics. Juan Flores describes immigrant writing as testimonial in form, dealing with the first changes and adjustments demanded by life in America (41). Gustavo Pérez-Firmat claims that immigrant writers intend to make America their home, their new *patria;* consequently, they generally write in English and tend to emphasize rebirth/conversion in their works (1987, 2).

   Most critics agree that ethnic literature, on the other hand, reflects bilingual and bicultural interaction, what Pérez-Firmat calls the "cohabitation of dissimilar cultures" (1987, 5). These standards nevertheless describe many works by first-generation immigrants as well. As I show in this chapter, immigrant writing frequently articulates an *ethnic* consciousness. For this reason, I do not consider the categories "immigrant literature" and "ethnic literature" to be mutually exclusive.

2. The case of Cuban immigrant writers in the U.S. is complicated by the conviction of many in the U.S. Cuban community that their people *are* exiles who will never consider America their true home (see chapter 3). David Rieff examines this phenomenon in depth in *The Exile: Cuba in the Heart of Miami.*

3. Classic assimilationist texts, with their optimistic message about the merits of Americanization, are Danish immigrant Jacob Riis's *The Making of an American* (1901) and Russian immigrant Mary Antin's *The Promised Land* (1912).

4. In addition to the novels already mentioned, other well-known examples of immi-

grant narrative are Upton Sinclair's *The Jungle* (1906), Willa Cather's *O Pioneers* (1913) and *My Antonia* (1918), Ole Rolvaag's *Giants in the Earth* (1927), and Henry Roth's *Call It Sleep* (1934). The corpus of American immigrant novels continues to expand with the inclusion of works by more recent immigrants from Asia (e.g., Maxine Hong Kingston, Bharati Mukherjee) and Latin America (Isabel Allende, Elena Castedo, and so on).

5. I will treat works by island-born Puerto Ricans who move to the mainland as immigrant literature, even though these writers are United States citizens. In spite of the pervasive Anglo-American presence in Puerto Rico, linguistic difficulties, discrimination, and conflict between the migrants' culture of origin and dominant American values cause Puerto Rican migrants' experiences to closely parallel those of other immigrant groups.

6. Nicholasa Mohr (*Nilda*, 1973; *El Bronx Remembered*, 1975; *In Nueva York*, 1977), Piri Thomas (*Down These Mean Streets*, 1967; *Savior, Savior, Hold My Hand*, 1972), and Edward Rivera (*Family Installments: Memories of Growing Up Hispanic*, 1982) are among the best-known New York Puerto Rican prose writers.

   Cuban immigrant writers Roberto Fernández (*Raining Backward*, 1988; *Holy Radishes*, 1995), Elías Miguel Muñoz (*Crazy Love*, 1988; *The Greatest Performance*, 1991), Virgil Suárez (*Latin Jazz*, 1989; *Havana Thursdays*, 1995), and Cristina García (*Dreaming In Cuban*, 1992), and Dominican-born Julia Alvarez (*How the García Girls Lost Their Accents*, 1991; *In the Time of the Butterflies*, 1994) are part of a generation of foreign-born Latina/o writers who were educated primarily in the United States. This, along with their use of English for their writing, differentiates them from other Latina/o immigrant writers such as Reinaldo Arenas, Antonio Benítez Rojo, Edmundo Desnoes, Isabel Allende, and Luisa Valenzuela.

7. Judith Ortiz Cofer was born in Puerto Rico and as a child migrated to New Jersey with her family. She has also published an autobiography, *Silent Dancing: A Partial Remembrance of a Puerto Rican Childhood* (1990), two books of poetry, *Terms of Survival* (1987) and *Reaching for the Mainland* (in *Triple Crown*, 1987), and a multigenre collection, *The Latin Deli* (1993).

   Julia Alvarez immigrated to the United States from the Dominican Republic at the age of ten. Her first book of poetry, *Homecoming*, was published in 1986, and her second collection is *The Other Side/El otro lado* (1995). Her second novel is *In the Time of the Butterflies* (1994), and her third is *¡Yo!* (1997).

8. Although the inhabitants of such communities are technically immigrants, the terms *immigrant* and *ethnic* are often used interchangeably.

9. Homi Bhabha also examines the racial drama that is played out in such societies. In "The Other Question: Stereotype, Discrimination and the Discourse of Colonialism," Bhabha maintains that

> [t]he difference of the object of discrimination is at once visible and natural — colour as the cultural/political *sign* of inferiority or degeneracy, skin as its natural "*identity*." (80)

The identity of many Latina/o immigrants in the United States is thus established on the basis of their visible difference from Anglo-Americans, before any other performative act has been perceived.

10. Wayne Koestenbaum examines the allure of the Jackie Kennedy "look" in his recent work, *Jackie Under My Skin: Interpreting an Icon* (New York: Farrar, Straus, and Giroux, 1995).

11. The primary reason for sending the girls to boarding school is to ensure that they associate with the "right" kind of Americans, that is, the children of wealthy families. The Garcías, who unlike most immigrants were part of their homeland's oligarchy, strive to associate with the American equivalent, the "old money" families of the East. This mentality underscores the widely diverging perspectives on issues of socioeconomic class presented by *García Girls* and *The Line of the Sun*, respectively.

12. In U.S. Latina/o communities, intentional use of *caló* and code-switching gives language the performative function of generating or reinforcing community solidarity. Rosaura Sánchez argues that for bilingual ethnic group members in the United States, the use of a minority language can be a sign of loyalty to the ethnic community and of defiance of domination (1983, 58). In a study of code-switching in Puerto Rican speech communities, Ana Celia Zentella calls code-switching a "badge of community membership" (54). Likewise, Susan Gal views code-switches as conversational tools to maintain or change ethnic group boundaries and personal relationships and as "symbolic creations concerned with the construction of 'self' and 'other' within a broader political, economic, and historical context" (247). U.S. Latinos with limited or no English ability, on the other hand, use Spanish out of necessity rather than choice.

13. Elmenhurst's obviously non-English heritage has not been an impediment to his family's success in the United States. His ancestors were most likely immigrants from northern Europe, a group whose "acceptability" in American society has historically been contested far less than that of nonwhite immigrants.

14. It should be noted that while for these writers (e.g., the Nuyorican poets) Puerto Rico offers a frame of reference for connection with ancestral "roots," the perspectives toward the *patria* that they present vary from reverence and acceptance to critique and rejection (Acosta-Belén 987).

15. While the (im)migrant characters in *Line of the Sun* and *García Girls* are not technically exiles—they could conceivably return to the homeland—they exhibit many of the behaviors and attitudes that Tabori considers typical of exiles. See *The Anatomy of Exile*, 11–38.

16. In general, the female characters in Ortiz Cofer's novel engage in nostalgic reverie and active maintenance of Puerto Rican traditions far more than their male counterparts. The insistence with which these women cling to their idealized view of the island hints at a connection between gender and immigrant nostalgia. Their culturally coded responsibilities as wives and mothers limit their mobility to the point that opportunities to learn English or acquire job skills are virtually nonexistent. These women are thus marginalized as a result of both their immigrant status and their gender-based lack of access to economic advancement.

17. Nuyorican writer Tato Laviera's poem "nuyorican" provides incisive commentary on both the powerful "American" influence on Puerto Rican culture and the Puerto Rican cultural elite's tendency to deny this phenomenon. As the poetic persona observes,

yo peleo por ti, puerto rico,
¿sabes? . . .
y tú,
me desprecias, me miras mal, me atacas mi hablar
mientras comes mcdonalds en discotecas americanas . . . (53)

[I fight for you, puerto rico,
you know? . . .
and you,
you scorn me, you look down on me, you attack
the way I speak
while you eat mcdonalds in american
discotheques . . . (my translation)]

18. The *campesinos*' reverence for the mysterious substance recalls the reaction of the inhabitants of Macondo when gypsies bring ice to the village in Gabriel García Márquez's *Cien años de soledad*. José Arcadio is left "[e]mbriagado por la evidencia del prodigio" ("[i]ntoxicated by the evidence of the miracle") and pronounces the ice to be "el gran invento de nuestro tiempo" (75) ("the great invention of our time," Gregory Rabassa's translation). Many passages in *Line of the Sun* that describe the narrator's mother's life in Puerto Rico similarly parody magical realism. The novel can thus be read as a subtle critique of the essentialized view of Latin America — homogeneously exotic and primitive — that circulates in American dominant culture.

   Mikhail Bakhtin observes that parody does not operate solely as critique, for it can convey perspectives ranging from reverence to ridicule (1981, 77). That is, parody can be deployed for different purposes, as indicated by its distinct uses in *The Line of the Sun* and the "magical realist" novels I discuss in chapter 5.

19. By reading El Building as parody, Marisol is critiquing dominant Puerto Rican culture even though she is a product (and a consumer) of that culture.

20. Arcadio Díaz Quiñones observes that members of the Puerto Rican elite support "una concepción monolítica y vertical del nacionalismo 'cultural'. . . . Se creen depositarios de la 'verdadera' identidad nacional" (153–54) ("a monolithic and vertical conception of 'cultural' nationalism. . . . They believe themselves to be trustees of the 'true' national identity" [my translation]).

21. Of course, nationalism is always a social construction. "Nation-ness" becomes far more tangible (and menacing) when this same "construct" facilitates the constitution, control, and oppression of transgressive subjects, as Foucault shows.

22. It is important to note that unlike the situation of Cubans and other exiles to the United States, contact with the *patria* is relatively available to Puerto Ricans inhabiting the mainland. As Edna Acosta-Belén points out, for Nuyorican writers their ancestral "roots"

   are not hidden in the memory of ancestors in the dark continent but possess the vitality of a present time because of the geographic proximity and continual migratory flow to and from the island. (987)

   Nevertheless, the seemingly endless adversity to which the residents of El Building are subjected (bitter New Jersey winters, discrimination, poverty) lends an aura of lost paradise to the island they left behind.

23. According to the *Harvard Encyclopedia of American Ethnic Groups,* from the fourteenth through the nineteenth centuries "ethnic" was used to signify pagan, heathen, or non-Christian. In the United States, the association of "ethnic" with "other" or "un-American" reflects the previous usage of the word to connote religious outsiders (Thernstrom 648).

24. In ethnic communities in general, traditions and beliefs brought from the homeland are protected and validated in order to bolster the ancestral culture against the onslaught of dominant American culture. Rieff's assessment of the protection of "Cubanity" by the predominantly conservative Cuban exiles in Miami supports this assertion. He claims that

> the Miami Cubans worried incessantly about the adulteration of their Cuban-ity. . . . And accompanying this had been the psychological hunkering down that has always been the hallmark of both the political refugee and the immi-grant, the sense that everything outside the enclave is dangerous. (140)

25. By referring to Yolanda as a Catholic *señorita,* the lover insinuates that her moral dilemma has a specifically Latina/o nature. However, the mandates of island Catholicism regarding female sexuality are similar to those imposed on Catholic women of other ethnic groups (Irish-Americans, Italian-Americans, and so on) as well.

26. In the case of Chicana/o literature, Bruce-Novoa proposes that the threat is of symbolic death through the disappearance of the ancestral culture:

> Assimilation into another culture is a form of death for those who fear losing their own culture. True, it can be seen as a necessary process for entering the receiving society, but those forced to change may not be convinced. The melting-pot ideal is fine for those who have forgotten the excruciating pain of being melted down and repoured into a different mold. (1982, 9)

These comments are relevant to the circumstances that motivate ethnic writing in general.

27. The title of Pérez-Firmat's *Life on the Hyphen: The Cuban-American Way* alludes to this in-between space of ethnic subjectivity. "Life on the hyphen" could serve as a metaphor for other ethnic cultures as well.

Chapter 5

1. "It was as if God had decided to put to the test every capacity for surprise and was keeping the inhabitants of Macondo in a permanent alternation between excite-ment and disappointment, doubt and revelation" (*One Hundred Years of Solitude,* translation by Gregory Rabassa).

2. The reviewer, Shelly Lowenkopf, claims that the novel's Brazilian setting, "lean" prose, and "subtextual anguish shouting like macaws in a tropical jungle" evoke this comparison (10).

3. In 1954 Angel Flores, the first critic to identify a common current of *realismo mágico* in twentieth-century Latin American fiction, argued that this new "phase" in Latin American literature was initiated by Borges's 1935 collection *Historia universal de la infamia* (21). In his 1988 article "El realismo mágico hispanoamer-

icano ante la crítica," Antonio Planells provides a comprehensive bibliography of criticism on magical realism that includes more than 125 entries.

4. "the view of man as mystery in the midst of realist details" (my translation).

5. This work won the second Quinto Sol prize and became the best-selling work of Chicano fiction. By 1975 *Bless Me, Ultima*, was read worldwide; Tonatiuh Press's senior editor at the time, Octavio Romano-V., declared that "[p]robably no other novel written by a Chicano has had such wide and varied acclaim as has Rudolfo A. Anaya's *Bless Me, Ultima*" (Preface to the novel).

6. See Alfonso Rodríguez, "Time As a Structural Device in Tomás Rivera's ... *y no se lo tragó la tierra*," *Contemporary Chicano Fiction: A Critical Survey*, ed. Vernon E. Lattin (Binghamton: Bilingual Press, 1986), 126–30; Daniel P. Testa, "Narrative Technique and Human Experience in Tomás Rivera," *Modern Chicano Writers*, ed. Joseph Sommers et al. (Englewood Cliffs: Prentice-Hall, 1979), 86–93; Catherine Bartlett, "Magical Realism: The Latin American Influence on Modern Chicano Writers," *Confluencia* 1, no.2 (Spring 1986): 27–37; Juan Bruce-Novoa, "Chicano Literary Production, 1960–1980," *Retrospace*, 75–90; Marvin Lewis, *Introduction to the Chicano Novel* (Milwaukee: Spanish-Speaking Outreach Institute, 1982); Charles M. Tatum, *Chicano Literature* (Boston: Twayne Publishers, 1982).

7. The extraordinary international success of Laura Esquivel's 1989 novel *Como agua para chocolate* and its film adaptation is evidence of the continuing popularity of the magical realism associated with Boom fiction.

8. "because of its virginal landscape, its formation, its ontology, because of the Faustian presence of the Indian and the Negro, the Revelation constituted by its recent discovery, and the fertile miscegenation for which it was favorable, America is very far from exhausting its abundant mythologies" (my translation).

9. It could be argued that certain Latin American writers have perpetuated cultural stereotypes; both José Lezama Lima and Carpentier wrote definitive treatises on the existence of a Latin American cultural essence. See Lezama Lima, *La expresión americana;* and Carpentier's prologue to *El reino de este mundo*. The three volumes of Eduardo Galeano's *Memoria del fuego*, on the other hand, deconstruct monolithic notions of Latin American culture by challenging official versions of history and giving voices to marginalized peoples (Afro-Hispanic, indigenous, etc.).

10. "no one knew for certain where the limits of reality lay" (translation by Gregory Rabassa).

11. An illustration of this is the way that the ethnic "excessiveness" of the Puerto Rican immigrants' spiritism in *The Line of the Sun* brings their outsider status into sharp relief (see chapter 4).

12. Pilar is hardly a devout believer in the spirit world. Her mother, on the other hand, is visited periodically by her deceased father, who "whispers to her through the oak and maple trees. His words flutter at her neck like a baby's lacy breath" (170). In response to her mother's claims that during these conversations Abuelo Jorge reports on Pilar's behavior, Pilar reacts like a typical American teenager: "Like what is this? The ghost patrol?" (136).

13. The irony of this tendency to attribute such narrative experimentation to Latin American Boom writers is that to do so ignores its rather obvious precursors, modernists Joyce, Faulkner, Woolf, and others.

14. "Many years later, as he faced the firing squad, Colonel Aureliano Buendía was to

remember that distant afternoon when his father took him to discover ice" (translation by Gregory Rabassa).

15. "The events that would deal Macondo its fatal blow were just showing themselves when they brought Meme Buendía's son home" (translation by Gregory Rabassa).

16. Reviews of Hijuelos's novel emphasize its magical realist bent; see Richard Eder's "Black Beans and Cabbage" and Lydia Chávez's "Cuban Riffs: Songs of Love." Eder claims that

> Hijuelos' magic-realist style is reminiscent of Gabriel Garcia Marquez's *Love in the Time of Cholera*. It is forced and honeyed, though, without the authentic wit and mystery of the Colombian writer. (8)

Chávez concurs, asserting that "readers will think of Gabriel García Márquez. . . . when they first encounter the magical realism in 'Fourteen Sisters' " (26).

17. "The concept of plagiarism does not exist: it has been established that all works are the creation of one author, who is atemporal and anonymous" (translation by James E. Irby).

18. Pineda's two previous novels are *Face* (1985) and *Frieze* (1986).

19. That is, a narrator who is also a character in his own narrative.

20. This conglomeration of interior decorating schemes recalls Fredric Jameson's analysis of the juxtaposition of unrelated styles in postmodern architecture. In his essay "Postmodernism, or the Cultural Logic of Late Capitalism," Jameson argues that this combination of styles from discrete historical periods is pastiche, which he considers to be the characteristic form of the postmodern aesthetic.

21. This is a technique that critics have noted in Alejo Carpentier's *Recurso del método* as well. Eugenio Matibag observes that "Carpentier's dictator is in fact a composite figure, a 'montage' of different characteristics drawn from a number of Latin American dictators" (154).

22. The American doctors' comment that "[t]hese people lack the most elementary hygiene" moves Bolívar to mention the United States' long history of exploiting his people in his final statement (189).

23. The novel's most direct critique of U.S. economic policy is found in its epigraph, Gina Valdés's poem "Working Women" (1986). The speaker refers to "this big cathouse U S A, que a todos nos USA" and characterizes herself as "una puta más in this / prostitution ring led by a heartless / cowboy pimp."

24. After discussing a series of earlier writers in whose works a Kafkalike sensibility can supposedly be found, Borges asserts that "if Kafka had never written a line, we would not perceive this quality; in other words, it would not exist" (201).

25. See my comments on repetition and the inaccessibility of essence in chapter 2, note 33.

26. Castillo's previous novels are *The Mixquiahuala Letters* (1986) and *Sapogonia* (1990). She has also published three poetry collections, *Women Are Not Roses* (1984), *The Invitation* (1986), and *My Father Was a Toltec* (1988), as well as a collection of essays, *Massacre of the Dreamers: Essays on Xicanisma* (1994).

27. Although the text offers no definitive proof of the narrator's gender, for the purposes of this reading (and at the risk of essentializing) I will assume that the narrator is female. Her intimate knowledge and understanding of the psyche of the novel's female characters, her interest in and commentary on traditionally feminine ac-

tivities (cooking, healing, child-rearing), and her sharp feminist critique all suggest that the narrator is a sort of omniscient Chicana storyteller.

28. No one seems surprised, then, when the spirits of the children of M.O.M.A.S. (Mothers of Martyrs and Saints) members appear at the group's yearly convention, bringing comfort to their mothers as well as news and advice for community agencies and local and federal governments.

29. This passage is a commentary on the real estate boom that is currently producing inflated land values in northern New Mexico. The "discovery" of Santa Fe by wealthy Anglo Americans and the resulting gentrification have caused property taxes to soar to levels that many longtime residents — primarily Chicanos — cannot afford to pay. In a recent article entitled "Culture Clash, Santa Fe Style," Bruce Selcraig observes that

> thousands of natives, many of whom trace their local ancestry to the 1700s, have seen property taxes on their homes rise 300% to 800% in the past decade. . . . Some children can't afford to inherit their parents' land, disrupting centuries-old tradition. (22)

30. This "fictional" problem points to contemporary issues of environmental racism. This far-reaching phenomenon includes the use of carcinogenic pesticides on crops harvested by migrant workers and the disproportionate number of toxic waste landfills in poor minority communities. See Richard Hofrichter, ed., *Toxic Struggles: The Theory and Practice of Environmental Justice* (Philadelphia: New Society Publishers, 1993); Bunyan Bryant and Paul Mohai, *Race and the Incidence of Environmental Hazards: A Time for Discourse* (Boulder, Col.: Westview, 1992); Robert Bullard, ed., *Confronting Environmental Racism: Voices from the Grassroots* (Boston: South End Press, 1993); and Robert D. Bullard, ed., *Unequal Protection: Environmental Justice and Communities of Color* (San Francisco: Sierra Club Books, 1994).

31. The protest reinforces *So Far from God*'s connection to a broader Latin American problematic by painfully evoking the demonstrations of the *Madres de la Plaza de Mayo* in Argentina. These women called attention to the abuses of the military regime by marching with photographs of their disappeared family members, *los desaparecidos*.

32. On the book jacket, Sandra Cisneros is quoted as describing *So Far from God* in this manner.

33. The recipes also allow assimilation-driven Fe to establish a connection to her ancestral culture. The cooking lessons that La Loca gives Fe function like Arden's tamale-making sessions with her mother in Ortiz Taylor's *Southbound* (see chapter 2). Through the lessons Fe acquires the knowledge and skills that she will need to continue performing this facet of *chicanismo* in her own home.

34. See chapter 1 and introductory comments in chapter 2.

35. *Webster's Ninth New Collegiate Dictionary* (1989) suggests the synonyms "potpourri" and "hodgepodge" for pastiche, both of which are apt descriptions of *So Far from God*. Jean Franco's use of the term is similar in her essay "Pastiche in Contemporary Latin American Literature." She takes pastiche to signify both imitation and a melange of styles, having "the notion of originality as its counterpoint" (95).

BIBLIOGRAPHY

Acosta-Belén, Edna. "Beyond Island Boundaries: Ethnicity, Gender, and Cultural Revitalization in Nuyorican Literature." *Callaloo* 15, no.4 (1992): 979–98.

Alarcón, Norma. "Chicana's Feminist Literature: A Re-Vision Through Malintzin/or Malintzin: Putting Flesh Back on the Object." In *This Bridge Called My Back: Writings by Radical Women of Color*, edited by Cherríe Moraga and Gloria Anzaldúa, 182–90. New York: Kitchen Table, Women of Color Press, 1983.

———. "Chicana Feminism: In the Tracks of 'the' Native Woman." *Cultural Studies* 4, no.3 (October 1990): 248–56.

———. "Conjugating Subjects: The Heteroglossia of Essence and Resistance." In *An Other Tongue: Nation and Ethnicity in the Linguistic Borderlands*, edited by Alfred Arteaga, 125–38. Durham, N.C.: Duke University Press, 1994.

Algarín, Miguel. "Nuyorican Literature." *MELUS* 8, no.2 (Summer 1981): 89–92.

Algarín, Miguel, and Miguel Piñero, eds. *Nuyorican Poetry: An Anthology of Puerto Rican Words and Feelings*. New York: Morrow, 1975.

Almaguer, Tomás. "Chicano Men: A Cartography of Homosexual Identity and Behavior." *differences* 3, no.2 (1991): 75–100.

Alvarez, Julia. *How the García Girls Lost Their Accents*. Chapel Hill, N.C.: Algonquin Books, 1991.

Anaya, Rudolfo A. *Bless Me, Ultima*. Berkeley: Tonatiuh-Quinto Sol International, 1972.

Antin, Mary. *The Promised Land*. Boston: Houghton Mifflin, 1969.

Anzaldúa, Gloria. *Borderlands/La Frontera: The New Mestiza*. San Francisco: Spinsters/Aunt Lute, 1987.

Argüelles, Lourdes. "Crazy Wisdom: Memories of a Cuban Queer." In *Sisters, Sexperts,*

Queers: Beyond the Lesbian Nation, edited by Arlene Stein, 196–204. New York: Penguin, 1993.

Argüelles, Lourdes, and B. Ruby Rich. "Homosexuality, Homophobia, and Revolution: Notes toward an Understanding of the Cuban Lesbian and Gay Male Experience." *Signs: Journal of Women in Culture and Society* 9, no.4 (Summer 1984): 683–99 (Part I).

Arias, Ron. *The Road to Tamazunchale*. Tempe, Ariz.: Bilingual Press/Editorial Bilingüe, 1987.

Arteaga, Alfred, ed. *An Other Tongue: Nation and Ethnicity in the Linguistic Borderlands*. Durham, N.C.: Duke University Press, 1994.

Augenbraum, Harold, and Ilán Stavans, eds. *Growing Up Latino: Memoirs and Stories*. Boston: Houghton Mifflin, 1993.

Bakhtin, Mikhail. *The Dialogic Imagination: Four Essays by M. M. Bakhtin*. Edited by Michael Holquist; translated by Caryl Emerson and Michael Holquist. Austin: University of Texas Press, 1981.

———. *Problems of Dostoevsky's Poetics*. Edited and translated by Caryl Emerson. Minneapolis: University of Minnesota Press, 1984.

Barthes, Roland. *S/Z*. Translated by Richard Miller. New York: Farrar, Straus and Giroux, 1974.

Bataille, Georges. *Visions of Excess*. Translated by Allan Stoekl. Minneapolis: University of Minnesota Press, 1985.

Beam, Joseph. "Brother to Brother: Words from the Heart." *In the Life: A Black Gay Anthology*, edited by Joseph Beam. Boston: Alyson, 1986.

Beaver, Harold. "Homosexual Signs (In Memory of Roland Barthes)." *Critical Inquiry* 8, no.1 (Autumn 1981): 99–119.

Bhabha, Homi K. *The Location of Culture*. London: Routledge, 1994.

Boelhower, William. *Through a Glass Darkly: Ethnic Semiosis in American Literature*. New York: Oxford University Press, 1987.

Borges, Jorge Luis. *Labyrinths: Selected Stories and Other Writings*. Edited by Donald A. Yates and James E. Irby. New York: New Directions, 1964.

Bruce-Novoa, Juan. *Chicano Poetry: A Response to Chaos*. Austin, Texas: University of Texas Press, 1982.

———. *Retrospace: Collected Essays on Chicano Literature*. Houston: Arte Público Press, 1990.

Brushwood, John S. "Two Views of the Boom: North and South." *Latin American Literary Review* 15, no.29 (January–June 1987): 13–31.

Burunat, Silvia, and Ofelia García, eds. *Veinte años de literatura cubanoamericana: Antología 1962–1982*. Tempe, Ariz.: Bilingual Press/Editorial Bilingüe, 1988.

Butler, Judith. *Gender Trouble: Feminism and the Subversion of Identity*. New York: Routledge, 1990.

———. "Imitation and Gender Insubordination." In *Inside/Out: Lesbian Theories, Gay Theories*, edited by Diana Fuss, 13–31. New York: Routledge, 1991.

———. *Bodies that Matter: On the Discursive Limits of "Sex"*. New York: Routledge, 1993.

Calderón, Héctor, and José David Saldívar, eds. *Criticism in the Borderlands: Studies in Chicano Literature, Culture, and Ideology*. Durham, N.C.: Duke University Press, 1991.

Cárdenas de Dwyer, Carlota. "The Development of Chicano Drama and Luis Valdez's *Actos.*" In *Modern Chicano Writers,* edited by Joseph Sommers and Tomás Ybarra-Frausto, 160–66. Englewood Cliffs, N.J.: Prentice-Hall, 1979.

Carpentier, Alejo. *El reino de este mundo.* La Habana: Editorial Letras Cubanas, 1984.

Castillo, Ana. "La Macha: Toward a Beautiful Whole Self." In *Chicana Lesbians: The Girls Our Mothers Warned Us About,* edited by Carla Trujillo, 24–48. Berkeley, Calif.: Third Woman Press, 1991.

———. *So Far from God.* New York: W. W. Norton & Co., 1993.

Chabrám, Angie. "Conceptualizing Chicano Critical Discourse." In *Criticism in the Borderlands: Studies in Chicano Literature, Culture, and Ideology,* edited by Héctor Calderón and José David Saldívar, 127–48. Durham, N.C.: Duke University Press, 1991.

Chabrám, Angie C., and Rosa Linda Fregoso. "Chicana/o Cultural Representations: Reframing Alternative Critical Discourses." *Cultural Studies* 4, no.3 (October 990): 203–12.

Chabrám-Dernersesian, Angie. "I Throw Punches for My Race, but I Don't Want to Be a Man: Writing Us — Chica-nos (Girl, Us)/Chicanas — into the Movement Script." In *Cultural Studies,* edited by Lawrence Grossberg, Cary Nelson, and Paula A. Treichler, 81–95. New York: Routledge, 1992.

Chávez, Linda. "Cuban Riffs: Songs of Love." Review of *The Fourteen Sisters of Emilio Montez O'Brien,* by Oscar Hijuelos. *Los Angeles Times Magazine,* 18 April 1993, 26ff.

Chin, Frank. "Come All Ye Asian American Writers of the Real and the Fake." *The Big Aiiieeeee! An Anthology of Chinese American and Japanese American Literature.* New York: Penguin, 1991.

Cliff, Michelle. *The Land of Look Behind.* Ithaca, N.Y.: Firebrand Books, 1985.

Codrescu, Andrei. "A Mad, Mad, Mad, Mad Mundo." Review of *Raining Backwards,* by Roberto G. Fernández. *New York Times Book Review* 93 (14 August 1988), 27.

Cortina, Rodolfo J. "Cuban Literature of the United States: 1824–1959." In *Recovering the U.S. Hispanic Literary Heritage,* edited by Ramón Gutiérrez and Genaro Padilla, 69–88. Houston: Arte Público, 1993.

de Certeau, Michel. *The Practice of Everyday Life.* Translated by Steven Rendall. Berkeley: University of California Press, 1984.

Díaz Quiñones, Arcadio. "Puerto Rico: Cultura, memoria y diáspora." *Nueva sociedad* 116 (noviembre-diciembre 1991): 153–58.

Doane, Mary Ann. *Femmes Fatales: Feminism, Film Theory, Psychoanalysis.* New York: Routledge, 1992.

Eder, Richard. "Black Beans and Cabbage." Review of *The Fourteen Sisters of Emilio Montez O'Brien,* by Oscar Hijuelos. *Los Angeles Times Book Review,* 14 March 1993, 8.

Epple, Juan Armando. "Hispanic Exile in the United States." In *Handbook of Hispanic Cultures in the United States: Literature and Art,* edited by Francisco Lomelí, 333–59. Houston: Arte Público Press, 1993.

Fernández, Roberta. *Twenty-Five Years of Hispanic Literature in the United States 1965–1990.* Houston: University of Houston Libraries, 1992.

Fine, David M. *The City, The Immigrant and American Fiction, 1880–1920.* Metuchen, N.J.: The Scarecrow Press, 1977.

Fischer, Michael M. J. "Ethnicity and the Post-Modern Arts of Memory." In *Writing Culture: The Poetics and Politics of Ethnography,* edited by James Clifford and George E. Marcus, 194–223. Berkeley: University of California Press, 1986.

Flores, Angel. *El realismo mágico en el cuento hispano-americano.* Puebla, México: Premia Editora, 1985.

Flores, Francisca. Introduction. *Regeneración* 1, no.10 (1971).

Flores, Juan. "Puerto Rican Literature in the United States: Stages and Perspectives." *ADE Bulletin* 91 (Winter 1988): 39–44.

Flores, Juan, John Attinasi, and Pedro Pedraza, Jr. " 'La Carreta Made a U-turn': Puerto Rican Language and Culture in the United States." In Juan Flores's *Divided Borders: Essays on Puerto Rican Identity,* 157–83. Houston: Arte Público, 1993.

Flores, Juan, and George Yúdice. "Living Borders/Buscando America: Languages of Latino Self-formation." *Social Text* 8, no.2 (1990): 57–84.

Foucault, Michel. *The Archaeology of Knowledge and the Discourse on Language.* Translated by A. M. Sheridan Smith. New York: Pantheon Books, 1972.

——. *The History of Sexuality.* Volume 1. Translated by Robert Hurley. New York: Pantheon Books, 1978.

Franco, Jean. "Pastiche in Contemporary Latin American Literature." *Studies in Twentieth-Century Literature* 14, no.1 (Winter 1990): 95–107.

Frase-Blunt, Martha. "A New Chapter." *Hispanic* (September 1992): 30–38.

Fuentes, Ileana. *Cuba sin caudillos: Un enfoque feminista para el siglo XXI.* Princeton, N.J.: Linden Lane Press, 1994.

Fusco, Coco. *English is Broken Here: Notes on Cultural Fusion in the Americas.* New York: The New Press, 1995.

Fuss, Diana. *Essentially Speaking: Feminism, Nature and Difference.* New York: Routledge, 1989.

Gal, Susan. "The political economy of code choice." In *Codeswitching: Anthropological and Sociolinguistic Perspectives,* edited by Monica Heller, 245–64. Berlin: Mouton de Gruyter, 1988.

García, Cristina. "Baroque Bordello." Review of *The Love Queen of the Amazon,* by Cecile Pineda. *Los Angeles Times Book Review,* 22 March 1992, 2ff.

——. *Dreaming in Cuban.* New York: Alfred A. Knopf, 1992.

García, Richard. *Chicanos in America, 1540–1974.* Dobbs Ferry, N.Y.: Oceana Publications, 1977.

García Márquez, Gabriel. *One Hundred Years of Solitude.* Translated by Gregory Rabassa. New York: Avon Books, 1971.

——. *Cien años de soledad.* Madrid: Espasa-Calpe, 1985.

——. "Latin America's Impossible Reality." Translated by Elena Brunet. *Harper's* 270, no.1616 (January 1985): 13–16.

Gomez, Jewelle. "Imagine a Lesbian . . . A Black Lesbian . . ." *Trivia* 12 (Spring 1988): 45–60.

González, Ray, ed. *Currents from the Dancing River: Contemporary Latino Fiction, Nonfiction, and Poetry.* San Diego: Harcourt Brace, 1994.

González Echevarría, Roberto. "Sarduy, the Boom, and the Post-Boom." *Latin American Literary Review* 15, no.29 (January–June 1987): 57–72.

Gordils, Yanis. "Island and Continental Puerto Rican Literature: Cross-Cultural and Intertextual Considerations." *ADE Bulletin* 91 (Winter 1988): 52–55.

Gutiérrez, Ramón, and Genaro Padilla, eds. *Recovering the U.S. Hispanic Literary Heritage*. Houston: Arte Público, 1993.

Hall, Stuart. "Minimal Selves." In *Identity*, edited by Lisa Appignanesi, 44–46. London: ICA Document 6, 1987.

———. "Ethnicity: Identity and Difference." *Radical America* 23, no.4 (October–December 1989): 9–20.

Herrera-Sobek, María and Helena María Viramontes, eds. *Chicana Creativity and Criticism: Charting New Frontiers in American Literature*. First published in *The Americas Review* 15, no.3/4 (1987): 1–190.

Hijuelos, Oscar. *The Mambo Kings Play Songs of Love*. New York: Harper & Row, 1989.

———. *The Fourteen Sisters of Emilio Montez O'Brien*. New York: Farrar, Straus and Giroux, 1993.

Horno-Delgado, Asunción, Eliana Ortega, Nina M. Scott, and Nancy Saporta Sternbach, eds. *Breaking Boundaries: Latina Writings and Critical Readings*. Amherst: University of Massachusetts Press, 1989.

Hospital, Carolina. "Los atrevidos." *Linden Lane Magazine* 5, no.4 (1987): 22–23.

Huerta, Jorge A. "Contemporary Chicano Theater." In *Chicano Studies: A Multidisciplinary Approach*, edited by Eugene F. García, Francisco Lomelí, and Isidro D. Ortiz, 135–50. New York: Teachers College Press, 1984.

Islas, Arturo. *Migrant Souls*. New York: William Morrow, 1990.

Jameson, Fredric. "Postmodernism, or The Cultural Logic of Late Capitalism." *New Left Review* 146 (July–August 1984): 53–92.

Kingsolver, Barbara. "Desert Heat." Review of *So Far from God*, by Ana Castillo. *Los Angeles Times Book Review*, 16 May 1993, 1.

Laviera, Tato. *AmeRícan*. Houston: Arte Público Press, 1985.

Leal, Luis. "El realismo mágico en la literatura hispanoamericana." *Cuadernos americanos* 26, no.153 (julio–agosto 1967): 230–35.

———. "Mexican American Literature: A Historical Perspective." In *Modern Chicano Writers*, edited by Joseph Sommers and Tomás Ybarra-Frausto, 18–30. Englewood Cliffs, N.J.: Prentice-Hall, 1979.

Lipsitz, George. " 'That's My Blood Down There': Strategic Anti-Essentialism in Popular Music." Paper presented at University of California Humanities Research Institute, Irvine, October 29, 1992.

Lomelí, Francisco, ed. *Handbook of Hispanic Cultures in the United States: Literature and Art*. Houston: Arte Público Press, 1993.

López, Natashia. "Trying to be Dyke and Chicana." In *Chicana Lesbians: The Girls Our Mothers Warned Us About*, edited by Carla Trujillo, 84. Berkeley: Third Woman Press, 1991.

Lowenkopf, Shelly. Review of *Face*, by Cecile Pineda. *Los Angeles Times Book Review*, 23 June 1985, 2ff.

Mailer, Norman. *The White Negro*. San Francisco: City Lights, 1957.

Manzor-Coats, Lillian. "Who Are You, Anyways?: Gender, Racial and Linguistic Politics in U.S. Cuban Theater." *Gestos* 6, no.11 (April 1991): 163–74.

Martínez, Eliud. "The Road to Tamazunchale: Cultural Inheritance and Literary Expression." Introduction to Arias's *The Road to Tamazunchale*. Tempe, Ariz.: Bilingual Press/Editorial Bilingüe, 1987.

Matibag, Eugenio. "Reason and the State: The Enlightened Dictator of Alejo Carpentier's *El recurso del método.*" *Dispositio* 18, no.44 (1993): 153–73.

Melville, Margarita B. "Los hispanos: ¿clase, raza o etnicidad?" *Hispanos en los Estados Unidos,* edited by Rodolfo J. Cortina and Alberto Moncada, 131–45. Madrid: Ediciones de Cultura Hispánica, 1988.

Moraga, Cherríe. *Loving in the War Years: Lo que nunca pasó por sus labios.* Boston: South End Press, 1983.

Moraga, Cherríe, and Gloria Anzaldúa, eds. *This Bridge Called My Back: Writings by Radical Women of Color.* New York: Kitchen Table, Women of Color Press, 1983.

Muñoz, Carlos, Jr. *Youth, Identity, Power: The Chicano Movement.* London: Verso, 1989.

Muñoz, Elías Miguel. *The Greatest Performance.* Houston: Arte Público Press, 1991.

———. "Into the Writer's Labyrinth: Storytelling Days with Gabo." *Michigan Quarterly Review* 34, no.2 (Spring 1995): 173–93.

Newton, Esther. *Mother Camp: Female Impersonators in America.* Chicago: University of Chicago Press, 1972.

Obejas, Achy. *We Came All the Way from Cuba So You Could Dress Like This?* Pittsburgh, Pa.: Cleis Press, 1994.

Ortiz, Ricardo. "Sexuality Degree Zero: Pleasure and Power in the Novels of John Rechy, Arturo Islas, and Michael Nava." In *Critical Essays: Gay and Lesbian Writers of Color,* edited by Emmanuel S. Nelson, 111–26. New York: Haworth Press, 1993.

Ortiz Cofer, Judith. *The Line of the Sun.* Athens, Ga.: University of Georgia Press, 1989.

Ortiz Taylor, Sheila. *Faultline.* Tallahassee, Fla.: Naiad Press, 1982.

———. *Spring Forward/Fall Back.* Tallahassee, Fla.: Naiad Press, 1985.

———. *Southbound.* Tallahassee, Fla.: Naiad Press, 1990.

Palumbo-Liu, David. *The Ethnic Canon: Histories, Institutions, and Interventions.* Minneapolis: University of Minnesota Press, 1995.

Patton, Cindy. "Power and the conditions of silence." *Critical Quarterly* 31, no.3 (Autumn 1989): 27–39.

Perera, Victor. "A Metaphor for Guatemala." Review of *The Long Night of White Chickens,* by Francisco Goldman. *Los Angeles Times Book Review,* 19 July 1992, 8.

Pérez-Firmat, Gustavo. "Transcending Exile: Cuban-American Literature Today." *Occasional Papers Series Dialogues* 92 (December 1987): 1–13.

———. *The Cuban Condition: Translation and Identity in Modern Cuban Literature.* Cambridge: Cambridge University Press, 1989.

———. *Life on the Hyphen: The Cuban-American Way.* Austin: University of Texas Press, 1994.

Pérez-Torres, Rafael. *Movements in Chicano Poetry: Against Myths, Against Margins.* Cambridge: Cambridge University Press, 1995.

Phelan, Peggy. *Unmarked: The Politics of Performance.* London: Routledge, 1993.

Pineda, Cecile. *The Love Queen of the Amazon.* Boston: Little, Brown, 1992.

Planells, Antonio. "El realismo mágico hispanoamericano ante la crítica." *Chasqui* 17, no.1 (mayo 1988): 9–23.

Poey, Delia, and Virgil Suárez, eds. *Iguana Dreams: New Latino Fiction.* New York: HarperCollins, 1992.

Quintanales, Mirtha. "I Paid Very Hard for My Immigrant Ignorance." In *This Bridge Called My Back: Writings by Radical Women of Color*, edited by Cherríe Moraga and Gloria Anzaldúa, 150–56. New York: Kitchen Table, Women of Color Press, 1983.

Rebolledo, Tey Diana. *Women Singing in the Snow: A Cultural Analysis of Chicana Literature*. Tucson: University of Arizona Press, 1995.

Rebolledo, Tey Diana, and Eliana S. Rivero, eds. *Infinite Divisions: An Anthology of Chicana Literature*. Tucson: University of Arizona Press, 1993.

Rechy, John. *City of Night*. New York: Grove Press, 1963.

———. *This Day's Death*. New York: Grove Press, 1969.

———. *The Sexual Outlaw*. New York: Grove Press, 1977.

Rieff, David. *The Exile: Cuba in the Heart of Miami*. New York: Simon & Schuster, 1993.

Risech, Flavio. "Political and Cultural Cross-Dressing: Negotiating a Second Generation Cuban-American Identity." *Michigan Quarterly Review* 33, no.3 (Summer 1994): 526–40.

Rivero, Eliana. "Hispanic Literature in the United States: Self-Image and Conflict." *Revista Chicano-Riqueña* 13, no.3/4 (Fall–Winter 1985): 173–91.

———. "Cubanos y cubanoamericanos: perfil y presencia en los Estados Unidos." *Discurso literario* 7, no.1 (II semestre 1989): 81–101.

———. "From Immigrants to Ethnics: Cuban Women Writers in the U.S." In *Breaking Boundaries: Latina Writings and Critical Readings*, edited by Asunción Horno-Delgado et al., 189–200. Amherst: University of Massachusetts Press, 1989.

———. "(Re)writing Sugarcane Memories: Cuban Americans and Literature." *The Americas Review* 18, no.3/4 (1990): 164–82.

Rodríguez, Richard. *Hunger of Memory: The Education of Richard Rodríguez*. Boston: David R. Godine, 1982.

Said, Edward. "Reflections on Exile." In *Out There: Marginalization and Contemporary Cultures*, edited by Russell Ferguson, Martha Gever, Trinh T. Minh-ha, and Cornel West, 359–66. New York: The New Museum of Contemporary Art, 1990.

Saldívar, Ramón. *Chicano Narrative: The Dialectics of Difference*. Madison, Wis.: University of Wisconsin Press, 1990.

Sánchez, Marta. "Revisiting Binaries of Race and Gender in Piri Thomas' *Down These Mean Streets*." Paper presented at University of California Humanities Research Institute, Irvine, March 2, 1993.

Sánchez, Rosaura. *Chicano Discourse: Socio-historic Perspectives*. Rowley, Mass.: Newbury House, 1983.

———. "Calculated Musings: Richard Rodríguez's Metaphysics of Difference." In *The Ethnic Canon: Histories, Institutions, and Interventions*, edited by David Palumbo-Liu, 153–73. Minneapolis: University of Minnesota Press, 1995.

Santiago, Esmeralda. *When I Was Puerto Rican*. Reading, Mass.: Addison-Wesley, 1993.

Sedgwick, Eve Kosofsky. *Epistemology of the Closet*. Berkeley: University of California Press, 1990.

Selcraig, Bruce. "Culture Clash, Santa Fe Style." *Los Angeles Times Magazine*, 5 September 1993, 20ff.

Shaktini, Namascar. "A Revolutionary Signifier: The Lesbian Body." In *Lesbian Texts and Contexts: Radical Revisions*, edited by Karla Jay and Joanne Glasgow, 291–303. New York: New York University Press, 1990.

Singh, Amritjit, Joseph T. Skerrett, Jr., and Robert E. Hogan, eds. *Memory, Narrative, and Identity: New Essays in Ethnic American Literatures.* Boston: Northeastern University Press, 1994.

Sollors, Werner. *Beyond Ethnicity: Consent and Descent in American Literature.* Oxford: Oxford University Press, 1986.

———. *The Invention of Ethnicity.* New York: Oxford University Press, 1989.

Sommer, Doris, and George Yúdice. "Latin American Literature from the 'Boom' On." In *Postmodern Fiction: A Bio-Bibliographical Guide*, edited by Larry McCaffery, 189–214. New York: Greenwood Press, 1986.

Sommers, Joseph, and Tomás Ybarra-Frausto, eds. *Modern Chicano Writers.* Englewood Cliffs, N.J.: Prentice-Hall, 1979.

Stavans, Ilán. "The Other Voice." *The Bloomsbury Review* (July–August 1992): 5.

———. Foreword of *Growing Up Latino: Memoirs and Stories*, edited by Harold Augenbraum and Ilán Stavans. Boston: Houghton Mifflin, 1993.

Steiner, Stan. *La Raza: The Mexican-Americans.* New York: Harper, 1970.

Tabori, Paul. *The Anatomy of Exile.* London: George Harrap, 1972.

Thernstrom, Stephan, ed. *Harvard Encyclopedia of American Ethnic Groups.* Cambridge, Mass.: Harvard University Press, 1980.

Trujillo, Carla, ed. *Chicana Lesbians: The Girls Our Mothers Warned Us About.* Berkeley: Third Woman Press, 1991.

Uslar Pietri, Arturo. *Letras y hombres de Venezuela.* Mexico: Fondo de Cultura Económica, 1948.

Vásquez, Mary S. "Family, Generation, and Gender in Two Novels of Cuban Exile: Into the Mainstream?" *Bilingual Review/La revista bilingüe* 16, no.1 (January–April 1991): 23–34.

Vidal, Mirta. "Women: New Voice of La Raza." In *Chicanos in America, 1540–1974*, edited by Richard García, 132–40. Dobbs Ferry, N.Y.: Oceana Publications, 1977.

Williams, Raymond. *Problems in Materialism and Culture.* London: Verso, 1980.

Yarbro-Bejarano, Yvonne. "From *acto* to *mito*: A Critical Appraisal of the Teatro Campesino." In *Modern Chicano Writers*, edited by Joseph Sommers and Tomás Ybarra-Frausto, 176–85. Englewood Cliffs, N.J.: Prentice-Hall, 1979.

———. "The Female Subject in Chicano Theatre: Sexuality, 'Race,' and Class." *Theatre Journal* 38, no.4 (December 1986): 389–407.

———. "Gloria Anzaldúa's *Borderlands/La frontera*: Cultural Studies, 'Difference,' and the Non-Unitary Subject." *Cultural Critique* 28 (Fall 1994): 5–28.

Zentella, Ana Celia. "Spanish and English in Contact in the United States: The Puerto Rican Experience." *Word* 33, no.1/2 (April–August 1982): 41–57.

INDEX